Law, Politics,
and Perception

Constitutionalism
and Democracy

GREGG IVERS AND
KEVIN T. MCGUIRE,
EDITORS

Law, Politics, & Perception

HOW POLICY PREFERENCES INFLUENCE LEGAL REASONING

Eileen Braman

UNIVERSITY OF VIRGINIA PRESS   CHARLOTTESVILLE AND LONDON

University of Virginia Press
© 2009 by the Rector and Visitors of the University of Virginia
Printed in the United States of America on acid-free paper

First published 2009

9 8 7 6 5 4 3 2 1

LIBRARY OF CONGRESS CATALOGING-IN-PUBLICATION DATA

Braman, Eileen.
  Law, politics, and perception : how policy preferences influence legal reasoning /
Eileen Braman.
     p.   cm. — (Constitutionalism and democracy)
  Includes bibliographical references and index.
  ISBN 978-0-8139-2829-6 (cloth : alk. paper) — (ISBN 978-0-8139-2837-1 (e-book)
  1. Law—United States—Methodology. 2. Judicial process—United States.
3. Political questions and judicial power—United States. 4. Law—United States—
Psychological aspects. I. Title.
  KF380.B6 2009
  340'.11—dc22
                                                                            2009005845

For my mother
and in memory
of my father

We may try to see things as objectively as we please. Nonetheless, we can never see them with any eyes except our own.

SUPREME COURT JUSTICE BENJAMIN N. CARDOZO

CONTENTS

FIGURES AND TABLES

PREFACE

In this book, I use theory and methods from psychology to explore legal decision making. I am far from the first researcher do this; indeed, chapter 1 details the strong influence of behavioral psychology in social science research on judicial decision making. What makes this book unique is its focus on cognition, or the mental processes that decision makers experience as they think about case facts and legal authority. I employ the concept of motivated reasoning to explain how decision makers reach conclusions consistent with their preferences while they are using objective decision criteria embodied in accepted norms of legal reasoning.

In developing my theory (and corralling evidence to support it), I draw from literature in three distinct fields: law, political science, and psychology. I have tried to keep concepts and language as accessible as possible, and it is my sincere hope that the book will appeal to students and researchers across disciplines. In fact, I hope that social scientists will pay special attention to chapters 1 and 2, which discuss legal socialization and doctrine, and that legal types will delve deeply into chapters 1, 3, 4, and 5, which describe the experimental logic, design, and results of my hypothesis testing. I realize this may move some readers out of their comfort zones, but I have tried to make the task as painless as possible, and I believe the payoff will be substantial in terms of encouraging creative research that takes into account the contributions and concerns of various perspectives relevant for understanding legal decision making.

A Note about Terminology

Even within disciplines, terminology can be confusing. Describing extralegal forces at work in legal decision making is no exception; so at the outset I'd like to make some simple distinctions. "Ideology," "attitudes," and "preferences" are all words that have been used to describe personal views that judges have about cases they are called on to decide. The three terms are related and have, on occasion, been used interchangeably in the literature on judicial decision making. It is important to understand, however, that they refer to distinct concepts. I discuss each term here as it is used in the context of research on judicial behavior.

In the judicial literature, the term "ideology" refers to political ideology, a coherent set of beliefs that individual judges hold about the proper role government in society. Ideology is usually operationalized in dichotomous terms; both judicial actors and case outcomes are categorized as liberal or conservative. Very generally, liberal judges favor more government regulation of the economy and less state interference in the lives of everyday citizens in civil liberties matters. Conservative judges have the opposite views. Because ideology involves a very general orientation toward the role of government, it covers a wide range of issues that judges may encounter in their decision making.

"Attitudes" are more specific than ideology. They describe positive or negative feelings judges have toward a particular target (McGuire 1985). Attitudes may be influenced by ideology (for instance, conservatives like tax cuts), but the relationship is not perfect. Judges can have particular attitudes that are inconsistent with their ideology. Moreover, attitudes can be shaped by factors other than ideology such as personal experience with a particular issue or class of litigant.

"Preferences" are outcomes that judges favor. Like attitudes, they are more specific then ideology; the term "preference" implies that judges are choosing from a set of alternatives in a particular choice domain (Velleman 1994). Individual judges may have preferences with regard to a given policy (such as when someone prefers tax cuts to tax hikes), or dispute (as when a judge prefers that the plaintiff prevail instead of the defendant).

An underlying assumption in judicial research is that judges prefer outcomes consistent with their attitudes and/or ideology. Ideology is often used to approximate judges' preferences in cases they are called on to decide. Sometimes researchers have more specific indicators of judges' attitudinal preferences with regard to cases involving particular issues. In this study, I use responses to specific policy questions to measure decision makers' attitudes about issues in cases they are considering. But judicial decision-making research is often done "at a distance," making ideology our most appropriate proxy in many cases.

Having clarified my use of these terms, I proceed to my inquiry of how political preferences can influence important aspects of legal reasoning. I hope readers who are interested in this topic from various perspectives will discover something worthwhile in the analysis and approach.

ACKNOWLEDGMENTS

There are many people to whom I am indebted for their help and support in researching and writing this book. Particular thanks go to three academic mentors I have harassed and exploited over the years. I thank Tom Nelson, from whom I have learned much as a teacher and collaborator, for the lessons in psychology, research design, and early professionalization; Larry Baum, whose theoretical insights helped to give this project form, for listening to my ideas and responding in ways that always make me think about things more carefully; and my advisor, Greg Caldeira, whose support from the earliest stages of my graduate training has been invaluable. I am especially grateful for their openness to new ideas and the latitude they indulged and encouraged in my thinking about ways to test them. The most valuable lesson I learned is to follow my instincts, but to allow for the very real possibility that those instincts are wrong. I thank them for helping me construct a research agenda that allowed me to do just that. I have learned much in the process.

I sincerely appreciate the assistance of the Center for the Study of Law and Social Policy at the Ohio State Law School, and more specifically Professors H. Camille Herbert, Peter M. Shane, and James Brudney in making possible my experiments with law students. This research was also supported by an Alumni Grant for Graduate Research and Scholarship and the Program for the Enhancement of Graduate Studies at Ohio State University.

Several years ago, in his presence, I referred to Jeff Segal as "my chief enabler and primary foil." I thank him and Harold J. Spaeth particularly for mentioning motivated reasoning in a 1996 article and subsequent work. Obviously, the insight has been important in shaping my own thinking and research on legal decision making. Additionally, I've been lucky to benefit directly from the insights of prominent political psychologists including Kathleen McGraw, Marilynn Brewer, Phil Tetlock, and various lecturers at the Summer Institute in Political Psychology for several years. Moreover, the input of Stephanie Maruska Boruda, Elliot Slotnick, Chuck Taber, Dean Lacy, Dan Simon, Greg Gwiasda, Wendy Watson, Kevin Scott, Margie Williams, Brandon Bartels, Paul Collins, Wendy Martinek, Sara Benesh, Nancy Scherer, Richard Pacelle, Steve Wasby, Richard Lau, Bridget Coggins, and Brent Strathman on particular aspects of this project has been invaluable.

I could not have made it though this process without the friendship and intellectual support of several dear friends and colleagues. Sara Dunlap Gwiasda, Charles Smith, Javonne Paul Stewart, Khalilah Brown-Dean, Mary Outwater, Yoav Gortzak, Paul Fritz, Yoram Haftel, Lorraine Katt, Chris DeSimone, Nagu Kent, Omar Lalani, Leena Bhatia, Nehal Dadamudi, Karen Jacobs, Donna Vitale Savoretti, Aaron Jacoby, and Michelle Bird all kept me sane and motivated at various phases of this project. Also, special thanks to members of my family including Janet, Steven, Evelyn, Andrew, and Jared Braman for their continuous and multifaceted support.

I am, of course, grateful to my Chair, Jeff Isaac, and colleagues at Indiana University in political science including Mike Ensley, Lauren Morris MacLean, Adbulkader Sinno, Ted Carmines, Jerry Wright, Bill Bianco, Margie Hershey, Regina Smyth, Yvette Alex-Assensoh, and Mike McGinnis. I have also benefitted from the friendship and advice of colleagues at the law school and several other departments at Indiana including Kevin Collins, Jeannine Bell, Ajay Mehrotha, Leandra Lederman, Ken Dau-Schmidt, Charlie Geyh (Law), Steven Jim Sheruman (Psychology), and Mike Grossberg (History). I have presented aspects of this research in talks for the Indiana Law School Faculty Colloquium Series, the Law and Society Workshop and the Workshop in Political Theory and Policy Analysis at Indiana University.

Some of the research in this monograph has been previously published in other incarnations. Specifically, the study described in chapter 3 was the subject of an article coauthored by myself and Thomas E. Nelson ("Mechanism of Motivated Reasoning?: Analogical Perception in Discrimination Disputes" *American Journal of Political Science* 51, no. 4 [2007]: 940–56). The study described in chapter 4 was published as "Reasoning on the Threshold: Testing the Separability of Preferences in Legal Decision Making," *Journal of Politics* 68, no. 2 (2006): 308–21, and is reprinted by permission. Both studies have been modified for presentation in this manuscript; some of the language/ideas in those articles appear in this book's first chapter, which introduces the concept of motivated reasoning. I am grateful to both journals (and Tom!) for granting permission for the appearance of that work in this volume. Each study was originally conceived as part of a larger whole, so I am especially pleased to see them published together with the book's other arguments and evidence.

I would like to express my sincere thanks to Kevin McGuire, Gregg Ivers, Dick Hollway, and the anonymous readers at the University of Virginia Press for their encouragement and help throughout the publication process. I am sure the book is much better for their input.

Finally, this book is dedicated to my parents. My father's influence is undeniable in everything I do. I thank my mom for her unwavering support. Finally, she has something tangible to show for it.

Law, Politics,
and Perception

INTRODUCTION

In the spring of 2004, citizens and legal scholars were watching the Supreme Court for a decision on whether the Pledge of Allegiance, including its phrase "one nation under God," could be recited in the nation's public schools. The case in which the issue arose, *Elk Grove Unified School District v. Newdow*,[1] had all the stuff of great drama. A young girl was caught in the middle of an acrimonious divorce between her Atheist father and Christian mother, with each parent claiming to have the child's "best interest" in mind.

The father, "ordained . . . in a ministry that 'espouse[d] . . . that the true and eternal bonds of righteousness and virtue stem from reason rather than mythology,'" had strong objections to the daily recitation that took place in his daughter's kindergarten classroom.[2] He filed suit against the Elk Grove school district, arguing that the ritual amounted to religious indoctrination in violation of the Constitution's prohibition on religious establishment and the Free Exercise Clause of the First Amendment. Following a highly publicized decision in California's Ninth Circuit, the girl's mother formally intervened in the litigation, stating that she did not object to the recitation of the Pledge in her daughter's classroom and questioning the wisdom of using the young girl to advance her ex-husband's political agenda.

The case also attracted third parties concerned about fundamental issues involving religious autonomy and love of God and country. Groups like the American Civil Liberties Union and the Christian Legal Society submitted legal briefs seeking to help lower federal courts reach the "correct" legal conclusion. The media exacerbated the tension surrounding the dispute by showing interest groups hurling competing sound bites at each other on the nightly news. By the time the nation's highest court announced it would take the case, emotions and expectations were high on both sides.

On June 14, 2004, when the Court released its decision, everyone was waiting with bated breath to see how the justices would come down on the issue. That evening, with decision in hand, television pundits found themselves having to explain that in the case that had been so highly publicized, the Supreme Court said *nothing* about the constitutionality of reciting the Pledge in the nation's public schools. The result was a resounding whimper rather than the anticipated roar by groups whose views would have been vindicated and/or repudiated by a decision on the merits. Legal experts collectively shrugged, while the general public was left somewhat confused by the decision. News organizations scrambled to explain that the Court did not decide the issue because of a legal "technicality." Game over, but stay tuned: a similar case may work its way up to the Supreme Court in the next few years.

What explains this outcome? Why did the Supreme Court shirk its responsibility to settle this highly volatile issue? Why were those in the legal community less surprised than the average citizen who had been paying attention to what was happening? Did the decision really have nothing *at all* to do with what the justices thought about reciting the Pledge in our nation's public schools? All of these are interesting and important questions. They go to the heart of what we, as citizens, expect from our legal system, how much we know about it, and what we are willing to "take on faith," leaving to experts specifically trained in the esoteric norms of legal discourse and decision making.

Explaining *Newdow:* Legal Justifications and Motivational Ambiguity

Simply stated, what was characterized by much of the media as a legal "technicality," represented for the bench and bar an important but familiar issue involving the appropriate use of federal judicial power. Far from being a procedural technicality, the "standing" issue that arose in the case goes to the heart of *how judges think about themselves* and the requirements necessary for them to exercise legitimate authority in our democratic system. It concerns whether the person bringing a particular cause of action is the proper party to litigate the claim. In legal jargon, it involves showing an "injury in fact" that is personal to the plaintiff and not shared by the population at large. The aim is to ensure the adverseness necessary for the proper exercise of judicial authority.

The fact that the issue arose in a case at the center of a national firestorm created public confusion when the Court decided that the non-custodial father was not the appropriate party to litigate his daughter's interests in view of a California court order giving the mother "sole legal custody" of the child. According to the majority in *Newdow*, the father, as a third-party litigant, or "next friend," could not raise the issue of his daughter's rights because it was not at all clear that their interests were consistent. Moreover, the Court could not rule on the important constitutional establishment issue without unduly interfering in domestic relations matters better left to state courts; any ruling regarding the father's individual parental interest would implicate the mother's custodial rights as well. For prudential reasons having to do with the appropriate division of state and federal authority, the Court declined to decide the merits of the case.

The *Newdow* case illustrates an important fact about our legal system—most cases are not simple or clear-cut. Litigation often involves multiple issues implicating competing legal claims. Sometimes the recognition of one legal right will mean that another will go without vindication, and perhaps, as in *Newdow*, without even being considered in an adversarial forum. Judges, with the aid of adversarial arguments presented by skilled litigators, are supposed to use their expert training to navigate this complex terrain. Accepted norms of decision making dictate that they must consider evidence and authority bearing on distinct legal issues independently, and we, as citizens, generally trust that they will do so in an unbiased manner.

But is this always the case? Did the justices' decision to dismiss the father's claim in *Newdow* have nothing *at all* to do with what the justices thought about reciting the Pledge of Allegiance in public schools? Obviously, we can never know for sure. All we have is their seemingly objective analysis of doctrine relating to the standing issue. But one could imagine a number of scenarios where their feelings about the ultimate issue in this high-profile case "shaded" their logic with regard to the preliminary standing question. For instance:

1. A judge sincerely hostile to the plaintiff's claim may have dismissed his cause of action on preliminary standing grounds.
2. Or, somewhat more strategically, a decision maker hostile to the plaintiff's establishment claim—which that judge felt he/she would have to decide in the plaintiff's favor under applicable law—dismissed the case on preliminary standing grounds.
3. Or, not wanting to appear unpopular by ruling against reciting the Pledge, he/she dismissed the case on the preliminary standing issue.

4. Or, not wanting an adverse decision, he/she dismissed the case on preliminary standing grounds based on a calculation of what the entire Court would do on the merits.

Given that the judges voting in the majority in *Newdow* were usually characterized as the more liberal members of the Rehnquist Court, arguably more sympathetic to Mr. Newdow's arguments about separation of church and state, if there was some sort of "interference" going on between feelings about the merits and standing issue in the case, the most likely scenarios would be 3 or 4, or some combination of the two. But all of the above are plausible accounts of how various judicial motives could have influenced the justices' apparently neutral decisions about the preliminary threshold question.

Exploring the Possibility of Motivated Reasoning in Legal Decision Making

Surprisingly, researchers know very little about how alternative issues raised in litigation influence legal decision processes. This is true although judges at all levels of our legal system suggest improper motives regarding how their brethren feel about the "merits" of politically charged cases are often driving threshold judgments[3] that deprive particular litigants of their "day in court."

As the majority decision in *Newdow* illustrates, however, when judges are deciding preliminary threshold issues in litigation, they never *say* they are dismissing claims because of how they feel about particular litigants or alternative issues; instead, they explain their decisions through the neutral analysis of doctrine relating to the threshold question. Moreover, judges become defensive when people accuse them of making threshold decisions on improper attitudinal grounds (Rowland and Carp 1996, 190; Edwards 1998). This sort of response belies the idea that judicial decision makers act strategically with regard to threshold issues. Instead, it suggests that judges themselves *believe* they are making threshold determinations based on their objective analysis of legal authority bearing on the threshold question.

That judges believe they are using legitimate sources of legal reasoning appropriately, however, does not end the inquiry into whether such decisions are entirely objective. Borrowing from cognitive psychology, Segal and Spaeth (1996b, 2002) suggest that judges may engage in "motivated reasoning," a biased decision process where decision makers are predisposed to find authority consistent with their attitudes more convincing than cited authority that goes against desired outcomes. Moreover, psychological research indicates that decision makers may not always be aware of how alternative motives influence their reasoning processes when engaged in the "objective" consideration of evidence (Kunda 1990; Lord, Ross, and Lepper 1979; MacCoun 1998).

The idea that legal decision makers may be subject to motivated biases is especially intriguing. Judges and attorneys are specifically trained to make arguments and decisions using accepted tools of legal reasoning including legal text, intent, and precedent. Indeed, the goal of legal training is to alleviate the role of attitudinal bias by elevating "reason" over "passion," or personal predispositions, in decision making. The legitimacy of judicial authority in our democratic system depends, in no small part, on judges' ability to be neutral third-party arbitrators of disputes between adverse parties. The suggestion that personal biases may impact their decision making, even if unintentionally, raises valid concerns about the fairness of distributive outcomes in our legal system.

Moreover, the idea that biases may enter into decision-making processes notwithstanding the use of decisional norms specifically invoked to attenuate their influence could have broad implications for *other* politically relevant domains where stylized decision rules and expertise are invoked to justify outcomes. Consider, for instance, foreign policy decision making and distributive allocations made by bureaucrats according to "neutral" decision criteria. Political scientists are just starting to investigate the relationship between democratic decision making and conceptions of "appropriate" behavior. Prominent scholars including Stone-Sweet (2002) and Sniderman (2000) have recently called for the incorporation of appropriate conceptions of behavior in models of decision making to investigate how norms and proscriptions influence politically relevant reasoning processes.

Legal decision making provides a rich context to undertake this inquiry. More than sixty years of behavioral research demonstrates a strong connection between judges' preferences and case votes. Put simply, empirical evidence demonstrates that judges tend to vote for outcomes consistent with their policy preferences. Liberal judges disproportionately vote for liberal outcomes in litigation, and conservative judges tend to vote for conservative outcomes. Most of our knowledge of the variables influencing judicial behavior comes from studies where researchers correlate some blunt measure of judicial predilections (like political party, ideology, or party of a judge's appointing president) with how judges vote in particular cases. Although this approach has significantly contributed to our understanding that policy preferences can and do influence judicial voting behavior, it cannot explain *how* such preferences come to bear on judges' decision processes.

Not much has been done to investigate the specific cognitive mechanism(s) by which judges, who say and probably believe they are using objective criteria, disproportionately reach conclusions consistent with their political preferences. This creates a significant puzzle that has been seldom and superficially addressed by behavioral scholars doing work on the courts: *If judges are applying objective rules of legal reasoning to decide cases, how do attitudinal forces exercise such a strong and consistent influence on their outcome choices?*

The failure to account for cognitive processes in the domain of legal decision making is especially problematic because scholars interested in judicial behavior have not resolved the tension between doctrinal and behavioral approaches to understanding legal decision making. Attorneys, judges, and legal academics function largely as interpretivists, conceiving of the law as it is portrayed in statutes and casebooks as a meaningful constraint on judges. Many judges and legal academics do not accept findings from behavioral studies or attitudinal theories of decision making (e.g., Edwards 1998). They act as if, and as if they believe, the law matters.

In contrast, political scientists who study the courts act more like critical theorists. Armed with evidence from research on judicial voting patterns, they argue that attitudes and policy preferences are at the root of judges' decision making. If legally trained academics, judges, and practitioners actually believe the law matters, they are woefully misguided about what really drives judges' decisional behavior.

As with most interesting questions, the answer to what influences legal decision-making behavior probably lies somewhere between these two extremes. In this book, I argue that in order to advance our knowledge, we need to move beyond the false "law/not law" dichotomy (Frank 1931a) toward a more complex understanding of how attitudes and legal factors *interact* to shape legal decision processes. Indeed, the time is ripe for such an argument. Today, the debates that exist between scholars in law and social science are largely about the degree and nature of attitudinal influence in judges' decisions, not the fact of such influence. We have finally reached a point in our knowledge where the vast majority of legal scholars and political scientists would agree that decisions are not determined by "wholly legal" or "wholly attitudinal" factors. But we need to move beyond this "all or nothing" distinction in our hypothesis testing as well as our rhetoric.

Here I argue that motivated reasoning is the best explanation we have to reconcile judges' affirmations that they are using objective legal criteria with strong and consistent findings of attitudinal influence in their decision making. Moreover, this psychological paradigm provides the most promising avenue for future research, allowing empirical scholars to test theoretically grounded hypotheses about the nature and extent of attitudinal influence in legal decision-making environments.

PLAN OF ANALYSIS

In making my case for using motivated reasoning to understand legal decision processes, I evaluate the claim that judicial actors may be subject to motivated biases in light of their specialized training and institutional surroundings. I argue that a more detailed understanding of the *specific role* that attitudes play in legal reasoning is necessary in light of psychological research on motivation in other decision contexts.

I present a theory of motivated reasoning that posits that the influence of attitudes in legal decision processes is real—but not without boundaries. I challenge the dominant assumption in social science literature that judges are primarily motivated by policy. In line with Baum's (1997) conception of mixed goals in judicial decision making, I offer an alternative characterization of motives based on the idea that those who are trained in the legal tradition come to internalize legal norms and "accuracy" goals consistent with idealized notions of decision making. The theory allows for the possibility, however, that "directional" (policy) goals may influence legal reasoning processes. Significantly, I suggest that objective case facts and norms of appropriate behavior can serve as a constraint on the ability of accuracy-seeking decision makers to reach directional conclusions consistent with their personal preferences.

To illustrate my conception of attitudinal influence, I show how norm-appropriate mechanisms of influence may operate in real-world cases by discussing a line of recent Supreme Court cases involving congressional commerce authority. I then test these intuitions using primary data from experiments with undergraduates and law students. My goal is to discover *how motivated reasoning occurs in legal decision making,* as well as to test the *limits* on biased decision processes.

Specifically, in the empirical chapters of this book, I test the two proposed mechanisms of influence: analogical perception and the separability of preferences in complex cases involving multiple issues. Drawing on theories of analogical reasoning from cognitive psychology, I investigate how case facts and policy preferences interact to influence perceptions of precedent. Using an experimental design, I compare how lay citizens and subjects with legal training make judgments about the similarity of case law cited as precedent in relation to a specific target dispute.

I also investigate the "*Newdow* scenario" in more detail. I test whether the policy preferences of legally trained decision makers affect how they decide preliminary threshold issues in complex cases. Here I draw on literature concerning separable preferences, conceiving of judicial reasoning as a nested decision process. The goal is to see if there are differences in the way legally trained individuals decide a threshold question depending upon how they feel about more divisive policy matters raised in a complex fact pattern.

Consistent with my theory, I find each hypothesized mechanism is a potential avenue of attitudinal influence in legal decision making. But there is also significant evidence of *constraint* in each study, demonstrating specific factors that can limit attitudinal biases in legal reasoning processes.

CHAPTER OVERVIEW

In chapter 1, I conduct a directed review of the literature demonstrating the importance of policy preferences in judicial decision making. I describe how theory and methods from psychology's behaviorist paradigm have influenced public law research so that our knowledge of the factors affecting legal reasoning has been shaped by a focus on judicial voting behavior. I discuss why judicial scholars never made the leap from behavioral to cognitive approaches for understanding decision making and describe my theory of motivated reasoning, detailing the basic assumptions underlying this conception of attitudinal influence.

Chapter 2 is a doctrinal analysis of recent Supreme Court cases on congressional commerce authority. In it, I discuss why existing models of sincere and strategic attitudinal influence provide inadequate accounts of decisional behavior. I argue that motivated reasoning explanations have significant potential to fill gaps in our understanding of judicial behavior. Using doctrinal evidence from this line of Supreme Court cases, I demonstrate how each of the mechanisms that I test in this volume can operate in real-world cases with important policy implications.

Chapter 3 is devoted to the investigation of the first hypothesized mechanism of motivated reasoning, analogical perception. I present a model of perception that accounts for the influence of legal *and* attitudinal factors in judgments of case similarity. Using an experimental design, I compare how lay undergraduates and subjects with legal training make judgments about the similarity of case law cited as precedent in relation to a specific target dispute. I test the hypothesis that decision makers will judge cases with outcomes that support their preferences as more similar to pending litigation than cases that do not support those preferences. I present a model in which the role of policy preferences in shaping perceptions is greatest in a "middle range" of cases that are neither very similar to, nor very different from, disputes that decision makers are currently considering.

In chapters 4 and 5, I investigate the second hypothesized mechanism of motivated reasoning, separable preferences. In chapter 4, I discuss the design of an experiment done exclusively with legally trained participants. The experiment is unique because it involves giving law students a realistic brief where case facts and legal arguments are controlled. The goal is to see how people with alternative preferences respond to identical legal arguments and authority in different decision contexts. By premeasuring participants' attitudes about a number of policy issues raised in a complex fact pattern, I discover not only *whether* preferences make a difference in the seemingly neutral judgment participants are asked to make, but also *which preferences matter* from a number of possible alternatives.

I conduct a content analysis of the legal justifications law student participants gave for their decisions in the experiment testing separable preferences in chapter 5. Specifically, I analyze closed- and open-ended questions about what facts and legal authority led law students to their decisions. In doing so, I take advantage of the control afforded by the experimental design to see what arguments were cited by people reaching alternative conclusions in support of their judgments.

I conclude in chapter 6 with a discussion of findings and what they suggest for future research. I argue that motivated reasoning represents an important empirical framework that scholars from multiple disciplines can use to investigate legal reasoning process. I suggest ways researchers can investigate motivated decision phenomena outside the laboratory using techniques that political scientists and legal scholars may be more familiar with. I argue that the approach has great potential to improve our understandings of the precise role of attitudes in legal behavior. Also, motivated reasoning explanations comport with decision makers' subjective experience better than do extant theories of attitudinal influence.

These benefits seem well worth pursuing; indeed, it is hard to understand how we have gone without a cognitive framework for understanding attitudinal influence in legal decision making for so long. This book attempts to fill that gap. I hope readers will proceed critically, but with an open mind.

The Case for Investigating Motivated Reasoning in Legal Decision Making

1

OUTLINING A THEORY OF MOTIVATED COGNITION IN LEGAL DECISION MAKING

Judges play a special role in our constitutional system. Federal judges, and many state judges, are not elected but appointed by other political actors. Judges do not have the same democratic authority as elected officials to act in accordance with their personal preferences. Neutrality is vital if judges' decisions are to be accepted and their distributive allocations are to be enforced with the authority of the state. This raises a critical dilemma because judges are, after all, human (Frank 1931a, 1931b). They are bound to have personal preferences, shaped by their ideology, attitudes, and experience, with respect to cases they are asked to decide.

The dilemma is addressed with reference to the unique knowledge judges acquire through their specialized training. We abide their substantial influence in our democratic system because of the *expertise* judges possess as interpreters of the law. On this view, judges are not free to decide cases according to their personal views because they are constrained by appropriate sources of legal reasoning and cannons of interpretation. Technical training in the tools of legal analysis enable judges to separate reason from personal biases in their deliberations, and it is the predominance of reason that endows judge-made law with legitimacy in our constitutional system.

Notwithstanding the extensive training they experience, there is substantial evidence that the policy preferences of judicial decision makers affect case outcomes. More than a half century of empirical research tells us that judges tend to decide cases in ways that are consistent with their policy predispositions. Indeed, the main thrust of much empirical research on decision making has been to demonstrate the substantial disconnect between what judges do (represented by case votes) and the objective criteria that judges say guides their decisional behavior. To make this point, political scientists researching the courts have borrowed extensively from theory and methods in a sister discipline, psychology.

The Psychological Tradition in Studies of Judicial Behavior

C. Herman Pritchett's 1948 investigation of justices on the Roosevelt Court represents the watershed study prompting judicial scholars to look at personal preferences as a major determinant of judges' voting behavior. The study is often cited as starting a "second generation" of research in political science, signaling a break between "judicial behavioralists" and those who studied legal decision making using more traditional, doctrinal, techniques (Shapiro 1993; Gibson 1991; Slotnick 1991).

Pritchett analyzed voting behavior of justices on the Court from 1937 to 1947. Classifying cases as involving "labor" or "free speech," he demonstrated that the justices could be systematically ordered in terms of their support for liberal outcomes in cases that were the subject of his investigation. The study was groundbreaking because it was first to analyze judicial voting behavior rather than explanations the justices authored themselves. It was also the first to explicitly link observed voting patterns to the ideology of the justices.

When it was published, Pritchett's study met with considerable criticism due to the challenge its findings posed to traditional portrayals of Supreme Court decision making. The most serious criticism came from legal scholars who argued that his approach was inadequate to capture the nuances of judicial reasoning. Legally trained scholars argued that merely looking at the way the justices voted, without considering the justification for their decisions, was not adequate to understand the complex process of case-by-case decision making. Early critiques emphasized the fact that legal reasoning is highly contextual—dependent on the facts and issues raised in particular cases. Critics also pointed out that judges on collegial courts often differ in their assessment of what authority should control legal analyses in cases involving multiple issues, rendering Pritchett's single-issue classification scheme too simplistic to capture the complexity of real-world decision making (Mendelson 1963; Tanenhaus 1966).

Despite these concerns, numerous scholars followed Pritchett's lead. There was a distinct rise in the number of behavioral studies of judicial decision making over the next two decades. This trend toward "behavioralism" was influenced by, but distinct from, the "behaviorist" movement that occurred in psychology (McGraw 2000). As part of this trend, researchers in political science continued to move away from legal doctrine, choosing to analyze case votes as the primary observable *response* to different classes of case *stimuli*.

This movement away from doctrine was partly strategic; it allowed judges' behavior to be analyzed across cases by focusing on the outcome choice common to all decisions. More significantly, it reflected a fundamental change in approach where case votes were viewed as a more accurate indication of judicial proclivities than the doctrinal justifications judges gave for their own decisions (Schubert 1962). Many judicial scholars came to view opinions written by judges as an imperfect account of decision making (Pritchett 1941; Spaeth 1961). They argued that the reasons decision makers gave for their outcome choices were subject to manipulation by judges concerned with self-presentation.

As political science broke away from doctrinal approaches to studying decision making, investigators increasingly relied on theory and methods from psychology. The first generation of behavioral studies focused on patterns of dissent and interagreement between justices on the Supreme Court. Findings from these studies showed that particular groups of justices voted together in cases, while others tended to vote in opposition. Judicial scholars explained the existence of identifiable "voting blocs" using extralegal factors. They argued analyses of case votes did not generate the type of random variation one would expect if the justices were engaged in unbiased application of their common legal training. Instead, observed patterns were taken as evidence of attitudinal decision making where like-minded justices voted in concert.[1]

Starting in the 1960s, researchers used "scaling" techniques explicitly developed in psychology to conduct more intricate analyses of judicial voting behavior. Originally attitudinal scales were developed as a series of questions in testing instruments to measure constructs like racial tolerance across survey respondents. One famous scale measured the degree of social interaction survey respondents were willing to accept between members of different races. Questions that described various levels of contact between people with distinct racial backgrounds were grouped together and ordered for analysis.[2] Typically, survey respondents manifested a "breakpoint"; as the behavior in questions became more intimate, responses would shift from "acceptant" to "not acceptant" of the interracial contact questions described. Different respondents manifested unique breakpoints. Individuals who demonstrated a willingness to accept a greater number of increasingly close interactions were categorized as having higher levels of racial tolerance (Bem 1972).

In studies of judicial behavior, researchers analyzed case votes rather than responses to survey questions, but the underlying logic was the same. According to this approach, cases involving different underlying issues represented distinct classes of stimuli. Similar cases could be grouped together and scaled like the questions on psychological testing instruments. Scaling studies demonstrated Supreme Court justices, like participants in psychological survey research, manifested unique breakpoints with regard to scaled cases involving similar legal issues.[3]

Schubert (1962) formalized the first attitudinal theory of judicial behavior to explain such findings. Explicitly borrowing from psychology, he posited that case outcomes were determined by where in an attitudinal "issue space" a dispute fell in relation to the justices' preferences. Later Murphy (1964) offered an explanation incorporating the concept of goal-directed behavior, suggesting that judges act strategically to obtain desired outcomes. Rohde and Spaeth (1976) took this idea further, adding the controversial insight that policy goals trump legal considerations in judges' decision making.

To date, Segal and Spaeth's "attitudinal model" (1993, 2002) is the most comprehensive statement of the role policy preferences play in judicial decision making. Their model builds on earlier theoretical works and adds substantially to them by offering a detailed account of how it is that judges are free to make decisions consistent with their preferences, in direct contrast to the role they are expected to play in our constitutional system.

Explicitly invoking stimulus/response (S-R) principles from behaviorist psychology, Segal and Spaeth argue that judicial voting behavior is driven by judges' attitudinal responses to differential case stimuli (1993, 215). Judges' choices are determined by their policy preferences concerning the issues raised in litigation. They argue that Supreme Court justices are free to act in accordance with their preferences because they are appointed for life and, therefore, they are not democratically accountable for their decisions.[4] In making this argument, Segal and Spaeth turn democratic theory on its head. They argue that the measures the Framers took to insulate judicial actors from politics so they could make decisions based on their expert interpretation of the law have the exact opposite effect, freeing judges to make decisions consistent with their political preferences.

According to these authors, the law does not constrain judicial actors in any meaningful way. Instead, the adversarial nature of our legal system facilitates policy-directed behavior because it allows judges to pick and choose authority from arguments made by competing parties. Thus, judges do not use legal authority to reason through cases; the law serves as a post hoc justification for choices consistent with their political policy preferences.

Like Pritchett's research, Segal and Spaeth's account of judicial decision making has met with resistance from some legal scholars (Kahn 1994; Cross 1997). For many political scientists, however, Segal and Spaeth's attitudinal model, and the substantial evidence they have amassed to support it, represents the culmination of fifty years of behavioral research on the role of attitudinal forces in legal decision making.

Current Trends and Lingering Questions

The role of policy preferences having been firmly established, political science seems to have moved on to a "third generation" of research (Shapiro 1993). Scholars who study the courts have been influenced by the trend that is occurring in political science more broadly. They are increasingly turning to game theory and utility maximization models to explain judges' behavior. As a result, current research is influenced more by economic theory than psychology (Epstein and Knight 2000; Bonneau and Hammond 2005).

Today most political scientists take for granted that attitudinal considerations predominate in judges' decisions. Investigating the law as a constraint on decision making has taken a back seat to looking at how other institutions shape judges' behavior. Rather than seeking to establish that personal preferences influence voting behavior, per se, judicial scholars are interested in understanding how forces like decision rules (Hall and Brace 1989), the preferences of other judges (Epstein and Knight 1998) or actors in other democratic branches (Spiller and Gely 1992) moderate the expression of judges' policy goals in decision making.

This shift toward explaining judicial behavior with rational choice models leaves a significant question scholars have not yet addressed, or, more accurately, have "skipped over" in the rush to assess the influence of institutional forces on judicial behavior: If judges say (and believe) they are using objective tools of legal analysis to decide cases, how is it that policy preferences exercise such a strong and consistent influence on their outcome choices?

Specifically, scholars who study judicial behavior have treated the process of legal reasoning like a "black box," remaining content with demonstrating a connection between attitudes and case votes without fully understanding the mental processes that underlie the relationship. The "black box" metaphor is borrowed from cognitive psychologists, who argued that their own discipline should move beyond the S-R paradigm to achieve a richer understanding of the mental processes underlying observed patterns of behavior. Starting in the 1950s, psychologists began to do just that, resulting in what is referred to as the "cognitive revolution" in psychology. Research on judicial behavior, however, never moved beyond the S-R paradigm. Instead, scholars continued to focus on judicial votes as the primary response to differential case stimuli without delving further into how judges arrive at those responses in the process of complex decision making.

In an especially thoughtful assessment of the contributions and limits of the behavioral paradigm, Rowland and Carp (1996) lament the failure of judicial scholars to make the leap from behavioral to cognitive approaches to understanding decision making: "Given the obvious implications of psychology's cognitive perspective for judicial decision making, one could have anticipated an explosion of inquiry that paralleled the parent discipline's more general inquiry into social cognition. . . . Unfortunately, however, the anticipated inclusion of cognitive processes into the attitudinal model never took hold in political science" (144).

There are several reasons judicial scholars did not make the transition from behavioral to cognitive approaches. First, investigating mental processes requires researchers to "get inside the heads" of individuals they are interested in studying. Judges, as elite decision makers, pose a knotty problem of access. Moreover, they are notoriously secretive about how they go about reaching decisions. Finally, strong norms discouraging judges from divulging policy views and rendering decisions in hypothetical cases make it highly unlikely that they would be willing participants in the kind of experimental studies widely utilized in cognitive psychology.[5]

To overcome similar obstacles, psychologists and political scientists have used content analysis techniques to investigate the reasoning processes of other elites studied at a distance.[6] Because judicial scholars remain highly skeptical of the doctrinal explanations judges give for their own decisions, however, few have engaged in the rigorous content analysis of case opinions.[7]

Finally, at precisely the time one might have expected scholars to delve deeper into decision-making processes, rational choice models took hold in the discipline (Shapiro 1993; Slotnick 1991). The assumption that judges were single-minded seekers of policy was calcified because it was convenient for scholars applying game theoretic models to judicial behavior. Consequently, the question of how judges arrived at those decisions seems to have been glossed over.

Taking Norms Seriously: A Theory of Motivated Reasoning in Legal Decision Making

One problem with much of the research on judicial behavior is that it fails to take seriously the idea that judges sincerely believe they are using appropriate legal criteria to reach decisions. Many behavioral scholars have assumed, from overwhelming evidence of attitudinal influence, that policy preferences are driving decision processes. They have failed to consider the possibility that such findings could be a reflection of the fact that there are many ways attitudes can influence legal reasoning as decision makers try to use legal criteria to achieve norm-appropriate ends.

Rowland and Carp argue, "if the study of political jurisprudence is to move beyond its current comfort zone, we must develop a theory of judicial behavior that can accommodate political and jurisprudential influences without assuming away the judicial reasoning process" (1996, 136). The time has come to get a more sophisticated understanding of how judges reach decisions that are consistent with their preferences in the context of using legal criteria they see as central to the appropriate exercise of their own authority. Toward this end, I suggest a different approach to studying attitudinal influence in legal reasoning. The goal is to see how attitudes affect the cognitive processes of decision makers as they make choices within the confines of accepted decisional rules. This book differs from others in that the main focus of the inquiry in on *legal decision making.* Although many of the intuitions guiding my hypotheses come from findings about judges, I am less interested in judicial behavior, per se, than in exploring how people *think* in the context of complex norms.

Borrowing Segal and Spaeth's intuition, I test the idea that individuals may engage in motivated reasoning when thinking about legal authority. Starting with the premise that decision makers believe they are employing appropriate tools of legal reasoning, I investigate how decision makers with different views make legal judgments given identical case information. I use experimental methods to investigate how policy preferences interact with case characteristics and the norms of legal decision making. The goal is to gain a more sophisticated understanding of the possible mechanisms for motivated reasoning and to discover their limiting conditions.

This conception of influence falls squarely on the "sincere" side of the debate about whether decision makers are sincere or strategic pursuers of policy outcomes. It has two main components that distinguish it from other theories of attitudinal influence. First, I posit that because legal decision makers have been subject to strong socialization emphasizing the importance of stylized rules of legal reasoning, they sincerely believe they are utilizing appropriate norms of legal analysis when making judgments. Indeed, their primary goal in making these decisions is to achieve "legal accuracy" within the confines of accepted decisional norms. Second, I allow for the influence of sincere preferences, positing that "directional" (policy) goals can influence legal reasoning processes in subtle ways such that decision makers themselves may be unaware of their influence. Consistent with evidence from psychology demonstrating limits on motivated decision processes, I propose that the law can inhibit attitudinal behavior where it prevents decision makers from constructing "reasonable justifications" for their attitudinally preferred outcome choices (Segal and Spaeth 1996b, 1075, quoting Kunda 1990).

To be clear, my approach to understanding legal decision making represents both an expansion *and* a significant departure from Segal and Spaeth's psychological account of legal behavior. Motivated reasoning is by no means central to Segal and Spaeth's theory of decision making. In fact, they do not mention motivated reasoning in their initial book on the attitudinal model (1993). It is first mentioned in a symposium where they pit the model against more traditional modes of decision making (Segal and Spaeth 1996a, 1996b).

Moreover, when they do introduce the concept, they do not fully commit to the idea. True to the vagueness about intentionality that has characterized attitudinal theories of decision making, they write: "we must never underestimate the ability of humans to engage in motivated reasoning. For all we know the justices actually believe that they resolve disputes by appropriate modes of legal analysis" (1996b, 1075). In subsequent work, they specifically state: "the attitudinal position on motivated reasoning is one of *agnosticism.* What matters is that the justices' ideology directly influences their decisions. Whether they do so with self-awareness . . . doesn't matter" (Segal and Spaeth 2002, 433, emphasis added). Despite their rather tepid treatment of the concept, Segal and Spaeth consistently mention motivated reasoning in work describing their model (1996b, 1999, 2002). Moreover, other judicial scholars have similarly invoked the concept of motivated cognition in accounts of judicial decision making (Rowland and Carp 1996; Baum 1997).

Far from treating this rich psychological paradigm as an afterthought, footnote, or post hoc explanation for observed patterns of behavior, I assign motivated reasoning a *central role* in my conception of how we should think about legal decision-making behavior. In exploring the cognitive mechanisms of attitudinal influence, I seek not just to describe, but to explain how decision makers may "get to" outcomes consistent with their policy preferences in the context of accepted norms. In doing so, I intentionally point out problems, gaps, and inconsistencies in existing accounts of attitudinal influence. Chief among these is that fact that extant strategic and attitudinal approaches have not been able to reconcile the subjective experience of legal decision makers with empirical evidence that tends to cast doubt on the justifications they give for their decisions.

Although attorneys and judges explicitly communicate in the language of law and decisional constraint, dominant accounts of attitudinal influence presume policy motivations are the primary determinant of judicial behavior. Existing attitudinal models are, at best, equivocal about whether judges act intentionally to secure desired outcomes. Perhaps worse, strategic accounts necessarily impute purposeful behavior on the part of judicial actors trying to achieve desired political outcomes; judges cannot act strategically to achieve policy goals without some self-awareness about what they are doing. Such accounts put little or no credence in the doctrinal explanations judges provide for their own decision making.

Motivated reasoning provides the key theoretical and empirical framework to bridge the significant gap that has developed between legal and attitudinal accounts of decision making. One clear advantage of the approach is its ability to answer questions about legal decision making *on its own terms* without assuming legal decision makers intentionally pursue what are, from a traditional lawmaking perspective, improper policy goals. As set forth further in the next section, the motivated reasoning account provides an explanation of attitudinal influence that is much more consistent with the realities of how practitioners construct, consider, and explain legal arguments and outcomes.

While some judicial scholars may think this is unnecessary, or that the discipline has "moved beyond" the need to do this, I argue that for political psychologists and cognitive scholars interested in the *process* of decision making, this is a puzzle well worth investigating. Moreover, legal scholars and practitioners who have so much invested in the legitimizing force of legal norms and expertise cannot be content with accounts of decision making that are, by their own terms, "agnostic" about whether judges intentionally flout accepted rules of decision making to reach political ends.

As Judge Harry T. Edwards writes, "serious scholars seeking to analyze the work of courts cannot simply ignore the internal experiences of judges as irrelevant or disingenuously expressed" (1998, 1338). Motivated reasoning allows for the influence of alternative goals in legal decision processes. Researchers do not have to assume that judges are exclusively seeking accuracy or that they are purely motivated by policy. The framework accommodates the distinct possibility that decisions are a result of a complex interaction between decision makers' conscious desire to "get things right" and their unconscious policy motivations. It provides a way for scholars to consider doctrinal accounts without having to take decision makers at their word *or* accuse them of being disingenuous.

Finally, motivated decision processes have been studied by psychologists for many years. Therefore, we have a rich field of knowledge from which to draw theoretical insights. Most importantly, these insights can be empirically tested. Instead of using motivated reasoning as an *ex post* account of observed outcomes, I argue scholars should adopt the motivated reasoning perspective *ex ante* in developing hypotheses about when and how policy attitudes are likely to influence legal decision processes. In this regard, the paradigm can lead to new testable questions stemming from insights that are firmly grounded in theory.

In this book I employ experiments, but using motivated reasoning as an empirical framework does not mean judicial scholars have to limit themselves to the laboratory or decision makers at the earliest stages of their legal training. I am confident that researchers concerned about the sacrifice in external validity experimental methods entail can think of creative ways to test hypotheses related to motivated decision processes with alternative methods and available decisional data in future research.

When using this framework, however, researchers will need to be more explicit about the mixture of conscious and unconscious goals in the minds of decision makers. They will need to acknowledge that pursuing some goals may interfere with the realization of others. Viewed in this light, following accepted norms of decision making in pursuit of "good law" may constrain decision makers' ability to make preference-oriented decisions. Alternatively, the predominance of directional policy goals can prevent decision makers from making legal judgments that are wholly objective if they are motivated to distinguish controlling legal authority and have the latitude to do so.

In the pages that follow, I flesh out the main aspects of the theory in more detail. I differentiate the motivated reasoning approach from other conceptions of attitudinal influence and argue that it is an empirical and theoretical framework worth adapting in our studies of legal decision-making behavior.

JUDGES SINCERELY USE APPROPRIATE NORMS IN DECISION MAKING

Over the years, behavioral scholars have been incredibly vague about whether judges are acting with volition or whether they are unwittingly influenced by their preferences. This may stem from a reluctance to argue that policy-directed decision making is intentional. Despite substantial evidence of attitudinal influence, accusations that judges are purposefully engaged in policy-oriented decision making seems to exceed the bounds of what existing evidence can reasonably support.

Within the confines of legal reasoning, there is plenty of room for biased perceptions and interpretation. Given the exact same facts and legal authority, different judges can, and often do, reach different conclusions. Gillman (2001) argues that rather than assuming that bare preferences drive findings of policy-oriented decision making, scholars should take seriously the idea that "ideologically influenced legal considerations" operate in judges' decisions (490). As he points out, the difference between the approaches is not "merely semantic." Gillman's conception of ideological influence acknowledges that judges use legal criteria in reaching and rendering decisions; the conclusion that many behavioral scholars draw from findings of directed behavior is that they do not (Spaeth 1963; Segal and Spaeth 1993, 2002).

At every level of our legal system, participants act *as if* the law matters. Lawyers fashion arguments in legal terms; judges invoke doctrinal explanations for their decisions; law reviews publish extensive analyses of individual cases and lines of authority assessing implications for future litigation. To suggest that judges intentionally disregard the law when making decisions would imply that all, or a significant subset, of the participants in the legal community are involved in a grand conspiracy to deceive the American people about the "true" nature of decision making. Moreover, if we were to take this idea seriously, it would mean admitting that the conspiracy has been largely successful, lasting more than two hundred years without significant defection or the lines of communication ever being discovered.

Moreover, there is every indication that judges *believe* they are reaching decisions through the objective application of legal doctrine. Evidence from behavioral studies shows that judges think they are using the law to reason through cases. Content analyses of legal briefs and judicial conference notes demonstrate that judges and attorneys speak about cases predominantly in legal terms (Spriggs and Wahlbeck 1997; Provine 1980; Knight and Epstein 1996; Epstein and Knight 1998). Studies based on judicial speeches (James 1968) and interviews (Gibson 1978; Rowland and Carp 1996) suggest that judges have a conception of the proper judicial role they play in our democratic system. Within this conception, individual judges may disagree about the extent to which courts should be involved in reviewing the acts of elected branches, or the desirability of relying on alternative sources of decision making such as legislative intent or precedent. But, one thing common to this conception is the belief that *judicial decisions must be based on the law;* judges sincerely believe that to the extent they stray from accepted sources of legal decision making, they exceed their authority in our democratic system.

Consistent with this characterization of their own authority, judges become defensive when scholars suggest that personal preferences drive decisions. Indeed, accusations of preference-driven behavior appear to be taken as a personal affront by judicial decision makers (F. Johnson 1976; Edwards 1998). The consistency and fervor with which judges assert their adherence to the law shows that they not only believe, but have *internalized* appropriate norms of decision making. The reason challenges to legal notions of decision making are taken so personally is because these deeply held beliefs dictate the standard to which judges hold themselves and each other accountable. Rowland and Carp (1996) report that district court judges were "indignant" in personal interviews when faced with the slightest suggestion that attitudes drive decision making (190). These strong reactions give additional weight to the idea that legally trained scholars believe judicial decisions should be grounded in appropriate sources of legal reasoning.

Epstein and Knight (1998) characterize representations that judges rely on the law made by judges themselves as inconclusive because judicial actors may be posturing, or trying to appear like they are using legal sources of decision making for the benefit of external audiences. Ironically, however, these authors provide some of the strongest evidence that judges internalize appropriate norms of decision making. Looking at the conference notes of Supreme Court justices, they discover that in the Court's private conferences the justices spend a substantial amount time arguing about the relevance of precedent (Knight and Epstein 1996; Epstein and Knight 1998). This behavior, which occurs exclusively among the justices, cannot be explained by the need to account to external audiences. Instead, it suggests the justices are speaking and thinking in legal terms because that is how they believe judges should decide cases. This is not too surprising as the justices, after all, are subject to the training and socialization common to all legal practitioners.

Socialization and Internalization

Traditional notions of legal decision making are rooted in two distinct but related concepts: first, the idea that judges, as third-party arbiters, must be *impartial;* and second, the notion that, as unelected officials, they have *limited authority* to decide disputes based primarily on their expertise. These ideas combine to form an often caricatured picture of judges using expert knowledge to discern what the law requires in particular cases. The prototype is often referred to as "legal formalism"; some use the more pejorative term "mechanical jurisprudence."

Legal formalism, in its strictest sense, is hard to defend but essential to understand for decision-making behavior. Few believe judges can perfectly separate their personal preferences from their reasoning processes, yet the "impartial judge" remains the ideal-type on which legal training is based and conceptions of appropriate behavior are grounded. Strong socialization inherent in the education and professional development of attorneys cause those in the profession to accept and internalize norms consistent with this idealized model of decision making. This has important implications for how those trained in this tradition think about the tasks they perform in our legal system. Thus, it is essential for those who study decision making to take these norms into account when considering the specific role preferences play in legal reasoning.

Those in the legal community take seriously the idea that the legitimacy of the judiciary is different from that of other government actors. To the extent that judges stray from accepted sources of decision making, they exceed their authority in our constitutional system. This basic assumption underlies all legal training. Because judges are constrained by text, intent, and precedent, those who want to join the legal profession must learn the appropriate rules of legal argument and analysis.

All citizens understand from an early age that judges should act impartially. Since they are referees between parties, their decisions should be guided by their reasoned interpretation of the law rather than personal feelings about particular issues or litigants. Those who choose to enter the legal profession not only understand this basic principle, they probably see some beauty in it. Thus, there is a *self-selection* process where people who are positively predisposed toward this notion of judicial authority start down the road to law school.[8]

Once they arrive, much of the training and early socialization that legally educated individuals experience is specifically aimed at *reducing* the role of personal attitudes in thinking about cases. Law school is not merely professionalization; it is a *resocialization* process where students' old ways of thinking are extinguished and replaced with reference to legally appropriate arguments and considerations.[9] The goal is to change the way students think about disputes between adverse parties. Students come to understand that the substance of legal argument is fundamentally different from other types of argumentation. It never involves a naked plea to a judge's sympathy or ideology; instead legal argument references relevant facts and controlling authority. Students learn the appropriate sources of legal decision making. They study how judges reason from case to case and develop lines of authority.

At the very earliest stages of this training, special attention is given to the fact that judges are constrained, not only by the law, but by the special roles they play in our constitutional system. Students learn that not all disputes meet the requirements for the exercise of judicial authority. The first week of Civil Procedure focuses on jurisdiction, limits on authority over particular persons or subject matters. First-year Constitutional Law covers justiciability concerns, grounded in the notion that disputes must meet specific criteria in order to be appropriate for judges to decide.

Students are steeped in conceptions of judicial restraint and deference to the popularly elected branches. They learn that judicial decisions should be narrowly tailored to the facts giving rise to a particular dispute so that judges do not exceed their authority by addressing more than absolutely necessary to resolve particular matters. Students also learn that there is a specific hierarchy of grounds that judges must consider when rendering decisions—commonly referred to as the *Ashwander* rules—so their rulings cause the least possible disruption to existing governmental forms. For instance, judges must not "reach," or address, constitutional issues unless it is absolutely necessary to decide a dispute. If there is a way to settle a matter by interpreting a statute written by some legislative body, judges must prefer those grounds to constitutional grounds in reaching their decision. This is because it is easier to revisit statutory interpretations than constitutional decisions in our democratic system.

All of these concepts are covered early in the legal socialization process, typically in the first semester of students' first year in law school. Over and above the primacy effect such early lessons are likely to have in shaping views of the judicial role, students are taught that issues related to judicial authority are *overarching* concerns that judges should consider in every dispute they are asked to decide. Unlike more narrow concepts that may be useful in specific legal domains, like contracts or criminal law, jurisdiction and justiciability issues are *always* relevant when parties seek the judicial resolution of disputes.

Concepts related to judicial authority are not only considered as an academic exercise in the first year of law school. Practitioners routinely use arguments related to jurisdiction and justiciability to argue on behalf of their client's interests. There are court rules, like Rule 8 of the *Federal Rules of Civil Procedure,* which require a party bringing a dispute to specifically state the grounds for jurisdiction in his or her complaint, thus, giving opposing parties the opportunity to challenge the purported grounds in their answers.

Thus, concerns about the appropriate exercise of judicial authority *start early* and *continue* throughout one's legal career. At first, learning the concepts and incorporating them into one's thinking may be necessary to get through a particular course in law school—later, they become instrumental as a tool practitioners can use on behalf of clients. From a psychological standpoint, the routine use and consideration of arguments related to the appropriateness of judicial authority is significant because such conduct has the potential to shape beliefs about judicial roles. Much of the work on attitudes that is done in political science explores how attitudes shape behavior. Psychologists who study attitudes, however, have discovered the directional arrow often goes in the opposite direction (McGuire 1985); that is, routinely making arguments about appropriate judicial behavior has the potential to shape what students, practitioners, and judges themselves believe about those roles.

Finally, the concept of "sunk costs" (Arkes and Blumer 2000) should not be underestimated in shaping practitioners' views of appropriate legal behavior. Learning the tools of legal reasoning involves a significant investment in doctrinal conceptions of decision making. Law students spend a good deal of time, money, and effort learning the appropriate modes of interpretation. Few who have been trained in the legal tradition would be willing to admit, even to themselves, that their substantial investment was wasted because the law does not matter in how judges reach decisions. More likely, the time and effort expended causes them to believe that legal norms actually matter in how judges reach and render decisions (see Stone-Sweet 2002 for a similar argument).

For all of these reasons, individuals in the legal community not only act as if the law matters, they sincerely believe it does. The socialization that starts in law school and continues throughout one's legal career causes those who are trained in this tradition to accept and internalize appropriate norms of decision making. These norms, in turn, become the standard to which judges and other practitioners hold themselves and each other accountable.

Implications for Studies of Decision Making

The most significant implication of this process for research on legal decision making is that it renders one of the assumptions behind existing studies subject to significant question: the idea that judges are primarily pursuing policy goals (Rohde and Spaeth 1976; Segal and Spaeth 1993; Epstein and Knight 1998). Put simply, this characterization of judicial motives is wholly at odds with how judges view themselves. It is not only inconsistent with traditional notions of what is appropriate in an adversarial context, but also directly contrary to conceptions of what unelected judges should be doing in our democratic system.

Baum's (1997) characterization of judges striving to achieve "good law" is more consistent with the processes outlined above. According to this view, strong socialization emphasizing formal notions of decision making instills the desire to make accurate legal judgments as a chronic goal in the minds of those trained in the tradition. Professional experience reinforces this idea as attorneys make predominantly legal arguments to judges. By the time decision makers reach the bench, conceptions of appropriate decisional behavior are well entrenched. Although other goals may be present in the way judges render decisions, the desire to make sound legal decisions is foremost in their awareness. It shapes the types of arguments judicial actors are willing to entertain and utilize in their decisions.

Posner (1995) presents a more pragmatic argument about why professional socialization leads judges to follow accepted norms. He argues that there is a purely consumptive value for judges voting in cases. According to Posner, this value is much like the value individual citizens derive from voting in elections, although the chances that they can influence outcomes are infinitesimally small.[10] He argues that judges are motivated to protect this value, which is based, in part, on their ability to call on their legal expertise when presiding over cases. According to Posner, judges take pleasure in the fact that professional norms differentiate them from ordinary individuals and other governmental decision makers:

> The pleasure of judging is bound-up with compliance with certain self-limiting rules that define the "game" of judging. . . . [I]t is by doing such things that you know you are playing the judge role, not some other role. . . . The judicial game has rules that lawyers learn in law school and then in practice or teaching. Both self-selection and the careful screening of federal judicial candidates help to ensure that most lawyers who become federal judges will be lawyers who enjoy this particular game. They are therefore likely to adhere, more or less, to the rules limiting the considerations that enter into their decisions. (1995, 131, 133)

Posner argues that the value of judging would be significantly diluted if judicial decision makers consistently eschewed legal rules in favor of their personal preferences. For the most part, judges sincerely follow accepted rules of decision making because that is part of what they enjoy about judging.

JUDGES' POLICY PREFERENCES CAN INFLUENCE LEGAL REASONING PROCESSES

If we take seriously the idea that judges feel constrained by norms of judicial behavior, an alternative way of explaining findings of policy-oriented decision making is that judges believe they are following the law, but somehow their preferences bias their reasoning processes. This explanation is wholly consistent with theories of motivated reasoning from cognitive and social psychology suggesting that the goals of decision makers can have a substantial effect on their mental processes. Particularly relevant is the finding that biases can come into play even when decision makers are trying to be objective in their evaluation of social information and various forms of scientific evidence and authority (Kunda 1990; 1999; MacCoun 1998).

In the motivated reasoning literature, there is a distinction between "accuracy" and "directional" goals. Research demonstrates that the nature of motivated decision processes depends on the goal of the individual making the judgment. In what is probably the most widely cited piece on motivated decision making, Kunda describes the distinction:

> The motivated reasoning phenomena fall into two major categories: those in which the motive is to arrive at an accurate conclusion, whatever it may be, and those in which the motive is to arrive at a particular directional

conclusion. . . . [B]oth goals affect reasoning by influencing the choice of beliefs and strategies applied to a given problem. But accuracy goals lead to the use of those beliefs and strategies that are considered most appropriate, whereas directional goals lead to the use of those that are considered most likely to yield the desired conclusion. (1990, 480–81)

Political scientists generally attribute directional goals to judges. They assume that judges seek to make decisions to influence policy in ways consistent with their personal policy preferences. As mentioned earlier, Baum (1997) argues that judges may not be as narrowly focused on directional policy goals as some scholars suggest; instead, judges are trying to achieve a mixture of goals. Citing the strength of legal socialization, Baum posits that one of the goals of judges in reaching decisions is the desire to achieve legal accuracy.

According to psychological theory, accuracy and directional goals are not necessarily mutually exclusive. Both types of goals can exist in the mind of an individual with respect to a particular decision. Moreover, decision makers are not necessarily aware of how alternative motives may operate to influence their decisions. For instance, a judge who identifies as a liberal Democrat may know that she favors affirmative action, but she may not be aware of whether (or how) that policy preference influences her interpretation of evidence and/or legal authority in cases involving that issue.

Consistent with judges' subjective accounts of decision making, I argue accuracy goals are foremost in the minds of decision makers when deciding cases. They sincerely utilize and cite appropriate legal authority in reaching their decisions. Psychological research demonstrates, however, that accuracy goals do not necessarily forestall motivated decision processes. Legal authority is not always determinative, because there is usually latitude in interpretation. There is often significant room for directional policy goals to influence the subjective evaluation of evidence and authority related to specific disputes.

Due to strong professional norms discouraging preference-based behavior, I argue that where policy preferences influence legal interpretations, their influence is largely unconscious. Specifically, motivated reasoning happens as decision makers choose determinative evidence, interpretations, and authority in the context of stylized norms, enabling decision makers to believe they are applying the tools of doctrinal analysis in an appropriately unbiased manner.

Although accuracy goals do not prevent biases from entering seemingly neutral decision processes, they do suggest an "outer limit" on the ability of decision makers to engage in motivated reasoning. Research tells us that when striving for accuracy, decision makers do not blindly accept evidence that supports their views, but seek out the decisional criteria that are *most appropriate* for the judgment they are making. For judges, this means looking to legitimate sources of legal reasoning. This characterization of motives suggests legal authority may be more of a constraint than envisioned by attitudinal theories of decision making. As Kunda writes: "people are not at liberty to conclude what they want simply because they want to. . . . [They] will come to believe what they want only to the extent that reality permits" (1990, 482–83). Presumably this applies to decision makers applying legal norms. Their ability to reach directional conclusions will not extend to choices the law can not reasonably support.

Segal and Spaeth's retort to this argument no doubt would be that because legal decision making happens in an adversarial context, there is appropriate authority to support whatever conclusion judges want to draw. This assumes, however, that all legal arguments are equal. Those who have been trained in the legal tradition would take issue with this assumption. Lawyers and judges are trained to recognize specific criteria that make some legal arguments more persuasive than others. When applying precedent, for instance, the best (most appropriate) authority is case law decided by a court whose opinions are directly binding on the presiding judge, with facts closely resembling those in pending litigation. Such authority, if it exists, should act as a constraint on accuracy-seeking judges despite the availability of alternative arguments.

Does Motivated Reasoning Happen in Legal Decision Making?

Although I have argued in this chapter for adopting a motivated reasoning perspective for understanding attitudinal influence in legal decision making, I want to make it clear that there are good reasons to be skeptical that motivated reasoning occurs in this particular domain. First, this explanation is entirely post hoc. Thus far, scholars have used motivated cognition to explain existing findings of attitudinal behavior without presenting any independent evidence that it is occurring in the realm of legal decision making. Second, they have failed to specify a precise mechanism by which judges would be influenced by their policy preferences in the context of legal decision making.

Reasons to Question Motivated Reasoning in This Context

The most serious reason to question whether motivated reasoning occurs is that behavioral scholars have, rather superficially, invoked what seems like a very attractive explanation for policy-oriented behavior, without taking seriously evidence suggesting that judicial decision making may not be the most hospitable environment for motivated cognition to occur. Specifically, judicial scholars have not adequately dealt with evidence demonstrating that when individuals are made aware of the way specific biases operate (Fischhoff 1977) or asked to consider that methods used in obtaining evidence may have resulted in opposite results (Lord, Lepper, and Preston 1984), the effects of motivated reasoning are attenuated.

This is significant because judges have what may be characterized as a chronic awareness of potential biases. They are cognizant that their own attitudes may inappropriately influence their reasoning, and *they are specifically trained to guard against such biases.* Although psychological findings suggest mere awareness of a potential bias may not be enough to forestall motivated decision processes (Lord, Ross, and Lepper 1979; Fischhoff 1977), the fact that judges have specific decision rules to help them reduce attitudinal influences suggests they may not be as vulnerable to motivated decision processes as some behavioral researchers suggest.

Literature in psychology documents a number of biases that can occur in a variety of contexts. Research on motivated reasoning embodies a broad range of psychological studies involving self-perception, interpersonal impression formation, and evaluation of scientific evidence (see Kunda 1990; MacCoun 1998; and Taber, Lodge, and Glathar 2001 for reviews of this substantial body of literature). Judicial scholars have not been careful about specifying which biases may be operating in legal decision processes. They have also failed to acknowledge that many of the biases documented have been explained by cognitive researchers as involving highly personal needs of decision makers to maintain a positive self-image (Cooper and Fazio 1984; Tesser and Campbell 1983) or consistent worldview (Lord, Ross, and Lepper 1979; Ross, McFarland, and Fletcher 1985). It is unclear whether the same ego-protective mechanisms are relevant for judges routinely engaged in adversarial decision making.

There are also institutional protections that should limit the role of unconscious policy motivations in judges' decision making. First, despite Segal and Spaeth's claim that judges are not accountable, they must justify their decisions to litigants, legal audiences, and the public. Lerner and Tetlock (1999) present evidence that accountability, specifically operationalized as having to justify decisions to others, causes people to engage in more detailed processing, making motivated reasoning less likely to be a factor in decisions. They find that decision makers evidence more "integrative complexity" when asked to explain their decisions: they are more likely to acknowledge and consider alternative arguments and viewpoints, thus diminishing the effect of unconscious biases in their judgments.

Also, the collective nature of decision making, especially the presence of dissent, is a strong institutional mechanism guarding against the operation of unconscious biases.[11] Having to convince others of their views increases the chance that judges will become aware of the potential role that policy preferences play in their decisional behavior. Other judges may explicitly make accusations of improper attitudinal motivations. Also, having to convince others thorough the utilization of appropriate norms and authority should reinforce accuracy goals and the constraining force of legal doctrine in judges' decision making.

For all of these reasons tending to cast doubt on the likelihood of motivated reasoning in this highly normative, institutionalized context, it is important that empirical scholars acquire *direct evidence* of its occurrence (and prevalence) in legal decision making. To date, judicial scholars have failed to corral such evidence. This study represents an attempt to fill that gap and advance our understanding of how policy biases can operate in the minds of decision makers to influence legal reasoning.

Using motivated reasoning as the central organizing paradigm, I develop hypotheses about how attitudes might influence decision makers in the context of thinking about cases using accepted legal norms. I test these hypotheses to determine (1) whether motivated reasoning occurs in legal decision making and, (2) if it does occur, how it happens. These are interesting and worthwhile questions that should greatly advance our understanding of attitudinal influence in legal reasoning. Specifically, addressing these issues will help us understand where legal training and expertise can have force in legitimizing the decisions of unelected judges, and where the requirements of objectivity in decision making may tax the limits of human capacity. Moreover, if motivated reasoning does occur in this domain, understanding the nature of the cognitive mechanism(s) at play could bring scholars closer to understanding the potential for attitudinal influence in other seemingly objective decision processes.

Debates on the Nature of Motivated Reasoning in Legal Decision Making

A final problem with the way motivated reasoning has been utilized in the judicial literature is that behavioral scholars have not done a very

good job of integrating motivated cognition into larger theories of decision making. Specifically, the concept of motivated reasoning has been
invoked in two distinct ways in the realm of judicial behavior. Segal and
Spaeth (1993, 2002) suggest a top-down process where outcome decisions come first and drive legal explanations that appear to, but do not
actually, dictate voting behavior. According to this characterization, legal
reasoning is more rationalization than deliberation, although judges may
convince themselves otherwise.

Other judicial scholars, including Baum (1997) and Rowland and
Carp (1996) have suggested a bottom-up, information-processing approach where attitudes act as information filters, exercising their influence by affecting microdecisions that occur in the process of legal reasoning. The information-processing approach is more compatible with
traditional characterizations of legal reasoning; it assumes judges really
do use the law in thinking through cases, though their preferences may
influence the kinds of arguments and evidence they are likely to accept.

As Baum states, "attitudes may serve 'as information filters or in-
termediaries that influence the cognitive processes of perception, [and]
memory' . . . rather than as direct basis for choice" (Baum 1997, 139,
quoting Rowland and Carp 1996, 150). Gillman's notion of ideologically
influenced considerations is decidedly bottom-up. Moreover, when legal
academics talk about attitudinal influence, they are usually referring to
a similar causal mechanism where preferences shade, rather than determine, decisions (Frank 1931a, 1931b; Lewellyn 1962).

Top-down models of judicial behavior are more of an affront to practitioners who adhere to traditional notions of decision making because
they posit that outcome choices come first and legal explanations follow
"in service" of those decisions. They conjure a picture of policy-oriented
judges doing exactly what they should not in the context of adversarial
decision making. This conception of attitudinal influence renders the
notion of constraint imposed by law illusory by characterizing judges'
reasoning processes as a post hoc justification, rather than a meaningful
basis for outcome choices.

The substantial disconnect between how top-down models portray
judicial decision making and how judges characterize their own reasoning processes is theoretically important. Judicial decision makers explain
how they reach decisions via appropriate legal criteria in decisions that
take up thousands of pages in case reporters. Top-down models of influence not only discredit such accounts, they are extremely vague in
explaining how judges construct these rationales that judges themselves

believe dictate their decision making. Segal and Spaeth, for instance, do not outline any cognitive process except to say that judges will use whatever authority gets them to preferred outcomes.

When judges decide which party is entitled to relief in an adversarial dispute, they make many legal judgments that presumably drive the outcome choice. Segal and Spaeth do not explain at what point in judges' decision making we are likely to see the effects of motivated bias. In a case involving more than one legal issue, for instance, judges must decide which issue is determinative and what legal authority should control their reasoning. Answering these questions usually involves making judgments about whether case facts resemble, or are distinguishable from, those in cases cited as authority, and to what extent a judge's own reasoning should be guided by decisions characterized by competing parties as more and less authoritative.

On Segal and Spaeth's account, it is not clear which of these choices is subject to motivational bias, especially where judges are not at liberty to ignore alternative evidence and arguments. Although judges do not have to make every decision that the parties request in litigation, they must, at the very least, address competing arguments (see Seudfeld and Tetlock [1977a, 1977b]), demonstrating that considering alternative arguments reduces the role of bias in decision making).

Presumably some of the decisions that judges "want" to make will be harder to justify than others given particular case facts and prevailing legal authority. Top-down theories assert that the availability of alternative arguments and legal grounds facilitates preference-driven behavior, but they fail to elaborate on how this happens. They do not state, for instance, whether judges, individually or collectively, have preferred avenues of motivated decision making, or specify what decision makers might do if such avenues are closed to them.[12]

Bottom-up models are only slightly better on this front. Baum (1997, 66) uses the distinction between "easy" and "hard" cases (Cardozo 1924, 60; Easterbrook 1982, 105–7) to argue that judges may have more latitude to make decisions consistent with their preferences when there is "ambiguity" in the law. Similarly, Posner (2008) describes a "zone of reasonableness" as enabling attitudinal behavior on the part of accuracy-seeking judges. These terms, however, defy concrete definition and have eluded effective operationalization in extant studies of judicial decision making.

Clearly, top-down and bottom-up portrayals of influence represent two very different conceptions of the role that preferences play in decision making. Both involve the concept of "motivated cognition," but they have very different implications for the potential of the law to act as a meaningful constraint in legal reasoning. Most significantly, although each characterization is entirely plausible, neither has been subjected to rigorous empirical investigation. The time has come to achieve a more so-phisticated understanding of how judges reach decisions that are consis-tent with their preferences in the context of complex decision making.

Studying Motivated Reasoning in Legal Reasoning

Notwithstanding the problems with how it has been used in the ju-dicial literature, motivated reasoning is the best explanation we have to reconcile findings of directed behavior with indicia that judges use, or believe they are using, legal criteria to make decisions.

I propose two mechanisms of motivated reasoning in the empirical section of this book and flesh out the theoretical underpinnings of each more fully in the chapters that follow. The intuitions are relatively simple. In chapter 3, looking at analogical perception as a potential mechanism of attitudinal influence, I test the idea that legal decision makers may actually perceive the similarity of case authority differently depending on whether it helps them achieve preferred policy goals. In the chapters on separable preferences, I test whether decision makers can compartmen-talize their reasoning when thinking about distinct issues in litigation.[13]

The hypothesized mechanisms come from aspects of legal reasoning that judges and legal scholars have been debating for years. Using moti-vated reasoning as an empirical framework, I am able to corral evidence that attitudes shape legal decision making in concrete ways, evidence that goes beyond anecdotal accusations that judges level against one another in isolated cases. Using experimental methods also allows me to test the *limiting conditions* of each hypothesized mechanism to get a better understanding of when attitudes are likely to influence decisions *and when they are not*. The result is a much richer understanding of not only how, but when, policy attitudes can influence individuals using ac-cepted norms of legal decision making. The aim is to introduce a unified theory of legal reasoning specifying the conditions under which each plays a dominant role.

My approach assumes that the best way to gain leverage on motivated decision processes is to look at how decision makers with alternative policy views respond to identical case information. I start with a doc-trinal analysis of three Commerce Clause decisions by the Rehnquist

Court. My logic is that each case provides its own controlled decision environment where the justices are responding to identical doctrinal authority. Moreover, looking at how Supreme Court justices respond to the same body of authority across situations provides some insight into how individual justices interpret the applicability of specific cases and legal arguments under different factual scenarios.

The cases I analyze provide a good example of the give-and-take that often occurs between judges with different views. There are forcefully worded majority and dissenting opinions about the controlling force of law using normatively appropriate tools of legal reasoning. The justices argue about which cases are most similar to facts in pending litigation; there are even allegations by some judges that improper political motives influence the analyses of others. My goal is to illustrate the plausibility of each of the mechanisms tested in the empirical chapters of this book and to illustrate their real-world significance. Simply stated, the analysis should give readers a strong sense of the intuitions underlying my hypothesized avenues of attitudinal influence.

I put these intuitions to the test in the empirical chapters that make up the heart of this inquiry using experimental methods. Although the virtues of experiments have been well documented in political science (Iyengar and Kinder 1987; Kinder and Palfrey 1993; Green and Gerber 2002), they have not been not commonly used by judicial scholars to study legal reasoning processes.[14] This is somewhat ironic because judicial decision making is, after all, decision making. It seems foolhardy to ignore the primary method psychologists use to study reasoning processes. Moreover, thinking of decision making in terms of testable cognitive processes allows judicial scholars to move beyond the simplistic stimulus-response paradigm toward a more sophisticated understanding of the *causal mechanisms* underlying patterns of observed behavior (Rowland and Carp 1996, 144).

Using experiments in the judicial context makes sense for several reasons. First, experiments provide a degree of *control* that has not been achieved in previous research. Most behavioral studies compare how judges vote across a large number of cases, each involving their own facts and legal authority. Experiments enable researchers to analyze judgments *holding facts and legal authority constant*. Comparing the decisions of participants with different policy views in this relatively closed system allows for greater confidence in our causal inferences about the role of attitudes in such judgments (Iyengar and Kinder 1987, 6).

Second, experiments enable us to manipulate aspects of the decision domain. This allows for the effective isolation of causal variables under different theoretically relevant circumstances. In the study on separable preferences, for instance, we observe how decision makers make the same threshold judgment—involving identical litigants, arguments, and case facts—where there is direct legal authority on the threshold question, *and where there is not.* Clearly, this would be impossible in the real world. Observing how participants make the same legal judgments under these counterfactual conditions provides a compelling test of the extent to which policy views affect decision makers acting under different levels of legal constraint.

Third, experiments allow researchers to take legal norms and decision-making environments into account when developing hypotheses. Thus, judicial scholars can move beyond the false choice between legal and attitudinal determinants of behavior toward a more sophisticated understanding of the "conditions under which" attitudes are likely to impact legal decision making.

Finally, because experiments allow for more precise measurement of policy preferences than do blunt observational indicia used in correlational studies, such methods have the potential to alleviate long-standing concerns about the adequacy of variables used to approximate attitudes in studies of judicial behavior (see Segal and Cover 1989).

Of course, experiments have their shortcomings. Researchers must be careful to address concerns about the extent to which participants differ from the decision makers we are most interested in understanding. We must be mindful of how differences between experimental settings and real-world decision contexts can limit the applicability of experimental findings. This is true for all experimental work, but especially important in a domain as complex as legal decision making.

Also, as mentioned above, there are real obstacles to studying judicial actors in this manner. Therefore, as I do here, researchers who use experiments will often need to rely on proxies who are familiar with stylized norms of decision making. Even where experimental researchers do not have access to judges, however, they can investigate important aspects of decision making that go to the heart of specialized techniques used by judicial actors. These studies may shed significant light on the mechanisms driving observed patterns of behavior and lead to the development of new hypotheses (Kinder and Palfrey 1993, 19).

Laboratory experiments have been criticized for distilling real-world phenomena into artificial conditions that bear little resemblance to the political concepts researchers are interested in understanding. I would argue that this is not *necessarily* the case. There are excellent examples of experiments in political science that strike an appropriate balance between the isolation of causal variables and the realistic simulation of information environments that decision makers encounter in the real world (Iyengar and Kinder 1987; Nelson, Clawson, and Oxley 1997).

I attempt to follow that tradition here by giving experimental participants realistic materials containing relevant case information and manipulations. Chapter 3 describes two experiments where undergraduate and law student participants are asked to read a *realistic journalistic account* of a dispute pending in the legal system. The results discussed in chapters 4 and 5 are from an experiment where law student participants are given real legal arguments in the context of an *adversarial case brief*. Because law students are specifically trained in the tools of doctrinal analysis, I am able to use arguments that are not "watered down" in any respect; indeed, they are quite like what a judge would encounter in a case implicating her ability to separate views on alternative issues in litigation.

Of course, it is important to remember that law students are not judges. Indeed, there are competing reasons to think they may be more *and* less attitudinal than judicial actors. For instance, because law students are relatively inexperienced in using tools of legal reasoning, one might expect attitudes to be more influential in their decisions. Also, they are not subject to the same accountability concerns as judicial actors faced with the threat of review. However, there are also reasons to think law student participants may be less attitudinal than judges in this context. For instance, their policy attitudes are presumably weaker than those of experienced judges who have been vetted through the political process.

These differences, however, should not give us much pause. The primary goal of this study is to test two potential mechanisms of attitudinal influence in legal reasoning. Because law students are trained in doctrinal techniques, they are an appropriate sample to use to test my experimental hypotheses. If findings demonstrate that attitudes influence participants' judgments the manner hypothesized, additional studies can be done to see if findings replicate in more sophisticated legal samples (see, for example, Becker 1964, 1966).

In short, as long as we are explicit about the costs and benefits of experimental methods, there is much to gain by including experiments in a pluralistic approach to understanding legal behavior. Consistent with the logic giving rise to this inquiry, I believe the benefits far outweigh the costs at this point in our collective knowledge. To advance our understanding of policy-oriented decision making, we need to "get inside the heads" of decision makers to discover how they reach decisions consistent with their preferences.

Moreover, to understand where to look for avenues of attitudinal influence, it is important to consider how decision makers actually think about evidence and authority when reasoning through cases. Therefore, I begin the inquiry with a look at Supreme Court justices' reasoning in three recent cases on congressional commerce authority to demonstrate the intuitions behind the mechanisms of motivated reasoning tested in this volume.

TWO

A MOTIVATED REASONING APPROACH TO
THE COMMERCE CLAUSE INTERPRETATION
OF THE REHNQUIST COURT

One might ask what the practical utility of a motivated reasoning approach is for understanding case outcomes. There are instances like *Newdow*, the Pledge of Allegiance case mentioned in the introduction of this book, where an argument can be made that judicial attitudes and motives influence legal reasoning processes in concrete ways. In *Newdow*, the justices' preferences concerning the separation of church and state, coupled with their desire to issue a public decision on the constitutionality of the Pledge, seem likely to have shaded one or more of the justices' interpretation of the standing doctrine deemed determinative by the Court.

But to *really know* if this was the case, one would need to delve more deeply into the minds of the justices. Ideally, we would need to know (1) how each justice felt about the constitutionality of the Pledge; (2) how each justice thought a majority of the Court would vote on the issue; and (3) whether or not they were willing to issue a public vote on the matter as a part of a binding decision. Armed with this information, we would also need to know (*a*) the legal basis of each justice's opinion on the standing question, along with (*b*) alternative interpretations each may have adopted with regard to the issue. And, of course, it would be helpful to have (*c*) past opinions of the justices in cases involving similar standing questions to see if their reasoning in *Newdow* represented a departure from previous interpretations.

Clearly, this is a tall order that is impossible for researchers to fill "at a distance." Still, we do have some insight into the reasoning of Supreme Court justices provided by case opinions authored by the justices themselves. "Conversations" often occur between judges via majority, concurring, and dissenting opinions, where they debate the relevance of specific authority. These exchanges can inform our understanding of how justices interpret authority in similar and different ways. Each Supreme Court case, in effect, provides its own controlled decision environment with an *N* of nine. Moreover, because the justices join opinions and/or write separately in successive cases involving similar issues, we can see how they interpret the same general body of authority under different factual scenarios. There is certainly less control in looking at the justices' opinions across cases, but often the fact that they are considering identical case and statutory authority across situations can provide insight into their individual reasoning processes—as when a judge concludes that a specific Supreme Court precedent applies in one instance, but not another.

In this chapter, using doctrinal evidence of the sort described above, I will illustrate how each of the mechanisms tested in this volume can operate in high-profile cases with practical policy implications. Specifically, I discuss a line of Supreme Court cases that has received a good deal of attention in recent years involving the appropriate division of authority between states and the federal government. I will focus on the majority, concurring, and dissenting opinions in three cases involving congressional authority to issue legislation under its commerce power in Article I, Section 8, *United States v. Lopez*, 514 U.S. 549 (1995); *United States v. Morrison*, 529 U.S. 598 (2000); and *Gonzalez v. Raich*, 454 U.S. 1 (2005) (hereafter referred to as *Lopez*, *Morrison*, and *Raich*, respectively).

I choose to analyze these cases for three reasons. First, they were decided by the same natural court, sometimes referred to as "Rehnquist 7" (1994–2005). This means the same nine justices participated in all three cases.[1] The decisions represent a tractable line of Supreme Court Commerce Clause doctrine where the cases are evenly spaced; each was decided about five years apart.

Second, besides touching on congressional authority, each of these cases involves a substantively interesting policy domain. *Lopez* concerns gun-control legislation; *Morrison* involves penalties arising from gender-motivated violence; and *Raich* is about the use of medicinal marijuana. Because these cases involve *both* federalism and substantive policy concerns, they, like *Newdow* and the case used to test the separability of preferences in chapters 4 and 5, are likely to evoke decision makers' political attitudes on multiple policy dimensions. Therefore, this particular line of authority is illustrative of the complexity that judges face when deciding real-world cases where legitimate democratic concerns compete for recognition in ways that do not neatly adhere to any single ideological dimension.

Finally, the votes in these cases suggest there is something interesting to explain beyond what existing models of legal decision making can tell us. In *Lopez* and *Morrison*, the court split five to four along what most judicial scholars regard as "straight ideological lines," with conservatives in the majority. The six-to-three *Raich* decision is different, not only because the liberals were in the majority, but because one moderate justice (Kennedy) and one conservative justice (Scalia) voted with them indicating differential justifications, not only across, but also *within* a previously cohesive ideological bloc.

In the remainder of this chapter, I first describe each of these Supreme Court cases, demonstrating why existing models of decision making lead to inconclusive and/or unsatisfactory explanations of the justices' behavior in this line of cases. I argue that approaches that focus on unidimensional preferences and judicial strategy miss some of the most interesting questions about judicial reasoning processes including how like-minded justices can reach conclusions that are distinct from one another *and also* distinct from conclusions that strategic justices lobbying for a majority may advocate.

Second, I show how the mechanisms of motivated reasoning tested in this book appear to be operating in this line of cases via a discussion of authority cited in the majority, dissenting, and separate opinions in each case. In line with chapter 3, investigating "analogical perception" in legal decision making, I demonstrate how justices across and within ideological blocs "see" identical precedents quite differently in relation to pending litigation. To illustrate legal-reasoning phenomena related to "separable preferences," I point to instances where the justices' opinions of the desirability of specific federal policy may influence their seemingly independent reasoning about federalism and the scope of congressional authority under Article I, Section 8. My goal is to provide context for readers who may be less familiar with the decisional norms that are the subject of this inquiry and to demonstrate their real-world significance.

Federalism, Ideological Ambiguity, and the Inadequacy of Existing Explanatory Models

The Rehnquist Court, through its Commerce Clause interpretation, revitalized a debate about congressional authority that had been largely dormant since 1937. Although the debate had been relatively quiet for almost sixty years preceding the Court's decision in *Lopez*, its origins date back to the nation's founding.

Without detailing the entire history of the Court's Commerce Clause interpretation, it is important to note that disputes about how to interpret that power are, essentially, about different conceptions of federalism, or how much power the national government should yield vis-à-vis the states. Traditionally, conservatives have been strong proponents of states' rights. They emphasize benefits like efficiency, innovation, and geographic autonomy in allowing state governments to deal with policy problems without excessive interference from Washington. Liberals generally envision a more expansive role for the national government in addressing matters of public concern; they cite collective active problems that can arise when states have different policy priorities. According to liberals, the very scope and breadth of some of our most serious societal problems necessitate centralized, coordinated federal action.

Federalism issues generally arise in litigation where state or federal governments are attempting to address some matter of public concern. The legal issue raised in these cases usually involves whether a particular governing body has the authority to take action with respect to a particular policy problem. This means that Commerce Clause cases typically involve at least two distinct issues: federalism and whatever substantive domain the government action at issue seeks to address. Sometimes decision makers' preferences for outcomes can be assumed to be consistent across multiple issue dimensions, but often they cannot. Attitudinal models have trouble dealing with such complexity because they assume judges vote along a single policy dimension (see chapter 4 for further discussion about this assumption of unidimensionality). *Lopez, Morrison,* and *Raich* effectively illustrate this phenomenon.

Assuming the usual package of liberal and conservative preferences, *Lopez* presents a case where the justices' ideological preferences should be consistent across issue dimensions. This is the easy case for attitudinalists. The case involves federalism in the context of national gun-control legislation. Ideologically speaking, conservatives are generally against the expansion of federal authority *and* they are also generally against gun-control measures. Both of these preferences in *Lopez* suggest that conservative justices on the Court will issue a ruling in favor of the defendant, striking down the gun-control legislation as an excessive exercise of congressional authority. Liberal justices should go the other way as their preferences are consistent in the opposite direction on both dimensions. Indeed, this is what happened in the case. The Court split along ideological lines with a majority of conservative justices voting to strike down the law.

Although the vote in *Morrison* five years later is exactly the same, the case presents a more difficult scenario for attitudinalists. Specifically, *Morrison* concerned whether or not the national government could impose civil liability on persons suspected of gender-motivated violence by allowing victims to sue individuals accused of such crimes. Here, again, conservatives should be against the broad exercise of congressional authority, suggesting an outcome preference for the defendant, with liberals voting in the opposite direction. But to the extent that conservative judges also tend to be strong law-and-order types, one might think they would be supportive of legislation allowing victims to recover from perpetrators of violent activity. This attitudinal dimension suggests the *opposite* preference in the case for conservative judges. It suggests they would vote in favor of the plaintiff and uphold the government's authority to provide additional remedies against criminal wrongdoers.[2]

Moreover, there is arguably a third issue dimension in the case, which involves the justices' attitudes on tort liability. To the extent that conservative justices are against the proliferation of civil litigation, they could be hostile to congressional efforts of this kind because civil liability lawsuits are likely to place an additional burden on the dockets of overcrowded federal courts.[3] This issue dimension predicts an outcome preference for the defendant accused of gender-motivated violence, consistent with the federalism dimension, but again, inconsistent with conservative attitudes on law-and-order issues.

Here the multidimensional nature of the case presents a problem for unidimensional models of decision making. Attitudinalists must either predict ahead of time which ideological dimension will be determinative (assuming it will operate consistently across all the justices), or they may implicitly presume some sort of averaging across dimensions (i.e., because two out of three dimensions yield preferences for the defendant, conservatives will vote for the defendant). Therefore, if we assume there are four possible attitudinal predictions for votes in *Morrison*—along the issue dimensions of (1) federalism, (2) law and order, and (3) tort reform, or (4) some averaging of these three issue dimensions—three out of four strategies yield predictions consistent with what happened in the case. Not bad, but still, *Morrison* illustrates potential shortcomings of the attitudinal approach to explaining case outcomes.

The *Raich* case, however, is most problematic in this regard. The case involved whether the national government could prosecute individuals for federal drug crimes where they were engaged in the medical use of marijuana sanctioned by state law. Because the case involves the appropriateness of criminal prosecution for traditional crimes, rather than the creation of civil liabilities for such activity, it presents the most direct conflict between ideological issue dimensions. Conservative justices are generally against the exercise of broad federal authority, but they are also in favor of criminal punishment for the sort of traditional drug crimes at issue in *Raich*. Indeed, it is not hard to imagine that liberal justices on the Court would be in favor of leniency toward the terminally ill defendants in the case, while conservatives would be less sympathetic to arguments that individuals should be exempted for liability for federal drug offenses.[4] These criminal justice preferences, however, stand in direct opposition to the justices' ideological attitudes on federalism. To hold defendants criminally liable in the case would be to endorse an expansive view of federal authority vis-à-vis conflicting state laws.

Unidimensional models of decision making have great difficulty with this sort of direct conflict. Again, the preferred strategy of attitudinalists in these cases is to choose issue dimensions. If the justices are voting in line with the federalism dimension, one might predict an outcome for the defendants consistent with what happened in *Lopez* and *Morrison*. If the justices are voting in line with criminal justice preferences, one would expect a straight ideological vote in the *opposite* direction, upholding the federal prosecutions as an appropriate exercise of national authority in combating drug-related crimes.

In fact, neither of these outcomes obtained. All the justices purported to vote on federalism grounds, but the vote in *Raich* was six to three with one moderate justice (Kennedy) and one conservative (Scalia) voting with the more liberal justices to uphold the national government's authority to prosecute drug crimes. The other conservative justices, who had previously been in the majority in *Lopez* and *Morrison,* were dissenters in *Raich*. Attitudinal models have a hard time accounting for this outcome. Specifically, attitudinal models have trouble explaining why Scalia and Kennedy, traditionally among the more conservative justices with respect to federalism and national supremacy issues (Segal and Spaeth 2002, 421), broke ranks and voted for federal authority in this particular case.[5]

Implicit in this observation is the idea that the standard attitudinal explanation—that these justices were somehow "closer" ideologically to the distant minority on federalism issues—is extremely unsatisfactory here. If it was ever an acceptable answer, we have long since outgrown it. Such a simplistic explanation tells us *nothing*, in itself, about how the facts and legal authority in this case allowed justices who previously agreed on federalism questions—and who were, in fact, much more similar in their legal philosophies and perspectives—to draw different conclusions about the appropriate outcome. Stated simply, there is some very interesting variance in this line of cases that extant attitudinal models of decision making do not sufficiently explain.

The specific alignment of votes and opinions in *Raich* also illustrates why strategic notions of decision making are not completely satisfactory in explaining judicial behavior. Justice Kennedy joins the majority opinion in the case. Justice Scalia does not; instead, he chooses to issue a separate concurring opinion detailing how his reasoning is different from conservative dissenters in the case *and is also* distinct from the justices in the majority. Arguably, the more liberal justices were able to convince Justice Kennedy of their version of the "law of the case," but not Justice Scalia. Why? What explains this difference? How did Scalia reach a conclusion that was distinct from how he had previously voted in similar federalism cases and also distinct from what justices lobbying for the majority advocated? He did not achieve any obvious strategic benefit in voting the way he did and writing separately. Of course, it is possible that Justice Scalia was swayed by arguments of the majority coalition. But here I argue that it is much more likely that there was something unique in how Justice Scalia viewed the facts and authority in that case that led him to his vote and opinion, something that strategic models of decision making do not effectively capture.[6]

To be clear, my point in this chapter is not to dismiss fifty years of behavioral research based on the justices' opinions in three recent cases, but rather to demonstrate that there is something here worth explaining that extant models of decision making do not address. The mechanisms of motivated decision making tested in this volume have great potential to fill in gaps left by attitudinal and strategic models of judicial behavior. It is only by looking at the interaction of facts, authority, and legal norms that we can fully understand how the justices are able to break from established voting patterns in a manner that is "reasonably supported" by their understanding of doctrine that has previously led them to opposite conclusions in similar cases. Similarly, it is only through this type of inquiry that we can understand how doctrinal arguments that sway some judges can simply miss the mark with others—even when their legal philosophies do not seem very different.

Judging, like baseball, can be a game of inches. Whether you "see" the ball as fair or foul often depends on which team you are rooting for. How you feel about the Red Sox winning their last game of the season could depend on whether it helps the Yankees' chances of making it to the playoffs. Judges are not immune to these effects. Justice Breyer may "see" a Commerce Clause precedent as controlling that Justice Rehnquist deems inapplicable in a case concerning federal gun-control legislation. Justice Scalia may have trouble striking down federal action as beyond congressional commerce authority where the effect of that ruling would be to inhibit the national government's ability to fight drug crimes. In such instances, the mechanisms I test and describe are likely at play. Moreover, the evidence cited here tends to illustrate that they can operate in subtle, unconscious ways as the justices reason through cases, allowing decision makers to reach conclusions consistent with their preferences while they adhere to the notion that they are using legal doctrine appropriately.

The remainder of this chapter illustrates how each of the mechanisms of motivated reasoning tested in this book actually operates in this line of Supreme Court decisions. To make my case, I need to discuss legal doctrine and the content of the justices' opinions more than is usual in social science studies of Supreme Court decision making. Luckily, however, I need not go beyond the basic understanding of the Commerce Clause doctrine taught in most undergraduate classes on government powers. Nor do I have to detail the entire history of Commerce Clause interpretation. After outlining the major contours of the legal debate, I start with post–New Deal understandings of the commerce power, detailing how the Rehnquist Court decisions I analyze have influenced those understandings in recent years.

The Legal Debate and Post–New Deal Understandings of Congressional Commerce Authority

Legally, the Commerce Clause debate is about the appropriate scope of federal power in our constitutional structure. The debate is rooted in the distinct nature of state versus federal authority. States existed as colonies and early manifestations of regional government before the Constitution was drafted. As such, they have what are called "police powers," which preexist the ratification of that document. States have the general authority to regulate for the health, welfare, and safety of their citizens. The powers of our national government are fundamentally different. Because the federal government, as we know it, was *created* in the Constitution, its powers are strictly provided for in that document. Therefore, when Congress acts to address some matter of public concern, it must draw on authority that is express or reasonably implied in the Constitution. Under the Supremacy Clause, where Congress acts pursuant to its legitimate authority, federal law will trump and/or preempt any conflicting state laws; but where Congress acts without authority, stretching its limits beyond what the Constitution can reasonably support, federal legislation will be deemed without legal effect.

Historically, many of the issues Congress has addressed in national legislation—from minimum-wage laws to the regulation of child labor—have involved economic activities occurring within and among the several states. Citing its authority to regulate interstate commerce, Congress has enacted laws regulating aspects of our everyday lives. Its power to do so has not always been uncontroversial. Although there has been significant ebb and flow in thinking about the commerce power over our two-hundred-year history, the general direction of Supreme Court doctrine has been to expand congressional authority as the economic fortunes of the states have grown increasingly interdependent and our national economy has become more and more complex.

Following significant debate about the scope of congressional authority to regulate under the Commerce Clause, the Supreme Court endorsed an expansive interpretation of that authority during the New Deal era in *National Labor Relations Board v. Jones and Laughlin Steel Corp.,* 301 U.S. 1 (1937). According to the Court's decision in that case, congressional authority to regulate interstate commerce was "plenary," that is, complete unto itself. As those who envisioned a strong role for the federal government argued, congressional commerce power was not limited by the Tenth Amendment to bar domains that had traditionally been the province of state regulation through their police powers. As long as Congress could reasonably assert activity involved interstate commerce, the national legislature would have the authority to make laws regarding that activity.

Five years later, in *Wickard v. Filburn,* 317 U.S. 111 (1942), the Supreme Court clarified just how broad that authority was. After *Wickard,* it was clear that the Supreme Court was willing to give Congress significant latitude in interpreting its commerce power in light of our increasingly complex economic system. The legal question in the case involved whether agricultural laws passed by Congress could constitutionally reach a farmer in Ohio who produced wheat for home consumption. The argument against the application of federal production limits in the case was that the farmer's activity occurred entirely *intra*state (within Ohio) and did not significantly affect interstate commerce as he was involved in selling only a very small portion of his crop to feed his livestock.

In a unanimous decision by Justice Jackson, the Court held that federal production limits could apply to the single family farmer because such production could conceivably affect national demand. More specifically, the Court reasoned that the "cumulative effect" of similar single family farmers producing for their own consumption could depress the overall demand for wheat. Therefore, Congress did not exceed the bounds of its authority under the commerce power in regulating such activity.

In *Heart of Atlanta Motel v. United States,* 379 U.S. 241 (1964), the Court likewise upheld legislation making discrimination by private business owners illegal under the 1964 Civil Rights Act. A unanimous court reasoned the act embodied a proper exercise of congressional authority under the Commerce Power in Article I, Section 8. The holding meant the power could extend to social regulation by Congress where that regulation was related to the movement of people, goods, and services among the states. Although the specific motel challenging the act was located in Georgia, did not advertise outside the state, and purported to serve a mostly local clientele, the Court reasoned that because it received goods from outside the state used for the comfort and consumption of its customers, Congress could reasonably regulate its activity.

Wickard and *Heart of Atlanta Motel* are often cited to demonstrate that since the New Deal the Supreme Court has taken a rather expansive approach in interpreting congressional authority under the Commerce Clause. Indeed, after these cases many legal scholars thought the Court would basically defer to Congress in its exercise of authority under Article I, Section 8. They reasoned that this line of cases meant that all Congress needed to do was cite its commerce authority and the Court would fall in line, approving the federal regulation of any activity that could be conceivably tied to economic behavior. And indeed, that's the way it looked for over a half century—until 1995, when a deeply divided Rehnquist Court announced substantive limits on congressional commerce power in *Lopez.*

Enter the Rehnquist Court

The central issue in *Lopez* was whether or not Congress had the authority to criminalize possession of firearms in a school zone. The Gun-Free School Zones Act of 1990 made it illegal, under federal law, "for any individual to knowingly possess a firearm at a place that the individual knows, or has reason to believe is a school zone" (*Lopez,* 514 U.S. 549 at 551). Congress passed the act under its commerce authority without making any explicit factual findings about how possessing handguns near schools impacted interstate commerce.

The defendant in the case, along with those who believed Congress exceeded the bounds of its authority in criminalizing such behavior, argued that there was no obvious connection between having a gun near a school and interstate commerce. Opponents of the law argued that if this law was found to be sufficiently tied to interstate commerce, then the federal regulation of *anything* that could be incidentally related to economic activity was possible.

Supporters of the law argued that even though Congress made no explicit findings about how the possession of firearms near schools was related to interstate commerce, it was not hard to see how members of the national legislature may have reasonably drawn such a connection. Most handguns have traveled through interstate commerce at some time; moreover, the proliferation of violence in and near our schools could be reasonably connected to students' feelings of security and ultimately to their academic performance. Any detrimental effects of firearm possession on our national system of education could reasonably be related to interstate commerce. As such, supporters argued, it was not for the Court to second-guess the judgment of Congress in criminalizing such behavior under its broad commerce authority.

A bare majority of the Supreme Court, in a decision by Chief Justice Rehnquist, held that without specific factual findings about the relation of gun possession near schools to interstate commerce, it was unwilling to hold that the Gun-Free School Zone Act was an appropriate exercise of congressional commerce authority. According to the conservative majority, the relationship between gun possession and interstate commerce was by no means obvious; mere possession of firearms was not commercial activity. There was not even the jurisdictional requirement, as had been the case in previous legislation, that the firearms at issue be transported across state lines.[7] In so holding, Rehnquist wrote for the majority, "to the extent congressional findings would enable us to evaluate the legislative judgment that the activity in question substantially affected interstate commerce, even though no substantial effect was visible to the naked eye, they are lacking" (*Lopez*, 514 U.S. 549 at 563).

After a half century of the Court universally upholding laws passed pursuant to congressional commerce authority, many legal experts were puzzled by the new scrutiny the Court seemed to be imposing on such legislation. Indeed, there was some question about the ultimate meaning of the Court's holding after *Lopez*. Justice Rehnquist's language only added to the debate. Some thought it meant that the Court wanted Congress to make explicit its factual findings about how legislation was connected to interstate commerce, and that as long as it did so, the Court would not interfere. Others took the majority at its word, concluding that the decision meant the Court would independently judge whether legislation "substantially affected" interstate commerce. They reasoned after *Lopez* that there was some zone of noneconomic activity that Congress would be unable to touch, at least through its commerce authority.

The Court clarified its meaning in *Morrison* a few years later. The law at issue in that case, providing a civil remedy for victims of gender-motivated violence, included detailed legislative findings about how such violence negatively impacted interstate commerce. Specifically, Congress noted the substantial incidence of domestic violence and rape across the nation; hearing reports included detailed studies tending to demonstrate that women often traveled across state lines to avoid the detrimental effects of gender-motivated violence. There were also findings regarding the impact of injury claims on the medical insurance industry tending to tie such violence to interstate commerce. Moreover, Congress noted that victims of gender-motivated crimes often lost their jobs as a result of having to cope with such violence.

Notwithstanding these findings, a majority of the Court struck down the legislation, reasoning that gender-motivated violence, in and of itself, was not sufficiently related to economic activity to justify the assertion of congressional commerce authority. The majority reasoned that to conclude that such behavior was substantially related to interstate commerce would require inferences the Court was uncomfortable with drawing between gender-motivated violence and interstate commercial activity. Moreover, the majority argued, as they did in *Lopez,* that drawing such a conclusion, and allowing Congress to do so, would set a dangerous precedent putting any behavior that could be arguably related to the economy within the reach federal lawmakers.

After the decisions in *Lopez* and *Morrison,* many Court watchers were expecting a similar decision striking down the exercise of federal authority in *Raich.* In *Raich,* the main question was whether federal authorities could prosecute persons for drug crimes who were engaged in the medically prescribed use of marijuana. The limited production and use of the drug for medical purposes was allowed by California state law. Those who argued that Congress could not criminalize the behavior of individuals engaged in the medical use of marijuana pointed to similarities between *Raich* and *Lopez.* If Congress could not regulate the "mere possession" of firearms near schools, the same logic should apply to the possession and sanctioned used of marijuana to alleviate pain associated with legitimate medical ailments; the behavior Congress sought to regulate was essentially noneconomic activity.

Those who argued that federal authority could extend to such behavior pointed to a different case, which had been the subject of lively debate between the majority and dissenting justices in its previous Commerce Clause decisions, *Wickard v. Filborn.* They argued that specific provisions of the California statute sanctioning the use of drugs by those with valid medical reasons made the cultivation and consumption of marijuana so like the home-produced wheat at issue in *Wickard* as to make that case, not *Lopez,* the appropriate controlling precedent.

In *Raich,* those who argued that the federal prosecution of drug crimes was an appropriate exercise of national authority won the day. The majority cited *Wickard* as controlling; the dissent argued it was not, pointing to *Lopez.* Justice Kennedy, who had signed on with the conservatives in two previous Commerce Clause cases, joined the majority opinion and voted with the liberal wing of the Court. Justice Scalia also voted with the majority, but for somewhat different reasons. Thus, two justices who were in the previously cohesive conservative majority broke ranks in *Raich*—but with different justifications.

Here I examine the opinions in the cases in more detail. In line with the theory of analogical perception tested in chapter 3, I demonstrate how the different perceptions of controlling case law had important implications in this line of Supreme Court doctrine. I also argue that the specific legislation at issue in *Raich* had a great deal to do with the vote in that case. Specifically, I suggest that the fact that the Court was reviewing the constitutionality of federal legislation related to traditional drug offenses made it difficult for Kennedy and Scalia to strike down the law on federalism grounds. To be clear, I am not arguing that these justices voted on criminal justice rather than federalism dimensions; indeed, the relevant opinions explicitly invoke Commerce Clause doctrine. Rather, my argument is that, consistent with findings on separable preferences presented in chapters 4 and 5, the specific interaction of facts, issues, and legal authority in the case caused the justices' feelings about criminal justice to interfere with their interpretation of Commerce Clause doctrine in such a way as to influence their previous voting patterns and change the outcome of the case.

Plan of Analysis

In looking at the Commerce Clause interpretation of justices on the Rehnquist Court, it is important to note the information that informs my analysis of the justices' reasoning. Each of the decisions I discuss includes several opinions. There is a "main" majority and dissenting opinion in each case. Chief Justice Rehnquist writes for the conservative majority in *Lopez* and *Morrison*. Justice O'Connor writes the main dissent for the conservative justices in *Raich*. The main dissenting opinions in *Lopez* and *Morrison* are written, respectively, by Justices Breyer and Souter. Justice Stevens writes for the majority in *Raich*. There are also several separate opinions.[8]

I focus on key differences between the main majority and dissenting opinions in discussing the mechanisms of motivated reasoning that allow justices to reach conclusions consistent with their attitudinal preferences. I also examine the legal rationale endorsed by Justices Kennedy and Scalia *across cases* to see what causes them to reach different legal conclusions about the appropriate exercise of federal authority in *Lopez* and *Morrison* versus *Raich*. Additionally, I am interested in how these justices reach conclusions in *Raich* that are different from the conservative justices with whom they have previously aligned.[9]

Close Cases, Close Calls: Legal Ambiguity and Indicia of Motivated Reasoning in *Lopez*

The *Lopez* decision is remarkable for at least three reasons that suggest the justices may be engaged in motivated reasoning processes. First, as detailed above, the case represents a significant shift in the Supreme Court's Commerce Clause interpretation. This transition is far from smooth; there is a closely divided case vote signaling doctrinal ambiguity that is significant enough to cause a substantial rift on the Court. Second, the Court, in its majority opinion, is fully cognizant of the fact that the new direction it is taking will be a surprise to many individuals in light of previous commerce authority. Indeed, the tone of Chief Justice Rehnquist's opinion is noteworthy because he seems to acknowledge the reasonableness of the alternative legal arguments offered by the U.S. government and endorsed by the dissenting justices in the case. Third, both the conservative and liberal justices take a position on the standard of review appropriate for exercise of legislative authority that is at odds with their usual stance. Conservatives argue for independent judicial review of whether congressional action is "substantially related" to interstate commerce, while liberals call for deference to congressional judgment in the exercise of its plenary commerce power. Viewed separately, each of these factors could be indicative of motivated decision processes at play in the justices' decision making. Taken together, they illustrate why *Lopez* is an ideal place to begin this inquiry.

Legal and behavioral scholars alike note that attitudes are most likely to come into play in judges' decision making where there is "ambiguity" in the law. Arguably, one of the best places to look for such ambiguity is when there is a shift in doctrine—when the Court veers right when it could go (or had been going) left. Under such circumstances, it is usually the case that reasonable judges can disagree about interpretation, making the mechanisms of motivated reasoning discussed in this book especially likely to operate. Clearly *Lopez* represents just such a moment in the Court's history.

Indeed, in announcing the standard of review the Court will apply in determining whether Congress can regulate activities under its commerce authority, Justice Rehnquist specifically points to ambiguity in this line of doctrine: "admittedly our case law has not been clear whether activity must 'affect' or 'substantially affect' interstate commerce in order to be within Congress' power to regulate it under the Commerce Clause. We conclude, consistent with the great weight of our case law, that the proper test requires an analysis of whether the regulated activity 'substantially affects' interstate commerce" (*Lopez*, 514 U.S. 449 at 559).

It is this sort of uncertainty that Court watchers often point to as enabling attitudinal choices. Clearly, the conservative justices in the majority should favor the stricter "substantial affects" test, all else being equal, because it narrows the appropriate range of federal authority. Consistent with motivated-reasoning processes, this is exactly what they do, bolstering their reasoning by citing "the great weight" of authority at the same time they acknowledge that Supreme Court doctrine has been unclear on this issue.[10]

Moreover, the majority in *Lopez* seems cognizant of the fact that the decision represents a departure from previous doctrine. Rehnquist concludes the opinion, acknowledging the significant shift that *Lopez* represents in the Supreme Court's Commerce Clause interpretation:

> To uphold the Government's contentions here, we would have to pile inference upon inference in a manner that would bid fair to convert congressional authority under the Commerce Clause to a general police power of the sort retained by the states. Admittedly, some of our prior cases have taken long steps down that road, giving great deference to congressional action. The broad language in these opinions has suggested the possibility of additional expansion, but we decline here to proceed any further. (*Lopez*, 514 U.S. 449 at 567)

This language stands out because it is atypical of the general tone of majority opinions. Most decisions of the Court are written in such a way as to convince interested audiences (i.e., litigants, attorneys, legal academics) that outcomes are dictated by the "state of the law" bearing on disputes. Dissenting justices are often characterized as "misled" in their interpretation of appropriate authority. Here, however, the majority seems to be acknowledging the reasonableness of alternative arguments in light of prior case law. Clearly, the majority does not agree with the dissenting justices' interpretation of Commerce Clause authority, but it seems clear that they understand how their colleagues could reasonably disagree. The acknowledgment serves as a second indication that motivated decision processes, where preferences for outcomes influence the way justices interpret doctrine in light of reasonable alternatives, could be at play in the case.

The third and final hint that motivated decision processes are at work in *Lopez* is that the justices seem to be taking positions on the appropriate scope of legislative review that is at odds with their usual position in cases where legislative authority is at issue. Liberals, as traditional guardians of constitutional rights, disproportionately argue in favor of independent judicial judgment in adjudicating the constitutionality of laws passed by Congress. Conservatives, who favor majority rule, usually argue for judicial deference to legislative judgments. Here the justices take the *exact opposite* positions. Liberals in the dissent argue for deference to the seemingly reasonable judgment of Congress that firearms near schools substantially affect interstate commerce. Conservatives argue it is appropriate for the Court to undertake its own independent review of that question. It is not clear why the justices switch their habitual reasoning on this issue. Under the circumstances, it seems likely that the justices' preferences for outcomes could be shading their analysis of appropriate congressional scrutiny, consistent with motivated reasoning phenomena.

Judging Substantial Effects: The Determinative Role of Analogical Perception in *Lopez* and *Morrison*

Once Justice Rehnquist announces in *Lopez* that the Court will undertake an independent review of whether the possession of firearms near schools is sufficiently tied to interstate commerce to justify the exercise of federal legislative authority, the main matter left for the Court to adjudicate is whether the activity Congress tried to regulate "substantially affects" interstate commerce. This is also the primary issue in the subsequent cases discussed here, *Morrison* and *Raich*. In each instance, the majority and dissent come to different conclusions about substantial effects.

Significantly, the key determinative factor in all three cases is the extent to which the justices viewed the activity Congress sought to regulate as analogous to the family farmer situation in *Wickard v. Filborn*. All the majority and dissenting opinions discuss relevant facts in light of authority in that case. This provides an excellent opportunity to consider how conservative and liberal justices treat identical case authority across factual scenarios.

It is important to note that a finding that regulated activity is similar to the behavior held to be within Congress' reach in *Wickard* weighs in favor of deciding that the use of federal commerce authority is appropriate; a finding that the behavior at issue is dissimilar, or distinguishable, from the scenario in *Wickard* weighs against finding an appropriate exercise of such authority. If motivated reasoning is occurring, we might expect to see a situation akin to the hypotheses tested in chapter 3, where there is an interaction between the preferences of the justices and the outcome in *Wickard,* causing the justices to "see" pending situations as more or less similar to that controlling authority. Thus, conservatives, who are against broad federal regulation, should focus on factors distinguishing *Wickard* from behavior Congress seeks to regulate, and liberals should emphasize similarities between proposed regulation and *Wickard.* Indeed, this is the pattern in all three cases.

Recall that the primary holding in *Wickard* was that the wheat production of a family farmer fell within the reach of congressional commerce authority because the "cumulative effects" of that farmer and all other similarly situated farmers producing for home consumption could substantially impact interstate commerce. The Court reasoned that this production could ultimately influence national demand when considered in the aggregate.

In *Lopez,* where the majority finds "mere possession" of firearms is essentially noneconomic activity, Chief Justice Rehnquist acknowledges the significant scope of *Wickard,* but distinguishes the case from activity regulated in the Gun-Free School Zone Act:

Wickard, which is perhaps the most far reaching example of Commerce Clause authority over intrastate economic activity, involved economic activity in a way that the possession of a gun in a school zone does not. Roscoe Filburn operated a small farm in Ohio, on which, in the year involved, he raised 23 acres of wheat. It was his practice to sow winter wheat in the fall, and after harvesting it in July to sell a portion of the crop, to feed part of it to poultry and livestock on the farm, to use some in making flour for home consumption, and to keep the remainder for seeding future crops. The Secretary of Agriculture assessed a penalty against him under the Agricultural Adjustment Act of 1938 because he harvested about 12 acres more wheat than his allotment under the Act permitted. The Act was designed to regulate the volume of wheat moving in interstate and foreign commerce in order to avoid surpluses and shortages, and concomitant fluctuation in wheat prices, which had previously obtained. . . .

Section 922(q) [The Gun-Free School Zone Act] is a criminal statute that by its terms has nothing to do with "commerce" or any sort of economic enterprise, however broadly one might define those terms. Section 922(q) is not an essential part of a larger regulation of economic activity in which the regulatory scheme could be undercut unless intrastate activity were regulated. It cannot, therefore, be sustained under our cases upholding regulations of activities that arise out of, or are connected with, a commercial transaction, which when viewed in the aggregate, substantially affects interstate commerce. (*Lopez,* 514 U.S. 549 at 560)

The majority's language is noteworthy for several reasons. First, in describing *Wickard,* they focus on characteristics of the case that make it different from the activity they are considering in *Lopez.* Justice Rehnquist chooses to specifically mention that the defendant in *Wickard* sold part of his crop and that the Agricultural Adjustment Act was aimed at controlling interstate and foreign commerce suggesting the activity in *Wickard* was within the appropriate scope of congressional commerce authority in a way that the activity sought to be regulated in *Lopez* is not.

Moreover, in holding the Gun-Free School Zone Act unconstitutional, the majority focuses mainly on the fact that the possession of handguns near schools is not commercial activity: "The possession of a gun in a local school zone is in no sense an economic activity that might though repetition elsewhere, substantially affect any sort of interstate commerce. Respondent was a local student at a local school. There is no indication that he had recently moved in interstate commerce, and there is no requirement that his possession of the firearm have any tie to interstate commerce" (*Lopez,* 514 U.S 549 at 567).

The dissent in *Lopez* sees things quite differently. Opinions from the case demonstrate that the dissenting justices are willing to look earlier (at the interstate transportation of firearms)[11] and later (at the detrimental effects of school violence) in the causal chain for evidence that guns near schools substantially affect commerce. Breyer's main dissent specifically cites *Wickard* as authoritative several times. He focuses on aspects of the case that make it similar to *Lopez,* strongly emphasizing language in the opinion tending to show that, notwithstanding the majority's characterization of determinative facts, justices on the *Wickard* Court did not see the defendant in that case as being engaged in economic activity:

> Although the majority today attempts to categorize . . . *Wickard* as involving intrastate "economic activity," The Cour[t] that decided . . . [*Wickard*] did not focus upon the economic nature of the activity regulated. Rather, they focused upon whether the activity affected interstate or foreign commerce. In fact, the *Wickard* Court expressly held that Filburn's consumption of homegrown wheat *"though it may not be regarded as commerce,"* could nevertheless be regulated—*"whatever its nature"*—so long as "it exerts a substantial effect on interstate commerce." (quoting *Wickard,* emphasis in *Lopez*) (*Lopez,* 514 U.S. 549 at 631 [Breyer J., dissenting])

Moreover, Breyer argues that Congress reasonably concluded that the "cumulative effect" of firearms in and near schools could have a substantial impact on interstate commerce because of the fear and havoc that guns wreak in our system of education. It is clear from Justice Breyer's opinion that the dissenting justices see the "cumulative effects" of potential gun violence on interstate commerce as akin to the aggregate impact that similarly situated family farmers could have on the national demand for wheat.

> In determining whether a local activity will likely have a significant effect upon interstate commerce a court must consider not only the effect of an individual act (a single instance of gun possession) but rather the cumulative effect of all instances (i.e. the effect of all guns possessed in or near schools). See e.g. *Wickard.* . . . [R]eports, hearings and other readily available literature make it clear that the problem of guns in and around schools is extremely serious. These materials report, for example, that four percent of American high school students (and six percent of inner-city students) carry a gun to school at least occasionally (citations omitted), that 12 percent of urban high school students have had guns fired at them, and 20 percent of those students have been threatened with guns. . . . Congress could therefore have found a substantial educational problem— teachers unable to teach, students unable to learn—and concluded that guns near schools substantially contributed to that problem.
>
> Having found that guns near schools significantly undermine the quality of education in our Nation's classrooms, Congress could also have found . . . that gun-related violence is a commercial as well as human

problem. Education, although far more than a matter of economics, has long been inextricably tied to the nation's economy. . . . [A]re the courts nevertheless to take *Wickard* (and later similar cases) as inapplicable, and to judge the effect of a single noncommercial activity on interstate commerce without considering similar instances of the forbidden conduct? However these questions are eventually resolved, the legal uncertainty now created will restrict Congress' ability to enact criminal laws aimed at criminal behavior that considered problem by problem rather than instance by instance, seriously threatens the economic as well as social well being of Americans. (*Lopez*, 514 U.S. 549 at 616, 619–20, 631 [Breyer J., dissenting])

Finally, Breyer makes it clear that the dissenting justices disagree with the majority's decision to second-guess the legislative determination based, in part, on the latitude the Court has been willing to extend to such judgments in previous Commerce Clause cases including *Wickard*:

In *Wickard* . . . this Court sustained the application of the Agricultural Adjustment Act of 1938 to wheat that Filburn grew and consumed on his own local farm because, in its totality, (1) homegrown wheat may be "induced by rising prices" to "flow into the market and check price increases," and (2) even if it never actually enters the market, homegrown wheat nonetheless "supplies the need of the man who grew it which would otherwise be reflected by purchases in the open market" and in that sense, "competes with wheat in commerce" (quoting *Wickard*). To find both of these effects on commerce significant in amount, the Court had to give Congress the benefit of the doubt. Why would the Court, to find a significant (or "substantial" effect) here, have to give Congress any greater leeway? (*Lopez*, 514 U.S 549 at 627 [Breyer J., dissenting])

These passages demonstrate that the justices in the majority and dissent in *Lopez* "see" the applicability of controlling authority in *Wickard* quite differently. Moreover, those differential perceptions enable decisions that are consistent with their ideological views on the federalism issue in the case.

As the commerce power debate evolves in *Morrison* and *Raich*, this general perceptual distinction persists. The conservative justices, having decided in *Lopez* against the exercise of congressional commerce power, are more likely to cite that case as authoritative (making occasional reference to the treatment of *Wickard* therein). Liberal justices on the Court continue to cite *Wickard* as directly controlling the question of whether the cumulative effects of regulated activity substantially impact interstate commerce.

In *Morrison,* the majority again focuses on the nature of behavior that is the subject of national legislation. In holding that Congress overreached in providing civil remedies for victims of gender-motivated violence, Chief Justice Rehnquist points to the fact that such behavior is essentially not economic:

> Since *Lopez* most recently canvassed and clarified our case law . . . it provides the proper framework for conducting the required analysis. . . . [A] fair reading of *Lopez* shows that the non-economic, criminal nature of the conduct at issue was central to our decision in that case. . . . With the[] principles [announced in Lopez] underlying our Commerce Clause jurisprudence as reference points, the proper resolution of the case is clear. Gender-motivated crimes of violence are not, in any sense of the phrase, economic activity. While we need not adopt a categorical rule against aggregating the effects of any non-economic activity in order to decide these cases, thus far in our Nation's history, our cases have upheld Commerce Clause regulation of intrastate activity only where that activity is economic in nature. (*Morrison,* 529 U.S. 598 at 609–10, 613)

Justice Souter, writing the main dissent, strongly disagrees with the majority's assertion that the noneconomic nature of the activity regulated puts it beyond the reach of congressional commerce authority. He draws an analogy between the implications of congressional findings in *Morrison* and two earlier cases in the Court's Commerce Clause jurisprudence, *Wickard* and *Heart of Atlanta Motel:*

> The legislative record here is far more voluminous than the record compiled by Congress and found sufficient in . . . prior cases upholding Title II of the Civil Rights Act of 1964 against Commerce Clause challenges . . . (citing *Heart of Atlanta Motel*). . . . [G]ender-based violence in the 1990's was shown to operate in a manner similar to racial discrimination in the 1960's in reducing the mobility of employees and their production and consumption of goods shipped in interstate commerce. Like racial discrimination, gender motivated violence bars its most likely targets—women—from full participation in the national economy.
>
> If the analogy to the Civil Rights Act of 1964 is not plain enough, one can always look a bit further. In *Wickard* . . . [t]he Commerce Clause predicate was simply the effect of the production of wheat for home consumption on supply and demand for interstate commerce. Supply and

demand for goods in interstate commerce will also be affected by the deaths of 2,000–4,000 women annually at the hands of domestic abusers . . . and by the reduction in the work force by the 100,000 or more rape victims who lose their jobs each year and are forced to quit [citations omitted]. Violence against women may be found to affect interstate commerce, and affect it substantially. (*Morrison,* 529 U.S. 598 at 635–36 [Souter J., dissenting])

Again, these passages demonstrate that conservative and liberal justices view the exact same body of precedential authority quite differently. By focusing on the nature of activity regulated and its recent decision in *Lopez,* the majority reaches a conclusion about the appropriate exercise of congressional authority very different from the conclusion of the justices in the dissent, who are willing to look further back in the Court's history of Commerce Clause interpretation to find what they see as more appropriate analogies.

Particularly relevant to this analysis, in *Morrison* Justice Souter accuses the justices in the majority of outcome-oriented decision making through a selective reading of Commerce Clause authority. Specifically, Souter argues the majority's view is unsupportable in light of applicable doctrine including *Wickard:*

If we ask now why the formalistic economic/non-economic distinction might matter today, after its rejection in *Wickard,* the answer is not that majority fails to see causal connections in an integrated economic world. The answer is that in the minds of the majority there is a new animating theory that makes categorical formalism seem useful. . . . Just as the old formalism had value in the service of an economic conception, the new one is useful in serving a conception of federalism. It is the instrument by which assertions of national power are to be limited in favor of preserving a supposedly discernible, proper sphere, of state autonomy to legislate or refrain from legislating as individual States see fit. The legitimacy of the Court's current emphasis on the noncommercial nature of regulated activity, then, does not turn on any logic serving the text of the Commerce Clause or on the realism of the majority's view of the national economy. (*Morrison,* 529 U.S. 598 at 645 [Souter J., dissenting])[12]

Although there is nothing in this language accusing the justices in the majority of intentional wrongdoing, Souter implies that if those justices refuse to see the "obvious" relevance of cases cited in his dissent, as he has characterized them, there is something other than "objective" analysis going on. Of course, in making this observation, Souter does not acknowledge that his own reading of the doctrine brings him (and the liberal justices on the Court) to a legal conclusion that is consistent with their own preferences on federalism; rather, it appears that Souter feels they have interpreted authority appropriately with legal "accuracy" as their primary goal. This language demonstrates that the dissenting justices, at least, show no self-awareness that their reasoning is anything other than objective. This is particularly interesting as the dissenters believe they have identified motivated decision processes in the reasoning of their conservative colleagues. The sort of asymmetric attribution the justices manifest in their roles as "actors" who themselves cast case votes, and as "observers" of their colleagues' behavior, is fully consistent with psychological research demonstrating that it is easier to see the role of improper influences on decision making in the behavior of others than it is in one's own behavior. (See, generally, the research on the "fundamental attribution error" [Heider 1958; Ross, McFarland, and Fletcher 1985] demonstrating that when people observe others they are likely to attribute behavior to internal, dispositional forces. When accounting for their own behavior, however, they are much more likely to cite external, situational forces.)

Thus, judges observing other judges who are acting in ways that may be classified as improper are likely to believe that observed decision makers are "bad judges" who are fundamentally policy-driven. Yet, they will sincerely account for similar patterns in their own decision-making behavior as dictated by the "state of the law" in the particular set of cases they are asked to decide.

Changing Votes, Shifting Alliances

Lopez and *Morrison* present what are perhaps "ideal" cases to look at ideologically based motivated reasoning phenomena. All the justices who have been characterized as conservative on federalism matters—the ones Segal and Spaeth refer to as the "Rehnquist Five" on states' rights issues (2002, 421)—vote in the majority in both cases. All the judges characterized as more liberal on the issue are consistently in the dissent. The six-to-three vote in *Raich* is somewhat more complex as two of the justices in the "Rehnquist Five" vote the other way. Again, we will see that analogical perception plays a decisive role in the Court's decision—at least one of the justices, Justice Kennedy, sees things quite differently than he did before. Moreover, Justice Scalia evidences a view of the case that is distinct from that of the conservative justices with whom he has previously aligned.

What can explain this outcome? Here I propose two possible alternatives. The first is that, consistent with the conceptual "continuum of similarity" used to test analogical perception in chapter 3, the scenario in *Raich* was simply objectively similar to facts in *Wickard*. This characterization is consistent with traditional legal explanations of decision making. In effect, it would mean that Justice Kennedy, at least, was constrained in his view of the case and that case facts compelled him to vote with the liberal wing of the Court under applicable law.[13] It is important to note that, even if one accepts this as the most logical explanation for Kennedy's vote, it does not preclude motivated perceptions in the minds of the other justices. Indeed, it may strengthen the case for motivated reasoning for some readers. What else could explain the dissenting justices' refusal to acknowledge the applicability of such "clearly controlling" authority?

An alternative explanation, which I suspect may be more attractive to political scientists who question the constraining force of law, is that the second hypothesized mechanism of motivated reasoning, involving separable preferences, is at play in *Raich*. On this view, the reason Kennedy and Scalia vote with the majority may have more to do with the content of the law they are reviewing than their "objective" analysis of Commerce Clause doctrine. In line with my argument about separable preferences in legal decision making, the fact that one (or both) of these justices did not want to inhibit the federal government's ability to fight traditional drug crimes could have shaded their reasoning on the federalism issue in the case.

Raich is an interesting decision on many levels. First, it deals with a politically charged issue where there is a clear tension between state and federal law. Second, as referenced earlier, the case presents the most direct ideological conflict between the justices' views on commerce authority and the desirability of the federal policy they are reviewing. Finally, the vote in the case reveals something "different" is going on in the minds of the justices in determining the appropriate scope of congressional commerce power than we saw in *Lopez* and *Morrison*. Because the facts of the case are particularly important in seeing how the justices navigate this complex terrain, I take some time to review them before delving into the opinions that provide some insight into the justices' reasoning processes.

Federalism and Marijuana as Medicine: Indicia of Ideological Conflict

In 1996, the voters of California approved a ballot initiative, Proposition 215, calling for the legalization of marijuana for "seriously ill" persons with medical authorization to use the drug. The purpose of the initiative was to allow limited use of marijuana to relieve chronic pain and other ailments associated with various medical conditions. The Compassionate Use of Act of 1996 was enacted by the state legislature pursuant to the vote. "The Act create[d] an exception from criminal prosecution for physicians, as well as for patients and primary caregivers who possess[ed] or cultivate[d] marijuana for medicinal purpose with the recommendation or approval of a physician" (*Raich*, 545 U.S. 1 at 5).

Although the Compassionate Use Act protected such persons from criminal prosecution under California state law, federal drug-enforcement officers argued that individuals were still subject to *federal* prosecution under the Controlled Substances Act (CSA), a "comprehensive regime to combat the international and interstate traffic [of] illicit drugs." Congress initially passed the CSA under its commerce authority in 1970 to "control the legitimate and illegitimate traffic in controlled substances." According to the Court's characterization of the facts in the case, "Congress was particularly concerned with the need to prevent the diversions of drugs from legitimate to illegitimate channels" (*Raich*, 545 U.S. 1 at 12–13). Critically, the federal law prohibited the possession and cultivation of various drugs including marijuana. Thus, the CSA specifically criminalized the sort of behavior that was sanctioned by California's Compassionate Medical Use Act.

There were two primary defendants in *Raich*. Both were seriously ill women who used marijuana on the advice of their doctors. One of the defendants grew her own marijuana at home. The other defendant relied on two caregivers, who provided her with the drug at no charge. In each instance, the drug was locally grown with seeds, soil, and water from California. Although the defendants did not challenge Congress' authority to pass the CSA under its commerce power, they did assert that their own behavior was beyond the reach of the law passed pursuant to such authority. Specifically, they argued, the federal government should be enjoined from prosecuting them for activities that were not commercial in nature and that occurred entirely within the state of California. In making their case, defendants pointed to the fact that that their cultivation of marijuana for personal consumption was too small to implicate the interstate market. Moreover, the voters of California specifically approved the use of medical marijuana; the state should be allowed to enact laws with the broad support of its citizens without undue interference from the federal government.

The argument for federal enforcement was that where Congress clearly had the authority to pass the CSA, it did not make sense to single out this distinct class of behavior as exempt from federal law enforcement. Marijuana cultivated for personal medical consumption could conceivably make its way into the interstate drug market. Moreover, when viewed in the aggregate, the effect of such drugs could substantially influence the market and interfere with federal efforts to combat the use and traffic of illicit substances. Supporters of federal authority argued the possession and cultivation of marijuana for personal medical use was akin to the small-scale wheat production in *Wickard* found to be within the reach of congressional commerce authority.

In deciding this case, both the majority and dissenting justices show signs that they are conflicted by having to rule on this particular policy in light of what they regard as controlling Commerce Clause authority. In upholding the federal prosecution, Justice Stevens implies that his sympathies are with the seriously ill defendants in the case: "The case is made difficult by respondents' strong arguments that they will suffer irreparable harm because, despite a congressional finding to the contrary, marijuana does have valid therapeutic purposes. The question before us, however, is not whether it is wise to enforce the statute under these circumstances" (*Raich* 545 U.S. 1 at 9). Justice O'Connor, writing for the dissent, expresses the opposite sentiment: "If I were a California citizen, I would not have voted for the medicinal marijuana ballot initiative; if I were a California legislator I would not have supported the Compassionate Use Act. But whatever the wisdom of California's experiment with medical marijuana, the federalism principles that have driven our Commerce Clause cases require that room for experiment be protected in this case" (*Raich* 545 U.S. 1 at 57 [O'Connor J., dissenting]).

These passages illustrate that the ideological tension suggested earlier between the justices' federalism and criminal justice attitudes is quite real—indeed, real enough that the subjective experience of conflict is acknowledged by a liberal justice writing for the majority and a conservative justice writing for the dissent. Of course, it is one thing to say the justices are conflicted; it is quite another to argue that the justices' feelings about one issue (criminal justice) interfere with their legal analysis on the other issue (federalism). But here I do suggest that such interference is a plausible explanation of the votes of Justices Kennedy and Scalia in the case, albeit in different ways.

In the sections that follow, I demonstrate how the justices in the majority and dissent again see *Wickard* quite differently in relation to *Raich*. I suggest that the fact that the case involves cultivation of an illicit drug may shade Kennedy's perception of similarity between *Raich* and *Wickard* in a manner that allows him to vote in favor of upholding federal prosecutorial authority. On this account, Justice Kennedy appears to be driven by the sort of bottom-up motivated decision processes discussed in chapter 1 and tested in the experiments on analogical perception in chapter 3.

I also delve into Justice Scalia's unique reasoning in the case. Scalia's vote is particularly interesting because although his justification does not seem very different from the justices in the majority,[14] he does not join the majority opinion in the case. He could have done so and *still* issued a concurrence detailing the differences in his rationale. Instead, rather than endorse the majority's logic, Scalia chooses to characterize controlling authority in his own way. Specifically, he deemphasizes *Wickard,* which plays a central role in the majority's opinion, and concentrates on language in *Lopez,* that when read in conjunction with the Necessary and Proper Clause, determines his vote in favor of federal authority in the case.

Thus, Scalia not only takes a different route than the dissenting justices with whom he has previously aligned, he also needs to do a bit more doctrinal maneuvering than the justices in the majority to get him to a justification that is "reasonably supported" by his analysis of relevant case law. This suggests that Scalia is not "strategically" convinced of the majority's view in *Raich;* he presents his own view of the case as he sees it. I argue Scalia's decision-making behavior is more consistent with motivated reasoning accounts than rational choice explanations. Moreover, it seems that Scalia's reasoning may be accurately characterized as a top-down process where his desire to uphold the federal prosecutions in *Raich* leads him to find authority enabling that decision.

Mechanisms in Concert? The Justices' Reasoning in *Raich*

The language the justices use in *Raich,* following and distinguishing *Wickard,* is perhaps the most interesting and strongly worded in this line of cases. According to Justice Stevens, "*Wickard* is of particular relevance" in the majority's analysis because "the similarities between [*Raich*] and *Wickard* are striking" (*Raich*, 545 U.S. 1 at 17–18). In contrast, Justice O'Connor, writing for the dissent, argues, *Raich* "is readily distinguishable from *Wickard*" (*Raich*, 545 U.S. 1 at 53 [O'Connor J., dissenting]). Thus, there is a stark difference between how the justices in each group perceive the controlling force of *Wickard* in adjudicating the appropriateness of federal authority to prosecute individuals engaged in the cultivation and use of medicinal marijuana.

The majority relies primarily on similarities between *Raich* and *Wickard* in holding that the prosecutions are an appropriate exercise of federal authority under Congress' commerce authority. Justice Stevens explains:

> Like the farmer in *Wickard*, respondents are cultivating for home consumption, a fungible commodity for which there is an established, albeit illegal, interstate market. Just as the Agricultural Adjustment Act was designed "to control the volume [of wheat] moving in interstate and foreign commerce in order to avoid surpluses" and consequently control the market price (quoting *Wickard*), a primary purpose of the CSA is to control the supply and demand of controlled substances in both lawful and unlawful drug markets. . . . In *Wickard*, we had no difficulty concluding that Congress had a rational basis for believing that, when viewed in the aggregate, leaving home-consumed wheat outside the regulatory scheme would have a substantial influence on price and market conditions. Here too, Congress had a rational basis for concluding that leaving the home-consumed marijuana outside federal control would similarly affect price and market conditions.
>
> . . . Given the enforcement difficulties that attend distinguishing between marijuana cultivated locally and marijuana grown elsewhere, and concerns about its diversion into illicit channels, we have no difficulty concluding that Congress had a rational basis for believing that the failure to regulate the intrastate manufacture and possession of marijuana would leave a gaping hole in the CSA. Thus, as in *Wickard*, when it enacted comprehensive legislation to regulate the interstate market of a fungible commodity Congress was acting well within its authority. . . .
>
> The exemption for cultivation by patients and caregivers can only increase the supply of marijuana in the California market. The likelihood that all such production will promptly terminate when patients recover or will precisely match the patients medical needs during their convalescence seems remote; whereas the danger that the excess will satisfy some of the admittedly enormous demand for recreational use seems obvious. . . .

Congress could have rationally concluded that the aggregate impact on the national market of all the transactions exempted from federal supervision is unquestionably substantial. (*Raich,* 545 U.S. 1 at 18, 22, 31–32)

Besides drawing these parallels to *Wickard,* the majority distinguishes *Raich* from *Lopez* and *Morrison,* the cases on which the dissenting justices rely most heavily. Echoing Justice Breyer's dissent in *Morrison,* Stevens argues that focusing on these recent Commerce Clause decisions is "myopic" because it "overlook[s] the larger context of modern-era Commerce Clause jurisprudence." Moreover, Stevens writes: "Unlike those at issue in *Lopez* and *Morrison,* the activities regulated by the CSA are quintessentially economic. . . . Because the CSA is a statute that directly regulates economic activity, our opinion in *Morrison* casts no doubt on its constitutionality" (*Raich,* 545 U.S. 1 at 23, 25).

In joining the liberal wing of the Court, it is clear that Justice Kennedy sees *Wickard* as controlling in *Raich* in a way he did not in *Lopez* or *Morrison.* Of course, the interesting question is, why? One possible explanation is that, consistent with the majority's opinion, the scenarios in *Raich* and *Wickard* are, indeed, very similar. It is important to note, however, that there is still enough latitude in perceptions that the dissenting justices are able to distinguish the case on several grounds they see as material, even though the justices in the majority do not.[15] An alternative explanation is that Kennedy's attitude about the desirability of preserving federal authority to prosecute drug offenses shades his perception of *Wickard;* his preference for that policy disposes him to see the precedent as more relevant to *Raich* than he did in previous Commerce Clause analyses. As referenced above, it is very hard to know what is going on in the minds of the justices "at a distance." Each of these is a plausible explanation for Justice Kennedy's apparent view of *Wickard* in relation to *Raich.*

Significantly, we can also look at Justice Kennedy's separate opinion in *Lopez* to get some insight into his reasoning. Interestingly, his concurrence in that case was joined by Justice O'Connor, who writes the main dissent in *Raich.* This might help shed some light precisely on how Kennedy differs from the dissenters with whom he has previously aligned. In *Lopez,* Kennedy writes separately to emphasize "two lessons" from the history of the Court's Commerce Clause analyses that are relevant to the new scrutiny the Court announces. First, Kennedy is concerned about "imprecision" in content-based restrictions the Court may impose on congressional authority. He implies that he does not believe that requiring the legislature to regulate "transactions of a commercial nature" will be problematic in that respect. Second, Kennedy states that he does not want to see the Court backtracking to distinguishing between interstate and intrastate commerce in announcing this restriction. As long as activity is economic in nature, Kennedy believes it can be regulated by Congress, even if it occurs within state boundaries. He writes, "Congress can regulate in the commercial sphere on the assumption that we have a single market and a unified purpose to build a stable national economy" (*Lopez,* 514 U.S 549 at 574 [Kennedy J., concurring]).

Assuming that Justice O'Connor agrees with this language that she has endorsed, it seems that the main perceptual difference between Kennedy and the dissenters in *Raich* (for whom O'Connor writes) is whether or not the cultivation and sanctioned use of medical marijuana is, in fact, commercial activity. If it is, Kennedy and O'Connor both appear to believe it can be regulated even if it occurs within state borders. If it is not, they agree that Congress cannot touch it.

As detailed above, the justices in the majority (including Kennedy) see the behavior regulated in *Raich* as essentially economic. Writing for the dissent, O'Connor clearly disagrees. Rather than *Wickard,* she argues that the most appropriate precedents involve the noncommercial activity at issue in *Lopez* and *Morrison:*

> The case before us is materially indistinguishable from *Lopez* and *Morrison* when the same considerations are taken into account. . . . The homegrown cultivation and personal possession of marijuana for medical purposes has no apparent commercial character. . . . *Lopez* makes it clear that possession is not itself commercial activity. And respondents have not come into possession by means of any commercial transaction; they have simply grown, in their own homes, marijuana for their own use, without acquiring buying, selling or bartering a thing of value. (*Raich,* 545 U.S. 1 at 45 and 50 [O'Connor J., dissenting])

Moreover, she distinguishes *Wickard* from the *Raich* scenario on numerous grounds:

> In contrast to the CSA's limitless assertion of power, Congress provided an exemption within the AAA [Agricultural Adjustment Act] for small producers. . . . [I]n this case the Government has made no showing in fact that all the possession and use of homegrown marijuana for medical purposes . . . has a substantial effect on interstate commerce. . . . Critically, [in Wickard] the Court was able to consider "actual effects" because

the parties "had stipulated a summary of economics of the wheat industry" (citing *Wickard*). (*Raich*, 545 U.S. 1 at 50–51 and 53 [O'Connor J., dissenting])

Finally, in some of the most strongly worded passages in the case, Justice O'Connor criticizes the Court's conception of economic behavior. She not only argues that *Wickard* is an inappropriate analogy, but offers analogies of her own, hinting at absurdity in the majority's rationale:

> The Court's definition of economic activity is breathtaking. It defines economic activity as any activity involving the production, distribution, and consumption of commodities. And it appears to reason that when an interstate market for a commodity exists, regulating the intrastate manufacture or possession of that commodity is constitutional either because that activity is itself economic, or because regulating it is a rational part of regulating its market. . . .
>
> . . . It will not do to say that Congress may regulate noncommercial activity simply because it may have an effect on the demand for commercial goods, or because the noncommercial endeavor can, in some sense, substitute for commercial activity. Most commercial goods or services have some sort of privately producible analog. Home care substitutes for daycare. Charades games substitute for movie tickets. Backyard or windowsill gardening substitutes for going to the supermarket. To draw the line wherever private activity affects the demand for market goods is to draw no line at all. . . . The Court suggests that *Wickard* . . . established federal regulatory power over any home consumption of a commodity for which a market exists. I disagree. . . . *Wickard* . . . did not extend Commerce Clause authority to something as modest as a home cook's herb garden. . . . *Wickard* did not hold or imply that small scale production of commodities is always economic and always within Congress' reach. (*Raich*, 545 U.S. 1 at 49–51 [O'Connor J., dissenting])

Obviously, there is some intentional irony in Justice O'Connor's choice of language. Not even the most ardent federalist would suggest the federal government should be involved in regulating private party games or windowsill gardening in an effort to control interstate markets. But to what extent does her desire to strike down federal regulation cause her to see these analogies as "closer" to medicinal marijuana than wheat production by a single family farmer?[16] To what extent might Justice Kennedy's desire to uphold federal authority over the use and cultivation of illicit drugs cause him to reject these analogies in favor of *Wickard* and vote with the majority? Of course it is impossible to know for certain, but the patterns of analogical perception in *Raich* and this entire line of cases certainly suggest that the differential perception of precedent by decision makers with different policy goals is fertile ground for motivated reasoning in legal decision making.

Moreover, as these cases demonstrate, the mechanism can have important policy implications when case outcomes turn on such perceptions. Legally speaking, Justice Kennedy did not move very far in changing his vote from *Morrison* to *Raich;* his position (and the majority coalition) depended on the differential perception of the applicability of a single case. Sometimes, however, the justices need to do more to "get them" to legal rationales that are consistent with their policy objectives. I argue that is the case with Justice Scalia's vote in *Raich.* If Justice Kennedy's perception of legal authority was "shaded" by his preference for upholding federal prosecutorial authority, it appears Justice Scalia's preference for the same outcome may be more accurately characterized as determining his legal justification in the case.

Getting to Yes: Justice Scalia's Reasoning in *Raich*

A very careful reading of Justice Scalia's concurrence in *Raich* reveals how his legal analysis is different from that of the justices in the majority, even though it brings him to the same conclusion with respect to federal government's authority to prosecute offenses related to medical marijuana. The main "sticking point" for Scalia appears to be that he sees the relevant provisions of the CSA as criminalizing "both economic (manufacture, distribution, possession with intent to distribute) and noneconomic activities (mere possession)" (*Raich* 545 U.S. 1 at 40 [Scalia, J., concurring in judgment]). For Scalia, this difficulty is compounded by the Court's decision in *Lopez,* which holds that the possession of firearms is not commercial activity.

The justices in the majority are not bothered by the distinction between possession and manufacture of marijuana; drawing on similarities between *Raich* and *Wickard,* they characterize both as essentially economic activity. The dissent is also not phased; according to O'Connor, none of the regulated activity is economic in nature. As referenced above, she implies that the small-scale cultivation at issue is too trifling to be regarded as commercial activity within the reach of congressional commerce authority.[17] Scalia sits between these positions. Apparently he would uphold federal authority to prosecute the cultivation of medical marijuana under prior Supreme Court precedents, but he seems less comfortable about upholding federal authority criminalizing its possession. Scalia could endorse this middle-of-the-road view, concurring (in part) and dissenting (in part) in the Court's judgment. He does not, presumably because holding that the federal government does not have the power to criminalize illicit drug possession does not sit well with his vision of what sort of drug crimes the federal government should be able to prosecute.

Yet, it is clear that Scalia's own reading of applicable doctrine requires that if he wants to uphold federal law criminalizing *possession* of medical marijuana, he needs to go further than the justices in the majority do in justifying the exercise of congressional commerce power over this sort of activity. This is exactly what he does by seeking out additional authority to justify this conclusion in the case.

The logic Scalia uses in his separate opinion is similar to that of the majority, but his doctrinal emphasis is very different. Concurring in the judgment, Scalia alludes to the fact that he agrees with the majority that much of the behavior at issue in *Raich* is essentially economic, hinting at similarities between the case and *Wickard*.[18] But significantly, Scalia never cites *Wickard* as controlling in his reasoning. Indeed, he only mentions that case once, very briefly, in a footnote. Instead, Scalia points mainly to *Lopez* as controlling his reasoning in *Raich*—but to a different part of that case than the dissenting justices deem applicable.[19]

To justify the assertion of congressional commerce authority over activity he sees as noneconomic, Scalia reasons that it is necessary to regulate possession of marijuana to make the provisions of CSA involving interstate drug traffic effective. Citing language in *Lopez* and the Necessary and Proper Clause, he explains his vote in favor of federal authority in this circumstance:

As we implicitly acknowledged in *Lopez* . . . Congress' authority to enact laws necessary and proper for the regulation of interstate commerce is not limited to laws directed against economic activities that have a substantial effect on interstate commerce. Though the conduct in *Lopez* was not economic, the Court nevertheless recognized that it could be regulated as "an essential part of a larger regulation of economic activity, in which the regulatory scheme could be undercut unless the intrastate activity were regulated." (quoting, *Lopez*).

As the passage from *Lopez* quoted above suggests, Congress may regulate even non economic local activity if that regulation is a necessary part of a more general regulation of interstate commerce. . . . That simple possession of marijuana is a non-economic activity is immaterial to whether it can be prohibited as part of a larger regulatory scheme. Rather, Congress' authority to enact all of these prohibitions of intrastate controlled-substance activities depends only upon whether they are appropriate means of achieving the legitimate end of eradicating . . . [illicit] substances from interstate commerce.

By this measure, I think the regulation must be sustained. (*Raich*, 545 U.S. 1 at 36 and 40 [Scalia, J., concurring in judgment])

Thus, by invoking the Necessary and Proper Clause, along with language from the Court's decision in *Lopez* (a case he and the other conservative justices have previously endorsed), Scalia avoids the emphasis the majority places on similarities between *Raich* and *Wickard*. It is worth noting that Justice Stevens, writing for the majority, also mentions the Necessary and Proper Clause and the same language from *Lopez* to bolster his reasoning—but without the care and specificity Scalia uses in citing that authority in his opinion. For the majority, it seems the similarities between *Wickard* and *Raich* are enough to justify congressional authority in this instance. For Scalia, those similarities are clearly not enough. This is why he chooses not to cite *Wickard* as authoritative in his opinion and declines to join the majority opinion in the case. He sees his reasoning as different, *in kind,* from the majority's view of the case.

Scalia's reasoning is a good example of the role of interrelated preferences in legal decision making. The fact that he takes the extra step to justify federal authority over possession of medical marijuana demonstrates that Scalia is not simply involved in the objective analysis of doctrine related to the Commerce Clause issue. If he were only concerned about the appropriate exercise of congressional authority, Scalia could have upheld the authority he saw as tied to interstate commerce (i.e., activities related to cultivation) and struck down the part of the regulatory scheme that, in his opinion, was not related to interstate commerce (i.e., mere possession). Instead, his attitudes about the appropriate use of federal authority to combat drug crimes appear to interfere with his Commerce Clause reasoning in such a way as to allow him to uphold the entire regulatory scheme. Unlike Justice Kennedy, who simply shifts his perception of relevant precedent, Justice Scalia has to actively seek out authority to support his position. His preference for upholding federal authority determines the invocation of doctrine to help him justify that result.

The fact that Scalia "reaches" to uphold the entire regulatory scheme suggests that his criminal justice preferences influenced his analysis of relevant Commerce Clause doctrine. Moreover, it is clear that Scalia is not strategically convinced to vote with the majority as rational choice theorists might conclude without considering the content of his opinion. Instead, it is his own distinct reading of relevant doctrine that leads him to his vote for federal authority in the case. Scalia's decisional behavior in *Raich* is wholly consistent with motivated-reasoning accounts demonstrating the influence of nonseparable preferences in legal reasoning in line with experimental evidence presented in chapter 4 and 5.

Explaining Susceptibility: Future Directions, Important Distinctions

Before leaving this line of Supreme Court doctrine, there is at least one question worth considering that may have already crossed the minds of some readers: Why were Justices Kennedy and Scalia subject to the interference of criminal justice preferences in their Commerce Clause analyses when the other justices appear not to have fallen victim to this particular mechanism of motivated reasoning in *Raich*? The honest answer is that I cannot be certain; indeed, looking at the justices' susceptibility to this sort of motivated decision process looks like fertile ground for empirical research. I can, however, offer some intuitions that highlight why it is important to discover the nature of attitudinal influence in decision making to improve our understanding of extralegal factors in judicial behavior.

One thing that researchers must pay more attention to is the inertia created by decisions makers' psychological need to be (or at least *appear* to be) consistent. This is especially true where individuals are deciding successive cases involving similar issues. Simply put, people are motivated to believe that they are themselves constant in their own thinking and reasoning processes. For legal decision makers, this means that the primary inclination is to stick to prior voting behavior and patterns of analysis, especially where they are "on record" as having made prior decisions according to specific jurisprudential philosophies using existing doctrine.

Of course, there is always the logic that each case involves its own unique set of facts, making individualized analysis and deviations from prior behavior normatively appropriate, and even laudable in some cases (as when a judge avers that the "state of the law" compels her to vote one way when her inclination is to decide a case in the opposite direction). But still, the overwhelming propensity in any "line" of cases where decision makers are personally involved is to be consistent. We see clear evidence of this in the Commerce Clause cases. Seven out of nine justices vote consistently in all three cases. Indeed, twenty-five of twenty-seven votes demonstrate consistency in the justices' reasoning processes.

There is even evidence in this doctrinal analysis suggesting that the desire for consistency influenced the justices' treatment of precedent. Recall the great lengths to which Justice O'Connor goes in distinguishing *Wickard* from *Raich*. Psychological research tells us that the need to be consistent in our thinking can cause us to change our personal beliefs or our beliefs about the relationship between objects to create psychological "balance" (Heider 1958). On this view, following their opinions in *Lopez* and *Morrison,* the dissenting justices were motivated to "see" *Wickard* and *Raich* as dissimilar to maintain consistency in their legal analyses. The arguably forced analogies that Justice O'Connor draws between small-scale drug cultivation and the federal regulation of party games and herb gardening help them to do just that. On her account, it is not only illogical, but potentially dangerous, to conclude that *Wickard* is controlling in *Raich,* notwithstanding the fact that six of the nine justices seem to view the cases as substantially similar.

Given this penchant for consistency, it is especially important that researchers attend to what enables attitudinal choices and deviations from established voting patterns in research on judicial behavior. Individual decision makers can live with inconsistency—it is just less comfortable (and potentially costly) to do so—especially where judges are subject to public scrutiny for their opinions. So where judges do stray from existing patterns, they often go to great lengths to justify why they vote the way they do to avoid the appearance of arbitrariness in their decisions. We see an example of such behavior in Scalia's concurrence in *Raich*.

Significant attempts have previously been made to explain individual patterns of decision making in federalism cases on the Rehnquist Court. In their most recent book on the attitudinal model, for instance, Segal and Spaeth provide evidence that of the "Rehnquist Five," Justices Scalia and Kennedy were the judges who voted least often for outcomes favoring states in cases involving national supremacy issues.[20]

One possible characterization of this pattern—the one usually advocated by those explaining votes with unidimensional issue preferences—is that these justices have weaker attitudes along the ideological continuum related to "federalism" cases. On this view, Kennedy and Scalia are less likely to support the exercise of state authority when it conflicts with federal power because they are somehow less committed to the plight of states in our constitutional structure than the other conservative justices on the Court. Critically, the content of the policy the justices are reviewing does not come into play in such explanations. Differences are understood as a matter of the justices' degree of support for states' rights outcomes.

An alternative explanation that fits better with the richness of multiple dimensions in legal decision making is that what attitudinal scholars characterize as a difference of degree is, at least in some instances, better understood as a preference for federalism outcomes in light of alternative policy objectives made relevant by the facts and authority in particular cases. On this view, the content of the policy the Court is reviewing is critical for understanding the nature of attitudinal influence in the justices' decision processes. Without taking such factors into account, our understanding of extralegal influences is, at best, incomplete and, at worst, incorrect.

Some may argue that this distinction is entirely semantic, that having "stronger" preferences for federalism outcomes implies a priority for those outcomes; therefore, a motivated reasoning account of the justices' behavior effectively collapses onto the existing attitudinal framework. This is not true for several reasons. First, characterizing the vote in *Raich,* for example, as being determined exclusively by the justices' federalism preferences clearly underestimates role of criminal justice preferences in that case. To ignore the influence of criminal justice attitudes in the vote of Justice Scalia, for instance, seems to mischaracterize his reasoning in some important respect.

Second, motivated reasoning explanations involve looking at the *process* of legal reasoning in a way that existing attitudinal explanations do not. The analysis presented in this chapter suggests that the justices' perceptions of *Wickard* and other Commerce Clause precedents *enabled* attitudinal choices in this line of Supreme Court cases. By looking at the specific interaction of facts, legal issues, and doctrine in litigation, motivated reasoning accounts provide an explanation of how justices reach decisions consistent with their preferences that are "reasonably supported" by the legal criteria they see as so central to their own decision-making authority. Extant accounts of attitudinal influence lack systematic mechanisms that comport with the subjective experience of decision makers.

Finally, this emphasis on cognitive process not only stresses specific mechanisms of influence, it suggests real *limits* on motivated decision processes consistent with the large body of evidence from psychology.

Although the Supreme Court is generally not the best place to look for the constraining influence of legal authority (Braman 2008), in this analysis we saw at least one instance where a Supreme Court justice may have been constrained in his ability to distinguish cases that were objectively similar. Existing models of influence tend to discount the potential for legal constraint. As we saw in *Raich*, however, this account of Justice Kennedy's decisional behavior is actually quite plausible.

Admittedly, using the sort of doctrinal evidence I do here to "get inside" the minds of the justices is not ideal. As is the case with Justice Kennedy's decision in *Raich*, it is impossible to tell which of two plausible explanations (objective constraint versus ideologically motivated perception in favor of upholding drug laws) determines his vote in the case by just looking at doctrine. More importantly, we *can not* tell from available case law whether the justices would have treated relevant authority the same way or differently if the outcomes of those cases had been otherwise. For instance, if the Court in *Lopez* had *upheld* the gun-control legislation at issue instead of striking it down, one might question whether the conservative justices on the Court would, nonetheless, have perceived the case as substantially similar to the facts giving rise to *Morrison* and *Raich* (and whether the liberal justices would have been so quick to distinguish *Lopez* from those cases). We may garner our suspicions—but we can not *definitively know* how the justices would have acted under this counterfactual scenario based on available evidence. This is where counterfactual conditions created by experimental manipulations are so useful. It allows us to see how decision makers with similar views perceive identical authority where the outcomes of those cases facilitate *and* hinder policy preferences triggered by a particular set of case facts.

Notwithstanding the limits of our ability to make causal inferences, exploring doctrinal justifications the way I do here is not *useless* either. Consistent with arguments in chapter 1, the analysis here highlights that behavioral scholars have ignored the content of legal opinions for too long. There is important information in explanations of judges for their own decisional behavior. Significantly, this does not mean researchers need to take legal decision makers at their word. Votes that are justified with Commerce Clause authority may actually be driven by criminal justice preferences; legal analysis of standing doctrine could be more closely tied to how judges feel about the merits of disputes currently before them. Systematically looking at the justices' reasoning in successive cases may help shed light on the operation of such "hidden" motivating factors in judicial behavior. Moreover, it can help us understand exactly how judges come to agree and disagree in important respects that determine case outcomes. These observations may lead to hypotheses that can then be tested with the sort of empirical evidence brought to bear in the experimental chapters of this book.

My purpose in presenting the doctrinal analysis of the Commerce Clause interpretation of justices on the Rehnquist Court was to demonstrate the plausibility of the mechanisms tested in this volume and to illustrate their real-world significance. I hope that readers also come away with a sense of the significant latitude that legal decision makers have in interpreting legal authority when reasoning through cases. The analysis also provides an appreciation for the seriousness with which the justices approach their task and the decisional norms they see as central to the appropriate exercise of their own authority. The words of the justices themselves may be the best evidence I have that we should take conceptions of "appropriate" behavior seriously in studies of legal decision making. This is exactly what I attempt to demonstrate in the empirical chapters comprising the heart of this inquiry.

Testing the Mechanisms   2

THREE

SEEING WHAT THEY WANT?

Analogical Perception in Discrimination Disputes

with Thomas E. Nelson

The analysis of the decision making of justices on the Rehnquist Court certainly implies that differential perception of precedent by judges with different policy views could serve as an avenue of motivated reasoning in legal decision making. Theory and findings from cognitive psychology illuminate how analogical reasoning may enable attitudinal choices on the part of legal experts and inform a concrete strategy to test the boundaries of motivated perceptions in legal reasoning processes.

Analogy and Legal Reasoning

Analogy is the logic of relations. Empirical studies demonstrate that humans have the ability to create mental maps of structural relationships from a very early age and that analogy is pervasive in the way we think about the world around us (Holyoak and Thagard 1995). Psychologists who study analogical reasoning believe it is adaptive behavior that plays an important role in learning and higher-level abstract thinking.

The classic analogical sentence from standardized testing instruments like the Scholastic Aptitude Test (SAT) is: *A* is to *B* as *C* is to *D*. Analogies always involve an aspect of similarity between relationships, although the nature of the relationship may differ. For instance, the verbal analogy "black is to white as hot is to cold" is valid in that each pair of concepts is related to one another in opposition. A different analogy, "happy is to glad as startled is to surprised" is also valid, but it conveys the opposite relationship because each pair of words is similar. Any number of relations may be the subject of analogy. For example, "large is to enormous as small is to minuscule" conveys a difference of degree; "subject is to king as servant is to master" involves a relationship of subordination.

Gentner (1998) defines analogy by emphasizing its functional role: "analogies are partial similarities between different situations that support further inferences. Specifically, analogy is a kind of similarity in which the same system of relations holds across different objects. Analogies thus capture parallels across different situations" (107). As her definition implies, analogies are useful because they help us make inferences about objects or situations based on our knowledge of familiar things that share the same structural relation. Analogies may start off as unfinished mental statements that we are motivated to complete in an effort to understand an object or relationship we have not encountered before. Alternatively, drawing new analogical connections between familiar things can lead to novel insights about relationships we thought we understood. Scholars have theorized that reasoning in this manner is especially important in the creative thought necessary for scientific innovation.[1]

Besides the general role it plays in learning and creative cognition, analogy has been of great interest to scholars in specific knowledge domains. Linguists study analogy because of the important role it plays in communication and metaphor (Gentner et al. 2001); students of international relations study how foreign-policy decision makers draw connections between historical conflicts and current crises to help them recognize and choose among available policy options (Khong 1992).

Perhaps the best-known domain where analogy operates is legal reasoning. Attorneys shape legal argument by citing precedent, or prior judicial decisions, as authority for the outcomes they seek. Norms of judicial decision making dictate that judges must use prior judicial opinions to guide their reasoning in current disputes. The Latin phrase expressing the authoritative force of previous case law is *stare decisis,* literally "let the decision stand." The phrase embodies one of the central tenets of legal decision making: to the extent that previous case law involves similar facts, litigants, and/or legal issues, judges adjudicating current disputes are bound to follow the rules and logic set forth in prior judicial pronouncements.

Although the operation of analogy is most evident when judges apply common law rules through case-based reasoning, analogy is also utilized in other aspects of legal decision making. In statutory construction, for instance, when the "plain language" of a disputed provision is ambiguous, judges often look to previous applications of the law, seeking to draw connections and/or distinctions between past and pending scenarios. Using analogy in this way helps judges make reasoned decisions about whether or not a particular rule should apply to circumstances giving rise to litigation. Moreover, when judicial decision makers engage in constitutional or statutory interpretation by delving into the intent of elected officials, analogy is also at work. Armed with legislative or constitutional histories, judges are charged with deciding whether some activity falls within the scope of behavior intended to be addressed by those who drafted the textual provision. Where language is unclear, judicial decision makers often use analogy to fill in gaps, deciding how "close" or "similar" a disputed action is to behavior drafters described in legislative or constitutional debate.

Analogy is not only a way that judges structure their decision making; it is also important to how they legitimize it. Legal scholars have detailed the benefits of reasoning by analogy at length (Sunstein 1993; Sherwin 1999). Deciding disputes in this manner ensures equal treatment of similarly situated litigants; and it helps to create expectations about the consequences of future behavior. Finally, analogy is important because it allows for the gradual evolution of doctrine based on the reasoned application of legal principles to new situations.

Ironically, the central role of analogy in American jurisprudence has been alternatively characterized as a virtue of our democratic system and a force that works to undermine it. At the center of these different characterizations is a fundamental disagreement about whether analogical reasoning acts as a meaningful constraint on the decisions of judicial actors. The debate, born out of the subjectivity inherent in case-based reasoning, is fundamentally important given the special role judges play in our constitutional democracy.

Case-based reasoning involves a complex form of analogical thinking where individuals reason between situations that share some features, but differ in respect to others. Judicial decision makers may disagree about which aspects of a situation are most important when choosing among analogical alternatives. Moreover, as we saw in the last chapter, even if decision makers agree about which aspects of a situation are important, they may disagree about whether or not case features are actually similar across situations. Therefore, the decision to accept a proffered analogy when reasoning from case to case is largely subjective.

Consider, for example, the dispute about the extent to which the government should be able to regulate the Internet. Litigants have offered competing analogies about what line of doctrine should guide judges when considering the constitutionality of content regulations. Civil libertarians argue that because the Internet involves written text, it should be treated like print media, which have been substantially free from content regulation because of the importance the Constitution assigns to a free press.

Those who favor stricter regulation of the Internet contend that it should be treated like broadcast media, which do not share the same privileged treatment. The federal government grants broadcast licenses, so it has more power to regulate content over the airwaves. Proponents of stricter regulation point to the fact that Web pages often involve moving pictures and that computer signals travel via phone lines much like TV signals travel over the airwaves. Ultimately, the extent of permissible content regulation will depend, in part, on which of these analogies judges chose to accept.

A MODEL OF ANALOGICAL PERCEPTION IN LEGAL REASONING

The study described in this chapter seeks to test empirically whether the differential perception of precedent by people with distinct policy views serves as a mechanism of motivated reasoning in the context of legal decision making. The goal is to set forth and test a model of analogical perception that attributes an important—but limited—role to policy preferences in shaping judgments of similarity. The underlying logic is based on findings from psychology demonstrating that our ability to engage in motivated reasoning is not boundless.

In the domain of legal reasoning, I hypothesize that the primary factor limiting motivated cognition is objective case similarity: the degree to which two cases share an identity of facts, parties, and legal issues. The logic is simple. Where cited precedent involves case facts that are very similar to facts in the pending litigation, all decision makers, regardless of policy views, should judge the cases as similar. Where case facts are very different, all decision makers, regardless of policy views, should conclude the cases are dissimilar. The role of policy preferences should be evident in a "middle range" of cases where there is ambiguity in deciding whether to accept a precedent as authoritative. In this middle range of cases, the preferences of decision makers should influence perceptions of similarity; decision makers should judge cases with outcomes that support their preferences in pending litigation as more similar to current case facts than cases that do not support their preferences, all else equal, and they should see cases that go against their preferences as less similar.

Because legal training and socialization should inhibit the role of policy preferences in making such judgments, my model predicts that the same pattern of judgments will be present but attenuated for decision makers with legal training. Figure 3.1 illustrates the model of analogical perception I propose and test in the experiments described in this chapter.

FIGURE 3.1 Model of analogical perception

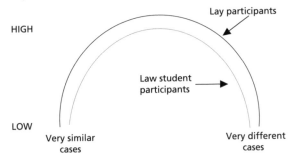

Clearly, the decision processes involved in making simple judgments of similarity are not the same as those involved in choosing which party is entitled to relief in a lawsuit, but they are related. Defining the zone of cases where attitudes operate in shaping simple perceptions may help us to understand where the law can serve as a meaningful constraint on the behavior of judicial actors and where policy preferences are likely to have the greatest impact in decision making.

TESTING THE MODEL

To test this model, I purposely choose two samples that vary considerably in their legal expertise: undergraduates (in Experiments 1 and 2) and law students (in Experiment 2). Obviously, undergraduates are not judges, and they are not attorneys. They have no legal training, and therefore are unlikely to be familiar with the complex decision rules that legal practitioners use when thinking about cases. Nonetheless, undergraduates are an appropriate sample to test this model of analogical perception. The decision tasks we are observing involve making simple judgments about the similarity of previous case law to a pending case. These decisions do not require special knowledge of complex decision rules. Moreover, such decisions are completely familiar to lay citizens. When reading media accounts of judicial decisions, for instance, citizen observers are likely to make mental judgments about the similarity of cases cited as precedent when assessing the quality of judicial outcomes. Although these judgments may never be communicated, they can affect evaluations of specific court outputs and, perhaps, more general orientations toward judicial institutions.

Moreover, testing the model on lay participants gives us a "baseline" to compare results with our legally trained participants. Drawing contrasts between lay and legally trained decision makers will help us determine whether legal education and socialization makes a difference in the role attitudes play in similarity judgments. Law student participants are an appropriate sample to use to draw such comparisons. Law students are familiar with decision-making norms. Starting in their first year of training, they are socialized to understand that attitudes should not play a role in legal decisions. They are specifically trained to apply tools of legal reasoning that practitioners use to guard against the influence of inappropriate biases in decision making. Moreover, finding effects in the law student sample is not wholly without significance. Throughout our legal system, a significant number of law clerks, many of whom have just finished law school, are given substantial influence in shaping judicial outcomes through the roles they play advising and assisting judges in decision making (Peppers 2006; Ward and Weiden 2006).

This model of analogical perception posits that there are three distinct classes of cases, characterized by how much they have in common with facts in the pending litigation: cases that are very similar, cases that are very dissimilar, and cases that fall between these two extremes. The lines between these categories are not fixed or obvious. Moreover, in the real world, it would be difficult to categorize a particular case as falling into one category or another. I propose, however, that the composite nature of legal disputes provides an opportunity to effectively operationalize and test this model in an experimental setting. By systematically manipulating the identity of parties and the nature of relationships in cases cited as precedent in relation to a specific "target" dispute, we can create a measure of "analogical distance" that will enable us to assess how policy preferences affect judgments in each of these categories of cases.

This was the specific strategy used in creating designs to test the model in two experiments. The structure of the experiments was identical, although the materials given to participants in each study described different legal disputes. Each experiment involved giving subjects a journalistic account of a discrimination dispute pending in the judicial system (the "target case"). Embedded in the mock article was also the description of a "source case," a prior judicial decision that the article stated "may guide the judges' reasoning" in the target dispute. Case facts and the outcome of the source cases were manipulated in order to assess their effects on judgments of similarity.

In the real world, cases can vary on any number of factual dimensions. Thus, the decision about which facts to experimentally manipulate is important. Holyoak and Thagard's (1995) theory of analogical reasoning was critical in shaping the manipulations and hypotheses for this experiment. Holyoak and Thagard suggest that three things are important in choosing to accept or reject a proffered analogy as authoritative: (1) *the similarity of the objects* in the target and source domains; (2) *the similarity of the relationship* between the objects in each domain; and (3) *the goal of the decision maker* making the analogy, or the purpose for which the decision maker wants to use the analogy.

In the realm of legal decision making, this theory presents a useful way to consider how case facts and policy preferences may interact to shape perceptions of precedent. First, one legal criterion that judges consider in assessing the applicability of precedent to a pending matter is whether the cited case involves a similar class of litigant. For instance, if a discrimination claim involves a gay man, all else equal, precedent cited involving other gay plaintiffs should be more influential than cases involving litigants complaining of other types of discrimination.

Second, the relationship between the parties to a dispute is another important legal consideration. A claim of discrimination by a gay man against his private employer is not the same as a claim against a government agency or a private membership organization. Even though each involves the same wrongful behavior (discrimination) toward the same type of individual (gay male), the legal obligations of the potential defendants are different because each has a different relationship with the claimant.

Finally, Holyoak and Thagard's third insight about how the goals of the decision makers shape perception provides a useful way to think about how policy preferences may come into play. If a decision maker wants to issue a ruling in favor of a particular party, the theory suggests she will be more likely to see precedent that supports that result as analogous to the case under consideration than cases that do not support that goal.[2]

Each experiment used a $3 \times 3 \times 2$ factorial design, where the target of discrimination, the entity accused of discrimination, and the outcome of the source case was manipulated. The first two manipulations combined to create nine distinct source cases varying in their objective similarity to the target dispute. The final manipulation varied the source case outcome to create cases that were consistent or inconsistent with participants' preferences in the target litigation. Based on the specific combination of facts in each source case, they were classified as close, medium distance, or far from the target dispute.

SPECIFIC HYPOTHESES

Manipulations of case facts regarding the target of discrimination and the relationship between the parties to the litigation are expected to each have significant effects on subjects' judgments of similarity. Moreover, there should be an interaction between subjects' policy preferences and the outcomes of cited authority such that subjects should be likely to view cases that support the outcomes they prefer in pending litigation as more similar to the target dispute than those that do not. Because objective case similarity is expected to act as a constraint on motivated perception, however, this interaction should occur only in the middle range of cases.

Finally, because legal socialization should inhibit the influence of attitudes in such judgments, the biasing influence of preferences should be attenuated in the legally trained sample compared to participants in the undergraduate sample. Stated more formally, the experimental hypotheses are as follows:

Hypothesis 1: Role of Legal Considerations

Manipulations of facts relating to the target of discrimination and the relationship between the parties will have significant effects on subjects' judgments of similarity. Generally speaking, cases designated as close should be judged to be most similar to the target case; those far away, least similar; and those in the middle, between these two extremes.

Hypothesis 2: Role of Attitudinal Considerations (Motivated Perception)

Subjects will be more likely to find cases that support their preferences similar to the target case than cases that do not. Specifically, we should see an interaction between the outcome of the source case and the policy preferences of decision makers such that subjects will be more likely to find analogous cases that support their views than those that do not.

Hypothesis 2A: Limits on Motivated Perception (Case Facts)

Motivated perception will be apparent in cases falling in the "middle" range of objective similarity.

Hypothesis 2B: Limits on Motivated Perception (Legal Socialization)

Participants with formal legal training will exhibit weak effects of personal policy attitudes on judgments of similarity.

If these intuitions are incorrect, two alternative patterns might obtain. First, case outcomes may not make a difference in judgments of similarity. If so, facts should drive perceptions in all categories. This result would be consistent with a legal model of decision making, suggesting that the law can serve as a meaningful constraint on all decision makers in the same way regardless of their policy preferences. Alternatively, if decision makers are entirely attitudinal, the interaction between preferences and case outcomes should occur in all categories, demonstrating perceptions motivated by policy preferences that are not tempered by the objective similarity of case facts.

Experiment 1

Experiment 1 was conducted with undergraduate participants. The purpose of this first experiment was to test whether judgments of analogical similarity were affected by personal attitudes, and also to see if the degree of bias would be most apparent for analogies that were moderately distinct from the target dispute on objective dimensions.

DESIGN SPECIFICS

In designing an experiment to test how lay citizens judge the similarity of prior case law, I sought to create a decision task that was relatively familiar to undergraduate participants. Most people do not encounter case briefs or judicial opinions in their everyday lives, so the case information was presented in the context of a journalistic account of a dispute pending in the legal system. My goal in choosing a target case was to select a dispute that undergraduates could readily understand, involving an issue about which they would have some opinion. It was also important to pick a legal issue that would allow for theoretically based manipulations of case facts to create analogical distance between source and target cases.

Supreme Court jurisprudence informed my choice. In June 2000, the Court decided *Boy Scouts of the United States of America v. Dale*, 530 U.S. 640 (2000). The case involved a clash of civil rights and civil liberties where a gay male claimed to be the victim of unlawful discrimination by a national scouting organization. Specifically, James Dale was relieved of his duties as youth leader and dismissed from the Boy Scouts because of his sexual orientation. He claimed that the conduct of the Boy Scouts was illegal under a New Jersey statute prohibiting discrimination against homosexuals in places of "public accommodation." In opposition, the

Boy Scouts argued that the Court should declare the New Jersey statute unconstitutional as applied to them because it violated their right to free association under the First Amendment. The Boy Scouts argued that despite its focus on civic values and its close connection with public education, it was not a public organization but a private membership organization. The Court, in an opinion by Chief Justice Rehnquist, agreed, holding that as a voluntary organization, the Boy Scouts' members had a right to "expressive association," which included the power to exclude people who did not share the values the organization sought to promote.

SPECIFIC MANIPULATIONS: CREATING ANALOGICAL DISTANCE

Boy Scouts of America v. Dale clearly involves a dispute about which most people are likely to hold an opinion. Moreover, because it involves a claim of discrimination on the basis of sexual orientation, this case provides an opportunity to create manipulations of facts that take advantage of theories of analogical perception.

Using Holyoak and Thagard's theory as a guideline, I created a 3 × 3 × 2 between-subjects factorial design in which the facts and outcomes in the source cases were experimentally manipulated. Specifically, I manipulated (1) the target of discrimination, so that each source case involved a claim of discrimination by either a gay male, a female, or a black male; (2) the entity accused of discrimination—subjects learned that the claim of discrimination was either against another scouting organization, an employer, or an insurance company for a denial of benefits; and (3) the outcome of the source case, so that half the subjects were told that the cases cited resulted in a finding of unlawful discrimination, and the other half, that the defendant was found to have "acted within its legal rights." The exact wording of the article and each manipulation appears in appendix A-1.

These manipulations generated nine source cases with distinct facts where there was either a finding of discrimination or no discrimination. Each of the nine cases was classified, a priori, into three categories based on their "analogical distance" from the target case. Table 3.1 summarizes the a priori classification scheme. As one moves down the chart and to the right, manipulations make it likely cases will be viewed as dissimilar.

There is currently a debate about exactly how individuals combine features to make analogical judgments (see Taber 1998 for discussion). The "gestalt" view holds that judgments are a reaction to the entirety of

TABLE 3.1 A priori classification of source cases' analogical distance from target dispute, Experiment 1

TARGET OF DISCRIMINATION	SCOUTING ORGANIZATION	EMPLOYER	INSURANCE COMPANY
Gay male	close	close	medium
Female	close	medium	far
Black male	medium	far	far

the analogue that cannot be explained by simple combinations of component features. In contrast, the "feature-matching" view maintains that judgments of similarity are more or less an additive combination of the extent to which individual features match (or do not match) across situations (Tversky 1977).

I classified each source case as "close," "medium distance," or "far" in objective distance from the target dispute based on the specific combination of facts in each case. In employing this scheme, I adopted a gestalt conception of analogical perception. My inclination to go with the gestalt view was based, in part, on how to choose the "best" cases from a legal perspective. Generally, cases involving an identity of target and relationships are most desirable, but having either in the legal world means you have a case you can use to argue your client's position.

The gestalt approach in creating distance categories was, informed, however, by a relative ordering of features. All else equal, I expected subjects would see source cases involving gay males and/or scouting organizations as most similar to the target case based on the identity of parties and issues involved. Also, I hypothesized that cases involving female targets of discrimination would be seen as more similar to the target dispute than those involving black male plaintiffs. This was the prediction I was most unsure of, especially in the context of a discrimination dispute where race may be especially salient. The intuition was guided by the fact that in legal analysis there is a hierarchy of standards that judges use in discrimination disputes. Distinctions based on sexual orientation are generally entitled to less scrutiny than racial or gender classifications. Gender classifications are entitled to what is called "intermediate" scrutiny, while distinctions based on race are subject to "strict" scrutiny because they are inherently suspect. Thus, gender is "closer" to sexual orientation in legal terms. Of course it is hard to say whether this technical classification scheme will translate to lay perceptions. Still, it seems quite reasonable to think that discrimination based on sexual orientation will be seen as substantially related to gender discrimination by lay participants. Finally, cases involving employment discrimination should be seen as more similar to the target case than cases involving claims of discrimination against an insurance company for denial of benefits.

Keeping this ordering in mind, I considered how particular combinations of facts would influence similarity ratings to create distance categories. Based on prior research demonstrating that the identity of relationship features across analogues tends to play a predominant role in perception (Gentner 1998), I emphasize the relationship manipulation in my classification scheme. For instance, two of the three cases in the "closest" category involve discrimination by scouting organizations (the specific entity accused of discrimination in the target dispute), and one involves discrimination by an employer. The case involving an employer in the closest category, however, involves a claim by a gay male (the specific victim of discrimination in the target dispute). Thus, I specifically hypothesize that it is the combination of features that shape judgments.[3]

PROCEDURE AND MEASURES

Two hundred and eight undergraduates were recruited from political science classes at a major midwestern university to take part in this experiment; all participants were given extra credit as incentive to participate.

The study was conducted using a computer program where participants were asked to read articles that appeared on an electronic monitor and answer questions about the information presented in those articles. Subjects were told that they were taking part in a study investigating how clearly news media presented information about legal disputes. All subjects in the experiment were given a mock newspaper article describing *Boy Scouts of America v. Dale* and stating that the matter was currently pending before the Supreme Court.[4]

Dependent Variable. After reading the article, subjects were asked to judge on a four-point scale how similar they thought the cited authority was to the target case. Higher numbers indicate that respondents saw the cases as more similar. The response to this question is the dependent variable in the analyses reported in this chapter.

Measuring Policy Preferences. To assess participants' views of the underlying issue in the target case, I asked them to rate the extent to which they viewed it as acceptable to have a gay man serve as a leader in the Boy Scouts. Responses were anchored at 1, "completely unacceptable," and 6, "completely acceptable." In conducting the data analysis, I split the sample at the median (4 on this measure) to create a variable to compare the responses of those who expressed substantial support for a gay scout leader to those who did not.[5]

Other Measures. To control for their influence on judgments of similarity, I measured several other variables including political ideology, partisan identification, race, gender, and level of political interest.[6]

RESULTS

Analysis of variance (ANOVA) is the main method of analysis used to test the effects of the manipulations and the influence of policy attitudes on judgments of similarity. First, I tested the influence of variables on judgments made by subjects in all treatment groups to assess the effect of manipulations on subjects' ratings of source cases. Second, because I expected an interaction between policy preferences and case outcomes only in the middle range of cases, I disaggregated the sample to test the effects of those variables in close, medium, and distant cases.

ANOVA Results: All Cases

I conducted univariate analyses of variance on subjects' judgments of similarity; specifically, the analysis considers the effects of four distinct variables: the target of discrimination in the source case; the relationship between parties in the source case; the outcome of the source case; and the policy preferences of the decision maker. Table 3.2 summarizes the observed main effects. Values in the table reflect the mean similarity judgments of participants for each case characteristic and political preference listed. Higher values indicate that, on average, respondents found characteristics more similar. Statistical tests for each variable indicate if it was a significant factor in participants' judgments of case similarity.

EXPECTED MAIN EFFECTS

Target of discrimination. Changing the target of discrimination had a significant effect on subjects' judgments of similarity [$F(2,206) = 3.5$, $p < .05$]. Although it appears that participants saw cases involving gay males most similar to the target case, followed by black males and then female targets of discrimination, I cannot interpret the substantive meaning of these relative ratings because the target manipulation is embedded in two significant higher-order interactions. Specifically, there is a two-way interaction between target and predisposition [$F(2,206) = 3.4$, $p < .05$] and a four-way interaction between all the factors investigated [$F(4,204) = 3.5$, $p < .01$]. Thus, we know that changing the target of dis-

TABLE 3.2 ANOVA results: Main effects of manipulations and policy preferences on judgments of case similarity (all cases), Experiment 1

TARGET	MEAN SIMILARITY
Gay male (*n* = 72)	2.63
Female (*n* = 74)	2.39
Black male (*n* = 62)	2.52
	$F(2,206) = 3.5^*$
Relationship	
Scouting organization (*n* = 68)	2.91
Employer (*n* = 77)	2.36
Insurance company (*n* = 63)	2.25
	$F(2,206) = 8.0^{***}$
Outcome	
Discrimination (*n* = 101)	3.36
No discrimination (*n* = 107)	3.65
	$F(1,207) = 6.2^{**}$
Policy preference	
Support gay scout leader (*n* = 102)	2.70
Oppose gay scout leader (*n* = 106)	2.33
	$F(1,207) = 6.0^{**}$
N	208
R-squared	.31
Adjusted R-squared	.17

$^*p < .05; ^{**}p < .01; ^{***}p < .001$ (two-tailed test)

crimination had some independent effect on similarity judgments (due
to the observed main effect), but we cannot interpret the substantive
meaning of the ratings because we cannot say what the effect would be
in the absence of the other factors manipulated that influence judgments
with respect to the target variable (Keppel 1983; Christensen 1997).

Relationship between the Parties. Altering the relationship between the
target and the entity accused of discrimination also had a significant
effect on ratings of similarity [$F(2,206) = 8.0, p < .001$]. Although the
relative position of the relationship ratings was as predicted, with cases
involving scouting organizations judged to be most similar, followed by
cases involving employers, and then cases with insurance companies as
defendant, again because the relationship manipulation is embedded in
higher-order interactions [$F(2,206) = 3.7, p < .05$ for relationship x out-

come; and the four-way interaction noted above], we cannot interpret the substantive meaning of this main effect.

UNEXPECTED MAIN EFFECTS

I hypothesized an interaction between outcomes of source cases and the preferences of decision makers in the middle range of cases. I did not expect a main effect for either of these variables. Yet, strong main effects obtained for both in judgments of similarity. These effects were not predicted and came as a bit of a surprise. For instance, subjects were significantly more likely to judge cases where there was no finding of discrimination as more similar to the target case than cases where there was a finding of discrimination. This was unexpected because there is no theoretical reason to expect that outcome, in and of itself, should affect ratings of similarity. Simply knowing that a court held in favor of the plaintiff or defendant should not have any influence on perceptions of similarity.

But again, it is important to note here that the unexpected main effects were embedded in the higher-order interactions noted above. So while we know that each of these factors had an independent influence on perceptions, we cannot interpret the substantive meaning of the relative ratings. When the sample is disaggregated by distance, however, the story becomes much clearer and is actually quite consistent with my hypotheses.

Disaggregating Results: Findings for Close, Medium, and Far Cases

MANIPULATION CHECK

Before testing the significance of the variables hypothesized to affect perceptions of source cases in the three categories, it is important to assess whether the a priori classification of cases as close, medium distance, and far from the target dispute adequately captured subjects' perceptions. Figure 3.2 sets forth the mean similarity ratings for each of the three categories of cases. The classification scheme did well. Cases classified as close were judged by subjects to be most similar to the target case (mean similarity rating = 2.68); cases classified as far away were judged to be least similar (mean similarity rating = 2.29); and cases designated as falling in between these two categories scored in the middle on similarity ratings (mean similarity rating = 2.52).

DISAGGREGATED ANALYSES

Because categories were built using manipulations of case characteristics, these factors drop out in the analysis of variance on close, medium,

FIGURE 3.2 Mean similarity ratings for cases designated as close, medium distance, and far from the target dispute, Experiment 1

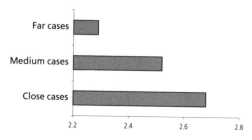

and far cases. Specifically, analyses look at the effects of outcome and policy predisposition on perceptions of source cases in each category. Table 3.3 sets forth the statistical results for the ANOVAs on similarity judgments in each class of cases.

In close cases, neither the outcome nor the policy predisposition of decision makers had a significant influence on judgments of similarity. Moreover, the interaction between the two was not significant. Thus, case facts seem to be driving the relatively high ratings subjects were giving to cases in this category.

The pattern of results for medium cases is as predicted. The interaction between preferences and outcome is statistically significant for judgments of similarity [$F(1,60) = 4.61, p < .05$]. There are no significant main effects for outcome or policy predisposition. Figure 3.3 shows the observed pattern of similarity judgments for decision makers with different policy preferences.

In medium cases, subjects who supported gay scout leaders found cases consistent with their preferences more similar than cases that were not (mean similarity rating for cases where there a finding of discrimination was 2.71; mean similarity for cases where there was a finding of no discrimination was 2.61). The opposite pattern emerged for participants who did not express substantial support for gay scout leaders, and the difference was more pronounced (mean similarity ratings for cases with no finding of discrimination was 2.85; similarity rating for cases with finding of discrimination was 1.93).

The pattern of results in far cases was somewhat surprising. I expected that all subjects would see cases in the same manner as relatively dissimilar to the target dispute. As predicted, there was no significant interaction between outcome and predisposition. Yet, it was in this category of cases

TABLE 3.3 ANOVA results: Effects of outcome and policy predisposition on judgments of similarity in close, medium, and far cases, Experiment 1

	CLOSE (N = 79)	MEDIUM (N = 61)	FAR (N = 68)
Outcome	$F(1,78) = .577$	$F(1,60) = 2.68$	$F(1,67) = 4.14^*$
Policy predisposition	$F(1,78) = .027$	$F(1,60) = 1.37$	$F(1,67) = 18.59^{**}$
Outcome × policy predisposition	$F(1,78) = .689$	$F(1,60) = 4.61^*$	$F(1,67) = .750$
R-squared	.017	.129	.258
Adjusted R-squared	−.022	.083	.223

$^*p < .05$; $^{**}p < .01$ (two-tailed test)

FIGURE 3.3 Similarity ratings in medium cases for decision makers with alternative views on gay scout leaders, Experiment 1

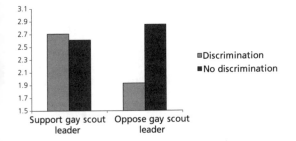

that the unexpected main effects for outcome and preferences were most evident. Findings were as follows:

Outcome. Subjects were significantly more likely to judge cases where there was no finding of discrimination as similar to the target case [$F(1,67) = 4.14, p < .05$].

As noted before, I was somewhat perplexed by this result. Perhaps my choice of a highly sympathetic defendant in the target dispute contributed to this effect. Unfortunately, I did not think to control for attitudes toward the Boy Scouts to test this hypothesis. Another possibility is that participants anticipated how a conservative Supreme Court would ultimately rule on this matter and made similarity judgments in line with that prediction.

Policy Predisposition. There was also an unexpected main effect for policy predisposition. Subjects who favored gay scout leaders were more likely to find *all source cases* similar to the target dispute, regardless of outcome [$F(1,67) = 18.59$, $p < .001$]. This result is easier to explain with the benefit of hindsight. People who favor gay scout leaders and gay rights in general may be more likely see judicial decisions as a legitimate source of rights. As such, they may use more lenient judgment criteria in assessing similarity of all cases than do individuals who don't believe the judges should be making these kinds of decisions.

If this intuition is correct, it would be evidence of an attitudinal bias I was not looking for, but one that is familiar to psychologists who study the influence of predispositions on decision making. Psychologists have written about the use of differential judgment criteria as a special form of motivated bias (see for MacCoun 1998). Moreover, if I am right about what is driving this result, it may be an artifact of my sample of lay decision makers. I would not expect this same result for legal sophisticates with different policy views who deal with judicial decisions on a routine basis. Experts are more likely to have a common evaluation metric that is less linked to feelings about the legitimacy of judicial intervention because they are used to thinking about courts as bestowers of rights and distributive outcomes.

Also, without reading too much into these unexpected main effects, it is very interesting that they are especially evident in the distant class of cases and not at all significant in judgments of similarity for cases that are most similar to the target dispute. It seems that, as one gets further from the specific facts of a dispute, there may be more latitude for attitudes to influence perceptions in ways I was not initially expecting.

Discussion—Experiment Number 1

What does this study tell us about analogical perception among lay citizens? First, in simple judgments of similarity, legal criteria seem to matter. Manipulations of the target of discrimination and the relationship between parties had significant effects on subjects' ratings of source cases. Second, it is equally clear that participants' policy preferences played a role in these judgments; as expected, there was an interaction between the outcome of cited authority and the predisposition of decision makers. Decision makers tended to perceive cases that supported their preferences as more similar to the target dispute than identical cases that did not support their preferences. Significantly, however, the interaction was not significant in all classes of cases, but only for a specific category of cases that were neither too close nor too far away from the target dispute.

Over and above these anticipated results, preferences seemed to influence judgments in other ways as well. First, people who supported gay scout leaders tended to use more lenient criteria judging all cases, regardless of outcome. And all subjects tended to see cases with outcomes involving no finding of discrimination as more similar to the target dispute than cases with discrimination outcomes. This may have been due to subjects' favorable views of this highly sympathetic defendant; unfortunately, I could not test this intuition with the data available from the experiment. Interestingly, both of the unexpected main effects were most prominent in the distant category of cases, suggesting that preferences may have more room to operate in these respects as cited authority gets further away from specific facts presented in a dispute.

Experiment 2

The purpose of Experiment 2 is to test my model with a different case and to discover if legal training further constrained motivated judgments. If so, legal norms proscribing judgments based on personal political views should weaken the impact of personal opinions on judgments of analogical similarity.

CHOOSING THE TARGET CASE

To test the hypothesis about the effect of legal socialization on motivated perception, I conducted another experiment with undergraduates and law students. The structure of the experimental design was identical to that used in Experiment 1, although the specific target case used in the second experiment was different. I was less confident that law students would not know of the *Dale* decision; it is commonly covered in first-year Constitutional Law and Civil Liberties classes. As a precaution, I decided to use a more obscure discrimination case.

The case I chose, *Wazeerud-Din v. Goodwill Home and Missions Inc.,* 737 A.2d 683 (N.J Super. AD 1999), involves the same New Jersey public accommodation statute that was initially at issue in *Dale,* although the context is somewhat different. *Wazeerud-Din* concerns the right of faith-based treatment services to exclude clients that do not share their religious views. Currently, the line between public and private assistance is becoming blurred with the introduction of programs like President Bush's "Faith-Based Initiative." The legal implications of these programs are, as yet, unsettled. Thus, *Wazeerud-Din* is a particularly useful case to use with the law student participants. Moreover, the case involves a value conflict similar to the one at issue in the *Dale* case—equal treatment versus free association.[7]

The plaintiff, Wazeerud-Din, was an Islamic man denied admission to a Christian-administered drug treatment program. Although the program received no direct government assistance, it accepted money from social security checks and food stamps issued by the government to its clients to subsidize costs. Wazeerud-Din argued that the program's refusal to admit him on the basis of his religious beliefs violated his right to equal treatment under New Jersey's public accommodation statute. The defendant, Goodwill Homes, argued that, as a religious-based program, it had a right to exclude individuals who did not share the organization's views. Goodwill Homes also asserted that successful participation in the program required "an openness to Christian teachings" that the plaintiff did not demonstrate. The Court ultimately held in favor of the defendant, ruling that under the facts of the case, the organization qualified for a statutory exemption as an "educational facility operated by a bona fide religious institution" (*Wazeerud-Din,*737 A.2d 683 at 687).

MANIPULATIONS: CREATING ANALOGICAL DISTANCE

Because I wanted to keep manipulations in each experiment as similar as possible, participants in Experiment 2 were also presented with a journalistic account of what they were told was a dispute pending in the legal system. I changed some of the facts of the case to suit experimental purposes and used more detail in the article than I did in Experiment 1 because participants were told it came from a legal trade periodical (see appendix A.1 for specific wording of the instrument).

In Experiment 2, manipulation of the target of discrimination involved telling participants that the plaintiff in the source case was either an Islamic man, a gay man, or a black man. The entity accused of discrimination was a religious treatment program, a community service organization (Kiwanis), or an insurance company. Once again, the outcome of the source case was manipulated so that half of the subjects were told that cited authority resulted in a finding of discrimination; the other half were told that there was a finding of no discrimination.

Again I classified the nine fact patterns created by manipulations, a priori, into three distinct categories based on their analogical distance from the target case. A summary of this classification scheme appears in table 3.4.

Once more the most challenging aspect of classifying cases was ranking the targets of discrimination on their relative similarity. Because the

TABLE 3.4 A priori classification of source cases' analogical distance from target dispute, Experiment 2

TARGET OF DISCRIMINATION	RELIGIOUS ORGANIZATION	COMMUNITY-SERVICE ORGANIZATION	INSURANCE COMPANY
Islamic male	close	close	medium
Gay male	close	medium	far
Black male	medium	far	far

target dispute involved religious discrimination closely related to belief systems and moral values, I expected participants to view claims involving sexual orientation as more closely related to the target case than claims of discrimination based on race. I also hypothesized that participants would view cases involving community service organizations as more similar to the target dispute than those involving insurance company defendants.

PROCEDURE AND MEASURES

Ninety-six undergraduate participants took part in the second experiment; their recruitment paralleled that of the undergraduate participants in Experiment 1. Additionally, seventy-seven law students at a major midwestern law school were offered twenty dollars to take part in this study and another experiment. Willing participants set up an appointment to do both studies, which typically took less than an hour. Each was administered through traditional paper-and-pencil techniques. Although I made a special effort to recruit students further along in their law school careers, I accepted all students who had *completed* at least one year of training (2LS and above). I set this as a minimum participation requirement because I wanted to make sure participants had been exposed to law school socialization, the brunt of which occurs during students' first year (Stevens 1983; Sheppard 1998).[8]

Undergraduate and law student participants were told they were participating in two distinct studies. Predispositions were measured via a pretest questionnaire. Participants were told that I was conducting a study to compare the views of professional and undergraduate students on campus. I embedded the critical measure of policy views concerning the relevant issue in the target dispute in a survey with other political questions. Participants indicated their agreement with the claim that faith-based organizations should have the right to restrict treatment or charitable services to clients who share their religious beliefs using a six-point scale anchored by "disagree strongly" and "agree strongly."

I then gave participants the article containing the manipulations, telling them that the purpose of the "second study" was to investigate how clearly legal periodicals reported cases pending in the judicial system. After reading the article, participants judged how similar the cited authority was to the target case using a seven-point scale. I measured participants' political ideology, party identification, race, gender, and level of political interest. I also asked participants how often they attended organized religious services.[9]

RESULTS

Full-Sample Analysis

Results of the full-sample ANOVA appear in table 3.5. As with Experiment 1, the analysis began by examining the similarity judgments of all participants in all cases as a function of the three manipulated features of the source case (target of discrimination, discriminating entity, and case outcome) as well as predispositions. The latter variable was created by dividing the sample at the median (3 on this measure), producing one group favorable to faith-based groups' right to restrict treatment to members of the faith, and another group opposed to such restrictions. Legal training (law student vs. undergraduate) was also included as a factor in the full-sample analysis. Its influence was highly significant [$F(1,172)$ = 26.52, $p < .001$]. Undergraduates were much more likely to judge cases as similar than were law students. Respective similarity ratings for the two groups in rating all cases were 4.78 and 3.55. At minimum, these results demonstrate that legal training sharpens attention to distinctions among cases, regardless of political attitudes.

EXPECTED MAIN EFFECTS

Target of discrimination. Changing the target of discrimination in cases cited as authority did *not* have a significant effect on judgments of similarity [$F(2,171)$ = .82, n.s.]. Moreover, undergraduates and law students responded to the target manipulations in different ways. The relative perceptions of undergraduates conformed to my hypotheses. Undergraduates rated cases involving Islamic targets most similar to the target dispute (mean similarity = 4.88); cases involving gay targets of discrimination next in terms of similarity (mean similarity = 4.79); and cases involving black targets of discrimination least similar (mean similarity = 4.24).

Law students, on the other hand, rated cases involving Islamic plaintiffs and black plaintiffs much the same way in relation to the target

TABLE 3.5 ANOVA results: Main effects, Experiment 2 (pooled analysis—all cases)

STUDENT TYPE	MEAN SIMILARITY
Undergraduate (n = 96)	4.78
Law (n = 77)	3.55
	$F(1,172) = 26.52***$
Target	
Islamic male (n = 60)	4.33
Gay male (n = 60)	4.12
Black male (n = 53)	4.05
	$F(2,171) = .82$
Relationship	
Religious charity organization (n = 52)	4.53
Community service organization (n = 60)	4.42
Insurance company (n = 61)	3.59
	$F(2,171) = 5.95**$
Outcome	
Discrimination (n = 82)	4.08
No discrimination (n = 91)	4.25
	$F(1,172) = .08$
Policy preference	
Support exclusion (n = 94)	4.13
Oppose exclusion (n = 79)	4.21
	$F(1,172) = .38$
N	173
R-squared	.48
Adjusted R-squared	.12

$**p < .01; ***p < .001$ (two-tailed test)

dispute (mean similarity ratings for cases with Islamic and black male targets were 3.74 and 3.62, respectively). Although contrary to my expectations, this finding is not too surprising for law student participants when viewed with the benefit of hindsight. As ascribed characteristics, religion and race are each subject to "strict scrutiny" for the purposes of discrimination analysis. Thus, the fact that law student participants rated Islamic and black targets of discrimination similarly could be taken as evidence that they were using legally relevant criteria appropriately.

Classifications on the basis of sexual orientation are subject to a different "rational basis" test. Yet law students rated cases involving gay men as only slightly less similar than the other categories (mean similarity rating of 3.38). Perhaps this is because, as predicted, participants viewed discrimination on the basis of sexual orientation as substantially similar to claims based on religion because both involve an organization excluding individuals based on their values.

Relationship between the Parties. Altering the entity accused of discrimination *did significantly affect* similarity ratings in the pooled sample [$F(2,171) = 5.95$, $p < .01$]. The relative position of the three entities was as predicted, with cases involving religious treatment programs judged to be most similar (mean rating of 4.52), followed by cases involving civic organizations (mean rating of 4.42) and cases with insurance company defendants (mean rating of 3.59).

The unexpected main effects observed in Experiment 1 for outcome and predisposition were not evident in Experiment 2. The interaction between outcome and predisposition, however, was highly significant in the full sample [$F(1,172) = 8.90$, $p < .01$]. As table 3.6 demonstrates, participants rated source cases with outcomes congenial to their predispositions as more similar than cases with outcomes that challenged their predispositions. The interaction emerged from the undergraduate sample [$F(1,95) = 2.58$, $p < .11$], but was considerably more powerful among the law students [$F(1,76) = 7.83$, $p < .01$). This pattern of results runs contrary to the prediction that legal training should check motivated perceptions. Moreover, it casts doubt on my hypotheses regarding the constraining influence of case facts on motivated perceptions. To adequately test this hypothesis, however, I again engaged in a disaggregated analysis of the factors influencing similarity judgments in close, medium and distant cases.

Disaggregating the Sample

The varying responses to the target manipulations across the two samples raises concerns about using my a priori classification scheme as a measure of distance. Indeed, the scheme works among undergraduates (similarity ratings for close, medium, and far cases were 5.20, 4.68, and 4.17 respectively), but the ratings of law student participants do not match my predictions (mean similarity ratings for close, medium, and far cases were 4.04, 3.15, and 3.54 respectively). Therefore, I decided to forego my a priori predictions that incorporated the problematic target manipulation in the analysis. Instead, I treat the relationship manipula-

TABLE 3.6 Marginal means for similarity judgments, Experiment 2 (pooled, undergraduate, and law student samples)

	DISCRIMINATION	NO DISCRIMINATION
Pooled analysis		
Favor exclusion	3.57	4.60
Oppose exclusion	4.43	3.90
Outcome × predisposition $F(1,172) = 8.90**$		
Undergraduates		
Favor exclusion	4.22	5.12
Oppose exclusion	5.13	4.71
Outcome × predisposition $F(1,95) = 2.58$		
Law students		
Favor exclusion	3.11	4.06
Oppose exclusion	3.96	3.13
Outcome × predisposition $F(1,76) = 7.83**$		

Note: Marginal means and reported interaction effects are from ANOVAs in each sample testing the influence of target, relationship, outcome, and predisposition. In the pooled analysis, participant type (law student vs. undergraduate) is also included as a factor.
$**p < .01$ (two-tailed test)

tion as the measure of distance for the disaggregated analyses. In essence, I am abandoning the "gestalt" conception of analogical perception in favor of a "feature-matching" approach with relationship as the predominant feature because it is clear the target manipulation did not influence perceptions as predicted (the manipulation involving the target of discrimination was not a significant determinant of similarity judgments in either sample). Under this revised scheme, all cases involving religious treatment services are classified as close; cases with civic organizations as defendants comprise the middle category; and cases with insurance company defendants are most distant from the target dispute.

FINDINGS FOR CLOSE, MEDIUM, AND FAR CASES

To get a better picture of how undergraduates and law students judged cases at the varying levels of objective distance, I disaggregated the sample by legal training and objective distance and conducted six two-way ANOVAs, testing the influence of outcome and predisposition on similarity judgments. The means appear in figure 3.4.

There is evidence of motivated reasoning in both samples, but the pattern is stronger and more consistent among the law students. While

FIGURE 3.4　Similarity judgments for undergraduate and law student participants in close, medium, and far cases, Experiment 2

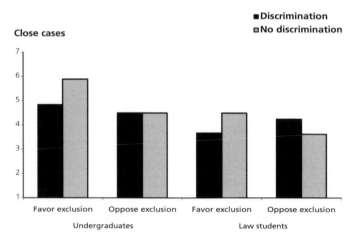

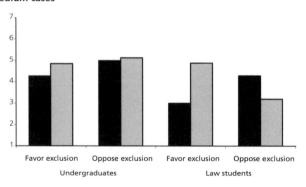

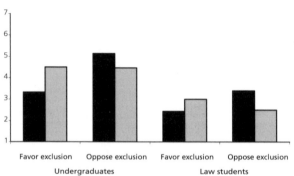

the previous analysis did not reveal a statistically significant moderating effect of objective distance, the pattern of results among law students matches my expectations. Motivated reasoning is apparent at every level of objective distance among the law students, but the effect is strongest in the middle category [$F(1,27) = 7.55$, $p < .01$], mirroring the results of Experiment 1. Indeed, this is the *only category* that returns a statistically significant interaction between predisposition and outcome. Thus, case facts *do appear to constrain* motivated judgments in a manner consistent with my hypotheses for law students in this experiment. The overall impact of attitudes is, however, contrary to my prediction that legal socialization should attenuate motivated judgments.

The pattern of results for undergraduates in this experiment is different than predicted. The interaction between outcome and predisposition is only significant in the most distant category of cases [$F(1,36) = 4.11$, $p < .05$], and rather weak in the other categories. Also emerging from the distant category was a marginally significant main effect for predisposition, with those opposing restriction of benefits more likely to judge cases as similar [$F(1,36) = 3.79$, $p < .06$]. These results, while not predicted, resonate with findings from Experiment 1. In the previous experiment, supporters of gay scout leaders saw more similarity between source cases and the *Dale* case, regardless of outcome; in Experiment 2, it is once again the opponents of discrimination (in this case, on religious grounds) who saw greater similarity between the analogues and the target case.

General Discussion

This study advances our understanding of how and when political preferences influence legal reasoning processes. The finding that opinions influence legal decision making may not be news to some, but we now have direct empirical evidence that points to one of the avenues by which such biases arrive. My results support the proposition that the differential perception of precedent by decision makers with varying policy preferences serves as a mechanism of motivated reasoning in legal decision making. Participants in both studies saw similarities in cited authority that supported outcomes consistent with their preferences in pending matters. In other words, participants with diverging opinions saw the very same cases in systematically different ways.

Moreover, objective case facts constrained motivated perceptions as predicted in Experiment 1, and for law student participants in Experiment 2. In each instance, the interaction between predisposition and outcome was *only significant* in the critical middle range of cases. Contrary to my prediction, undergraduates in Experiment 2 evidenced motivated perception in the most distant category of cases. The familiar scenario raised by the *Dale* case may have enabled undergraduates to make finer distinctions between categories than in the less familiar case involving restriction of benefits on the basis of religious orientation. In the second experiment, it could be that undergraduates saw the first two categories as substantially similar to the target dispute and the third as moderately similar. In essence, my operationalization of distance may not have gone "far enough" to effectively capture what undergraduates would categorize as "distant" in relation to this novel scenario, especially where it was presented in the context of a relatively authoritative trade periodical. Indeed, there was evidence that law students were more skeptical in making similarity judgments for all cases in Experiment 2, suggesting that they were more sensitive to distinctions between cases. This, of course, is part of the difficulty in doing an experiment with participants with different levels of expertise—but the possibility that each sample was using a different "metric" of distance is an intriguing notion that could lend itself to future investigation.

Law students as well as undergraduates demonstrated motivated perception. While these results invite cynicism about legal decision makers, I hasten to add that *nothing I have found suggests a conscious effort to twist the law to serve one's opinions.* In fact, participants were probably unaware that their views shaded the judgments I asked of them. Across the board, law students saw less similarity than did the undergraduates between the target case and the analogue, suggesting that, at a minimum, legal training attunes the student to subtle but meaningful distinctions among cases. The results further suggest, however, that these heightened sensibilities can serve political preferences.

In this study, I was looking for one very specific type of motivated perception, an interaction between case outcomes and policy predispositions. Findings indicate, however, that attitudes influenced judgments in ways I was not anticipating. In the sample of lay decision makers, there were significant and marginally significant main effects for outcome (in Experiment 1) and predisposition (in Experiments 1 and 2). These effects were most evident in cases that were furthest away from the target dispute, suggesting that attitudes may be most likely to influence judgments in these respects where there is substantial latitude for them to operate. Significantly, neither of these unexpected main effects was present in the sample of legally trained decision makers. This could be because legal training helps to prevent such biases, but it could also be a function of the particular cases used in the study.

Taken as a whole, I believe this study demonstrates the utility of adapting theory and methods from cognitive psychology to studies of legal decision making—for both disciplines. From a psychological perspective, these findings are noteworthy in at least two respects. First, the observed influence of policy attitudes in this context provides empirical support for Holyoak and Thagard's (1995) argument about the effect of decisional goals on analogical reasoning. Second, consistent with previous studies of analogical reasoning, both experiments demonstrated that manipulations of the relationship between the parties affected judgments more powerfully than did target manipulations (Gentner 1998).

Results also reinforce my contention that research regarding perception of legal precedent can be informed by theory and methods from psychology. Findings not only tell us that analogical perception is a potential avenue of attitudinal influence in legal decision making but suggest there are *real limits* on motivated decision processes. Judicial scholars have, thus far, failed to systematically investigate mechanisms and limits of attitudinal influence in the context of decisional norms actively used and subjectively experienced by decision makers they are studying. Motivated reasoning provides a major advance in this respect.

Analogical reasoning is clearly a fundamental aspect of legal decision making. But as detailed earlier, the differential perception of precedent is by no means the exclusive avenue by which attitudes can influence decision makers in the context of accepted legal norms. With this in mind, the following chapters investigate an entirely different avenue of motivated reasoning, the separability of preferences in cases involving multiple issues, to further examine whether and how policy preferences can influence seemingly neutral legal decision processes.

FOUR

REASONING ON THE THRESHOLD

Testing the Separability of Preferences
in Legal Decision Making

Litigation often implicates multiple policy dimensions. In chapter 2, we looked at Commerce Clause cases touching on federalism and other contested policy issues. But Commerce Clause cases are not the only ones that raise the possibility of interrelated preferences in legal decision making. In this chapter, I test the idea that how decision makers feel about one issue can influence their legal reasoning with respect to another. Specifically, I investigate whether "threshold" decisions are influenced by decision makers' feelings about the "merits" of a dispute using intuitions from economics about separable and nonseparable preferences.

Embracing Complexity in Studies of Legal Behavior

Legal reasoning is complex reasoning. Although our judicial system requires that judges make a dichotomous choice between adverse litigants, this seemingly simple decision is often embedded in complex fact patterns where several issues are raised that each could serve as the basis for deciding a case one way or the other. Cases with multiple issues are common in our judicial system because litigation arises from complicated real-world situations and attorneys are trained to present all legal arguments favoring their client's position. Attorneys routinely "argue in the alternative," or emphasize different aspects of a case at different points in their argument, even if doing so seems inconsistent. The goal is to provide judges with as many legal grounds as possible to make a decision favorable to their client's interests.

Surprisingly, much of the social science research on decision making treats cases as if they were unidimensional. Scaling studies, for instance, assume that cases involve a single "dominant" issue and that outcomes can be explained or predicted by ordering the justices' preferences along that dimension (Schubert 1962; Rohde and Spaeth 1976; Segal and

Spaeth 1993). Critics of scaling techniques raise questions about studying judicial decision making in this manner. Tanenhaus (1966) argues that, at best, scaling techniques lose information about alternative issues that judges may consider, and that, at worst, they can result in the mischaracterization of votes judges cast for other reasons. Mendelson (1963) echoes this sentiment. Citing an instance where Justice Brandeis cast his vote on procedural rather than substantive grounds in a case that was included in Pritchett's (1948) analysis of First Amendment decisions, he wrote, "to count that vote as against free speech is to pretend that red is green" (595).

Treating cases as if they involve a single issue also ignores the possibility that there is a *connection* between issues in litigation. How decision makers view one legal issue may influence their reasoning with respect to another. This possibility is especially intriguing in the context of disputes involving "threshold" matters that often accompany substantive disputes between parties. A threshold issue is one the court must decide before it can consider a matter or invoke a particular mode of analysis. Some threshold issues, including jurisdiction and the family of issues relating to justiciability, concern the appropriateness of using judicial authority to resolve particular disputes.[1] Other threshold questions involve preliminary matters that judges sometimes need to address to determine what rules will guide the analysis of substantive claims in litigation, as when a judge decides if a claim falls under a specific statutory scheme or requires a certain standard of review. Norms of decision making dictate that threshold issues must be decided first in litigation, before judges consider the "merits" or substance of a claim.

Decisions on threshold issues are fundamentally important in determining outcomes. The preliminary decision about whether to apply a particular standard of review can substantially tip the scales in favor of one side or another. Moreover, decisions on threshold issues often determine whether litigants are entitled to the judicial resolution of disputes that they are seeking. If a court decides it does not have jurisdiction to hear a matter, the only thing for the court to do is dismiss the claim. Under such circumstances, the plaintiff will not get the relief she is seeking or even the opportunity to have her complaint heard in an adversarial forum.

An assumption in traditional characterizations of judicial decision making is that judges' reasoning across issues is independent. How a judge views a claim on the merits *should not* affect her reasoning on threshold issues involving jurisdiction or justiciability. Given the potential for decisions on threshold matters to shape outcomes, however, it is not unreasonable to think judges' preferences on threshold issues may be related to how they view other issues raised in litigation. Judges who look favorably on a plaintiff's substantive claim may be more likely to conclude that the plaintiff meets the requirements necessary to litigate the matter; conversely, decision makers who sympathize with the defendant on the merits may be more likely to dismiss the matter on preliminary threshold grounds.[2]

The potential for such behavior in judges' decision making is problematic. Threshold matters are generally classified as "procedural" or technical issues; they do not attract a great deal of attention compared to substantive claims in litigation. It has been suggested that the ability of judges to dispose of controversial claims with which they disagree on such technical grounds may be a tempting way for judges to make decisions consistent with their preferences while flying "under the radar."

Segal and Spaeth (1993) are among scholars who have argued that the availability of different lines of authority facilitates attitudinal decision making on the part of judges. Without conducting any empirical analysis on the subject, they assert that Supreme Court judges use threshold issues to allow them to reach the merits in cases involving issues they want to address and avoid doing so in cases they do not.[3] Epstein and Knight (1998) have also suggested that judges may use alternative legal issues to achieve policy goals. In their analysis of the strategic behavior of justices on the Supreme Court, they explicitly state "interjection of an additional dimension to a case can be a rational course of action for policy-oriented justices" (89).

Judicial reasoning does not occur in a vacuum. The complexity of decision making increases with the number of contentious arguments in litigation, but so do the justifications that decision makers can use to support their outcome choices. Viewed in this light, the nested nature of decision making in cases with threshold issues represents an opportunity for decision makers seeking to justify distributive outcomes.

Characterizations of judges actively using alternative lines of authority to justify policy outcomes, however, are directly at odds with traditional portrayals of judicial decision making in cases involving multiple issues. Legal accounts maintain that the professional training that judges experience enables them to use appropriate rules of legal reasoning; one of these rules involves strict adherence to the norm that judges should separate their personal feelings about particular claims or litigants from their reasoning about disputes—another involves the well-established rule that distinct issues in litigation should be considered independently.

Even judges, however, acknowledge the potential for issues to "bleed" into one another in the process of legal decision making. One does not have to look too hard, or too long, to find judicial accusations suggesting improper motives concerning their colleagues' views of substantive claims in litigation drive threshold decisions that deprive particular parties of their "day in court." Given rules of decision making that dictate threshold matters must be considered first in litigation and the potential for threshold issues to shape outcomes, there is no question that judges could act to avoid substantive questions in this manner. Whether they do so intentionally is another matter.

The experiment I discuss here investigates the relationship between issues in complex litigation. Specifically, I test whether decision makers' preferences with regard to substantive policy issues influence their decision on a seemingly neutral threshold question. My aim is to gain a more sophisticated understanding of a second possible mechanism of motivated reasoning in legal decision making and discover its limiting conditions.

Theoretical Underpinnings: Considering the Separability of Preferences in Legal Decision Making

In considering how policy views may affect decision makers, I draw on the concept of separable preferences from economics and political science. Separable preferences involves the notion that the preferences of citizens and public officials may be related across choices. The concept of separable preferences has been employed by political scientists to explain the behavior of voters (Hinch and Munger 1997), citizens responding to political surveys (Lacy 2001), and members of Congress (T. Schwartz 1977).

Separable preferences has also been invoked the judicial literature. Edward Schwartz (1992) developed a formal model of judicial decision making based on his intuition that judges' preferences for policy outcomes are related to how much precedential authority they want cases to have. According to his model, judges who agree with outcomes in particular cases want those cases to yield substantial authority in future litigation involving similar issues. Likewise, judges who disagree with results seek to limit the application of those cases to future litigation. Schwartz's insight about the relation between policy preferences and the authoritative force judges want cases to have is extremely compelling, but it is distinct from how I use the concept of separable preferences here. Specifically, this study looks at the separability of preferences across issues in complex litigation. I conduct an empirical investigation of the extent to which policy preferences may influence decision makers as they consider issues assumed to be independent in legal accounts of decision making.

Preferences are separable if "a decision maker's preferences along any particular issue dimension does not depend on her preference along any other dimension" (E. Schwartz 1992, 220). This characterization of the relationship between preferences comports with how legally trained scholars characterize decision making in cases involving multiple issues. Distinct issues are to be considered independently in litigation in terms of relevant facts and authority that judges bring to bear on their decisions. Moreover, according to traditional notions of decision making, policy preferences should not affect judicial reasoning processes. So, how a decision maker feels about the parties or alternative claims raised in litigation should not come into play when deciding independent threshold matters.

In practice, decision makers may fall short of this ideal. Here, I propose a mechanism of motivated reasoning involving the relationship between issues in multidimensional cases. The boundaries between distinct issues may be more permeable than traditional characterizations of decision making suggest. I employ an experimental design to test whether the decisions of legally trained participants regarding a hypothetical threshold issue are influenced by their views on other policy matters concurrently raised in a complex fact pattern. Again, this mechanism of attitudinal influence does not necessarily impute improper motives to legal decision makers; instead, it allows for the very real possibility that attitudinal considerations can influence seemingly objective reasoning processes as decision makers use tools of legal analysis to achieve norm-appropriate goals.

Design Specifics: Basic Intuition

Standing is a threshold issue that involves whether the person who files a complaint is an appropriate party to litigate the matter. As mentioned in the introduction, this requirement means that the injury the plaintiff claims to have suffered must be an "injury in fact" that is personal to the plaintiff and not commonly shared by others in the population.[4] Standing is especially useful for an experiment like this because it can arise in a variety of factual contexts. Whenever it is raised, the question of standing is always embedded in a larger substantive dispute. Moreover, from a legal standpoint, how a judge views the substantive issues raised in litigation should not affect the determination of the standing question. Although there are several "subparts" to the standing doctrine, the most important for the purpose of understanding the design used in this experiment is the requirement that the alleged injury be "personal" to the plaintiff.

THE MOCK BRIEF

To test the relationship between issues in complex litigation, I drafted different versions of a hypothetical case brief, or Mock Brief, involving a standing issue that has been the subject of conflicting rulings by federal circuit courts. Law student participants were presented with this brief in which case facts and legal arguments related to a standing issue were experimentally controlled.

The model for the case described in the Mock Brief was a decision from the United States Court of Appeals for the Eighth Circuit: *International Association of Firefighters v. City of Ferguson*, 283 F.3d 969 (8th Cir. 2002). The case involved a local ordinance with provisions akin to the Hatch Act restricting the political activity of public employees. The city ordinance stated that municipal employees would be subject to disciplinary action or dismissal if they were involved in supporting candidates for municipal office directly or indirectly.[5] In *City of Ferguson*, the wife of a city firefighter challenged the provision when her husband's job was threatened after she tried to run for municipal office. Her claim was that the ordinance improperly restricted her political conduct because she was fearful her husband could lose his job on account of her activities.

The defendant city employer raised the issue of standing, arguing that because the provision did not threaten the plaintiff directly, but only *indirectly* through the loss of her *husband's* employment, she did not have standing to challenge the ordinance. The Court of Appeals for the Eighth Circuit decided the issue in favor of the plaintiff; it held that the fireman's wife suffered a legally cognizable injury that was personal to her because it was her own political expression that was inhibited by the operation of the ordinance. The court reasoned that she had a reasonable apprehension that her husband could lose his job, which would cause economic harm to her entire family.

In ruling for the plaintiff on the standing issue, the Eighth Circuit reversed the decision of a Missouri federal district court. It also contradicted the decisions of two other federal circuit courts that have decided the same standing issue, *Biggs v. Best, Best and Krieger,* 189 F.3d 989 (9th Cir. 1997) and *Horstkoetter v. Department of Public Safety,* 159 F.3d 1265 (10th Cir. 1998). Each of these cases also involved challenges to restrictive ordinances raised by spouses of public employees. In both cases, the circuit court specifically held that harm alleged by the plaintiff was "too indirect" to confer standing to challenge the ordinance at issue.

The issue raised in this line of cases presents an excellent opportunity to test the separability of preferences in a concrete legal dispute. Experimental conditions were created where participants were given identical legal authority to make a decision on the standing issue in different contexts. Significantly, from a legal standpoint, variations in the fact pattern across treatment conditions should not influence participants' reasoning on the standing issue, although they may significantly alter how participants view the larger dispute in which the threshold issue is embedded.

All participants were given a "Summary Legal Brief," which they were told was a new format that some jurisdictions were considering to promote timely motion decisions. This brief was a ten-page document setting forth the facts and legal arguments submitted by each side to a hypothetical dispute, *Denise Brunell v. City of Gayson and Rick Humphry, City Manager.* Each side submitted arguments regarding the defendants' Motion to Dismiss. The basis of the defendants' motion was a standing issue similar to the one raised in the federal cases described above.

The brief described a dispute in which a city ordinance prohibited public employees from supporting local candidates for mayor or city council. The plaintiff was the wife of a city firefighter; her husband was threatened with disciplinary action after she posted a campaign sign on their property in the midst of a "hotly contested" campaign for city council that "centered on the controversial issue of abortion." After she discussed the matter with her husband, the couple removed the sign, but the plaintiff brought an action challenging the ordinance as an improper restriction on her right to political expression.

The experiment involved a 2 × 2 factorial design in which the content of the political expression was manipulated. Half the participants read a brief in which the plaintiff expressed support for the pro-life candidate in the election for city council; the other half read a brief in which she expressed her support for the pro-choice candidate. The jurisdiction in which the case was pending was also manipulated. Half the participants read a brief indicating that the matter was pending in a district court in the Eighth Circuit, where there is direct legal authority in favor of the plaintiff (*City of Ferguson*); the other half read a brief that stated that the case came from a district court in the Third Circuit, in which no federal case law is directly on point but the weight of authority goes in the opposite direction (i.e., cases from three other federal courts that have decided the spousal-standing issue including *Biggs* and *Horstkoetter*).

A copy of the brief with alternative wordings appears in appendix B. After a rendition of the facts, the brief presents the legal arguments on each side on the standing issue. The authority each side cited in support of its position was identical across conditions; the only differences in the facts given to subjects in each treatment involved the content of the message on the campaign sign and the state in which the hypothetical city of Gayson was situated (in order to locate the dispute within the geographic jurisdiction of each relevant circuit).

Traditional notions of legal decision making suggest that decisions on multiple issues in complex cases should be independent, so there should be no difference in how participants make decisions, provided relevant case facts and controlling authority on the standing issue are identical. Systematic differences across conditions would suggest evidence of motivated reasoning, demonstrating that participants' views on other issues raised in the hypothetical fact pattern shaded their reasoning on the standing issue.

Because the alleged "injury" to plaintiff and the authority bearing on that question is identical across conditions, the standing analysis should be *the same* regardless of the content of the plaintiff's political expression. The critical question this experiment is designed to answer is whether participants are more likely to conclude that the plaintiff has standing when the content of the political speech she expresses is consistent with their views on abortion. There are behavioral studies that indicate that judges disproportionately decide cases in favor of parties with whom they are ideologically aligned (Sheehan, Mishler, and Songer 1992). From a legal perspective, this should not happen. By ascertaining whether there are systematic differences in the way people with alternative views decide the standing issue, we will be able to make valid causal inferences about the extent to which participants' abortion attitudes influence their decision-making behavior.[6]

Although the manipulations relate most directly to opinions on abortion, the hypothetical case raises two other policy issues that could also influence participants' view of whether the plaintiff has suffered an injury sufficient to challenge the ordinance. Participants who support the type of government action at issue—the ordinance restricting the speech of public employees—may be less likely to conclude that the plaintiff has suffered an injury sufficient to allow her to challenge the ordinance. Conversely, those who support free speech, in general, may be more likely to conclude that she has standing regardless of whether or not they agree with the specific content of the political message she is expressing. By measuring participants' attitudes on each of these potentially relevant dimensions, as well as the abortion issue, we can determine not only whether policy preferences influence decision-making behavior but also which preferences influence decisions on the standing issue from a number of plausible alternatives.

Finally, legal accounts of decision making suggest the law should be a limit on the ability of decision makers to make decisions consistent with their preferences. Yet, judges often operate under different levels of constraint. The fact that the standing issue has been the subject of conflicting rulings by the federal circuits creates an opportunity to test how preferences influence legal reasoning under different levels of constraint. By manipulating the jurisdiction where the case is pending, we can observe how preferences operate in constrained versus relatively unconstrained conditions. In the Eighth Circuit, there is direct controlling authority on the spousal standing issue, suggesting that the plaintiff should have standing; in the Third Circuit, there is no direct authority on point but the weight of authority is in the *opposite direction.* As set forth more fully below, three alternative patterns of behavior were hypothesized based on competing theories of how the law acts to constrain legal decision-making processes.

EXPERIMENTAL HYPOTHESES

Attitudinal Hypotheses

The questions of interest are whether and how participants' views on abortion, ordinances restricting the political activity of public employees, and free speech influence their decision on the standing issue. The "attitudinal" hypotheses are as follows:

1. Participants should be more likely to find the plaintiff has standing to challenge the ordinance when the content of the message on the campaign sign is consistent with their views on abortion.

2. Participants who oppose restrictions on the political activities of public employees should be more likely to find standing regardless of content.

3. Participants who support free speech should be more likely to find standing to challenge the ordinance regardless of content.

All or none of the foregoing hypotheses may gain support. A finding of no systematic differences would show that decision makers were able to separate their preferences on issues, in line with traditional notions of legal decision making; significant differences would suggest evidence of motivated reasoning, in that participants could not strictly separate their preferences on the standing issue from the other issues raised in the fact pattern.

Hypotheses Regarding the Law as a Constraint on Motivated Decision Making

There are three alternative patterns of behavior that may be observed based on a legal model, an attitudinal model, and a "constrained attitudinal" model of decision-making behavior. Specific hypotheses and a graphic illustration of the pattern of the behavior each model predicts are set forth below.

PURE LEGAL MODEL PREDICTIONS

Legally, decision makers should be less likely to make preference-based decisions where there is direct controlling authority limiting their ability to do so. Under conditions in which there is direct controlling authority (the Eighth Circuit conditions), it favors the plaintiff. As a matter of law, then, subjects should decide in her favor under those conditions. It is also important to keep in mind that the authority in the brief is "stacked" in favor of the defendants. Most of the legal authority in the Mock Brief is on one side—three federal court cases to one holding that spousal plaintiffs do not have standing to challenge ordinances restricting the political speech of public employees. Thus, where there is no direct authority on point (the Third Circuit conditions), legal models of decision making would predict a decision in defendants' direction (against standing) because the weight of authority goes in that direction.

PURE ATTITUDINAL MODEL PREDICTIONS

Alternatively, according to attitudinal models of decision making, the law should not inhibit preference-based judgments. We should observe behavior in line with the attitudinal hypotheses set forth above in both the constrained (Eighth Circuit) and unconstrained (Third Circuit) conditions.

FIGURE 4.1 Alternative hypotheses for legal, attitudinal, and constrained at-titudinal models in Third and Eighth Circuit conditions

Legal model prediction, Eighth Circuit

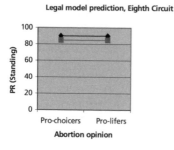

Legal model prediction, Third Circuit

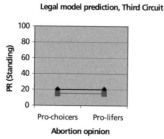

Attitudinal model prediction, Eighth Circuit

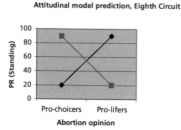

Attitudinal model prediction, Third Circuit

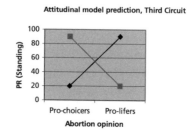

Constrained attitudinal model prediction, Eighth Circuit

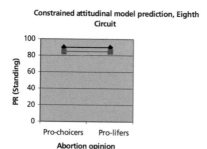

Constrained attitudinal model prediction, Third Circuit

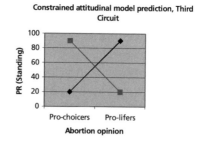

CONSTRAINED ATTITUDINAL MODEL PREDICTIONS

There is a third possibility, a "constrained attitudinal" conception of legal decision making. According to this model, decision makers should follow their attitudes where they are relatively free to do so and resist the temptation to make preference-based decisions when they are not. This conception predicts decision making consistent with legal hypotheses in the constrained condition (Eighth Circuit) and patterns of behavior consistent with the attitudinal model in the unconstrained condition (Third Circuit).

Procedure

Experiments were conducted in June and September 2003. All students who successfully *completed* their first year of training at a major midwestern law school were contacted via an email solicitation and a table in the lobby of the law school. There were 115 law students participating in this study; a summary of sample characteristics appears in appendix B.

Participants were paid twenty dollars to participate in what they believed were two distinct studies. Participants were told that "Study A" was a survey that was being conducted to compare the political views of various graduate and professional students on campus. The survey included eight policy questions and measures of background characteristics. The three questions that were used as the relevant policy measures were embedded in the survey. Participants indicated, on a six-point scale, the degree to which they supported statements concerning abortion, restrictions on the political activity of public employees, and criminal sanctions for flag-burning, which was used as the general measure of support for free speech. Exact wordings of the questions are included in appendix B.

After completing the survey, participants moved on to "Study B." A cover story was embedded in the instructions stating that the purpose of the study was to get feedback on a new "Summary Brief" format that some jurisdictions were considering to expedite motion practice. Participants were informed that under the new format, adversarial parties made legal arguments in a single document with strict page limits. Participants were also told that the brief was an actual legal document submitted to a federal district court in either Missouri (situated in the Eighth Circuit) or Pennsylvania (situated in the Third Circuit).

To put participants in a decision-making mode, they were asked to read the brief "as if they were the judge responsible for rendering a decision on the motion." Moreover, they were instructed, "[a]t the end of the brief you will be asked how you would decide the motion and what information from the Summary Brief led you to your decision." Thus, participants knew they would be asked to justify their decisions as judges do when choosing between parties.

Participants then read the brief containing the experimental manipulations. Each brief cited identical legal authority on the standing issue. At the end of the brief, participants were asked a series of closed- and open-ended questions including how they would decide the standing issue, how confident they felt in that judgment, and what facts and legal arguments in the brief led them to their decision.[7] Exact wording of the instructions, "Summary Brief," and questions in "Study B" appear in appendix B. After they completed the instrument, law students were debriefed as to the true nature of the study and compensated for their participation.

Summary Statistics with Appropriate Caveats

To present a general idea of results, I briefly summarize statistics describing the distributions for the standing decision and relevant measures of preferences in this study. Table 4.1 summarizes the distribution on the standing question in each of the treatment conditions.

In this sample, 75 percent of participants (86 out of 115) indicated that the plaintiff should have standing and 25 percent (29 of 115) said that she should not.

At first glance, these results, which demonstrated that participants were three times more likely to conclude that the plaintiff had standing than not, were quite surprising and a bit troubling. There was a concern that the brief itself may have biased results in favor of the plaintiff. According to participants' answers to questions concerning the clarity and objectivity of the document, however, the brief does not appear to have had this unintended effect. Ninety-five percent of participants said the information in the brief was presented clearly; 67 percent stated the facts were presented objectively; and 91 percent said the legal arguments were balanced. These responses suggest that something other than the way the brief was drafted may have driven the pattern of observed results.

TABLE 4.1 Distribution of standing decisions across treatment conditions

CONDITION	STANDING	NO STANDING	TOTAL
Eighth Circuit/Pro-life content	24	5	29
Eighth Circuit/Pro-choice content	20	9	29
Third Circuit/Pro-life content	20	9	29
Third Circuit/Pro-choice content	22	6	28
Total	86	29	115

TABLE 4.2 Distribution of relevant opinion measures

	FLAG-BURNING SANCTIONS	HATCH ACT REGULATIONS	ABORTION REGULATIONS
Disagree strongly	53	32	52
Disagree somewhat	18	29	17
Disagree slightly	15	21	13
Agree slightly	11	20	7
Agree somewhat	13	10	8
Agree strongly	5	3	18
Total	115	115	115

Indeed, the distribution of two of the policy measures suggests that participants may have been sympathetic to the plaintiff on attitudinal grounds. Table 4.2 summarizes the distributions of the three policy measures relevant to this study. There was strong evidence of support for free speech in this sample; 75 percent of participants said they disagreed with criminal sanctions for flag burning. Moreover, 71 percent of participants expressed opposition to governmental regulations that limit the political activities of public employees. The substantial level of support for free speech and opposition to regulations that limit political expression suggest, at least on the surface, that participants' preferences may be underlying the pattern of aggregate results observed in this sample.

Participants' views on abortion, in and of themselves, do not suggest any particular direction on the standing question without taking into account the content of the speech in the condition to which they were assigned. The distribution on the abortion variable, however, is especially important for understanding the pattern of results in this study. Most of the participants in the sample expressed pro-choice views. Specifically, 71.3 percent (82 out of 115) expressed opposition to the idea that the government should have substantial authority to regulate women's access to abortion services. Not only were there fewer participants in the sample who expressed pro-life views (33 out of 115), but unfortunately they did not distribute as evenly as they might have across treatment conditions.

Table 4.3 shows how pro-lifers and pro-choicers were distributed across the four treatment conditions. Although subjects were randomly assigned to conditions, the significant skew in this variable resulted in smaller Ns for pro-lifers—especially in conditions where the plaintiff was expressing pro-choice views. This is a problem in a study like this for

TABLE 4.3 Distribution of participants with pro-life and pro-choice views across treatment conditions

	PRO-CHOICE VIEWS	PRO-LIFE VIEWS	TOTAL
Eighth Circuit/Pro-life content	18	11	29
Eighth Circuit/Pro-choice content	26	3	29
Third Circuit/Pro-life content	17	12	29
Third Circuit/Pro-choice content	21	7	28
Total	82	33	115

two reasons. First, the unequal size of the treatment groups impedes our ability to find significant results because differences between groups must be quite large to register as statistically significant. Second, where differences are large enough to achieve significance, there may be a concern that results are driven by outliers in the small treatment groups who are not representative of the larger population we are tying to learn about (in this case people with pro-life views).

This is addressed in the ANOVA analysis by collapsing subjects with different views into a single variable indicating whether the content of the campaign speech in the condition to which they were assigned was consistent or inconsistent with their own view on abortion.[8] Collapsing the predisposition variable with the speech content variable in this manner allows me to investigate their influence in a manner wholly consistent with testing my experimental hypotheses. Moreover, it provides more participants in each group, lessening concerns that results may be driven by outliers.

In a logit analysis, however, where I attempt to make finer distinctions about how people with different views react to content, the small Ns are associated with large standard errors for predictions involving pro-lifers, especially in the conditions where the plaintiff is expressing support for the pro-choice candidate. This impedes my ability to say whether some of the observed differences, which look quite substantial, are, in fact, significant. I elaborate on this in more detail below as I describe the specific analyses used to test experimental hypotheses.

Testing Hypotheses

To test the hypotheses about the separability of preferences in cases involving multiple issues, data were analyzed in two ways. First, to assess whether subjects were more likely to decide the plaintiff had standing when she was expressing views consistent with their own, I conducted an analysis of variance to see how participants responded to messages that were consistent and inconsistent with their views on abortion in each circuit. Second, I conducted a logit analysis of the standing decision to test the influence of the other potentially relevant policy attitudes and additional control variables.

ANOVA ANALYSIS

The dependent variable for the ANOVA was a scaled version of the standing decision that was created by combining participants' responses to the standing question with reports of how confident they were in that judgment.[9] This scale ranged from one to six, with the lowest values for subjects who were extremely confident in their decision that the plaintiff did not have standing to challenge the ordinance and high scores for those who were extremely confident in their decision that she did have standing.

Two variables were used in the analysis. The first captured whether participants were in a condition where the content of the political message on the campaign sign was consistent, or inconsistent, with their own views on abortion;[10] the second, the jurisdictional condition where the decision was made (Eighth vs. Third Circuit).

Relevant means and the results of F tests from the ANOVA appear in table 4.4. There was a significant interaction between speech consistency and circuit [$F(1,114) = 3.37$, $p < .05$].[11]

Figure 4.2 illustrates the observed interaction. In the Eighth Circuit, participants decided the standing issue similarly when the plaintiff expressed views that were consistent with their opinions on abortion and when she expressed views that were inconsistent with their views. In fact, the mean for the standing/confidence variable is slightly higher where the view the plaintiff expressed was inconsistent with decision makers' view on the issue.

In the Third Circuit, more of a difference is evident. Participants were more likely to decide that the plaintiff had standing when the view she expressed was consistent with their own. The mean for the standing/confidence variable was 4.72 where speech was consistent, and 3.71 where speech was inconsistent with participants' views [$t = -2.6$ ($Df = 55$), $p < .01$, one-tailed test].

Moreover, the results demonstrate that participants treated the plaintiff differently when she expressed a view on abortion that was inconsistent with theirs, depending on the jurisdiction where the case was pending. In the Eighth Circuit, participants were more likely to find

TABLE 4.4 ANOVA results for Separable Preferences Experiment

ANOVA FACTOR	MEAN OF STANDING/ CONFIDENCE VARIABLE	F-TEST RESULT	SIGNIFICANCE
Speech consistency			
Consistent	4.60		
Inconsistent	4.11		
		2.41†	0.06
Circuit condition			
Eighth Circuit	4.52		
Third Circuit	4.30		
		1.07	0.15
Speech consistency × Circuit condition			
Eighth Circuit/Consistent	4.49		
Eighth Circuit/Inconsistent	4.57		
Third Circuit/Consistent	4.72		
Third Circuit/Inconsistent	3.71		
		3.37*	0.04

†significant at .10 level; *significant at .05 level (one-tailed test)

FIGURE 4.2 Observed means for standing decision across treatment conditions

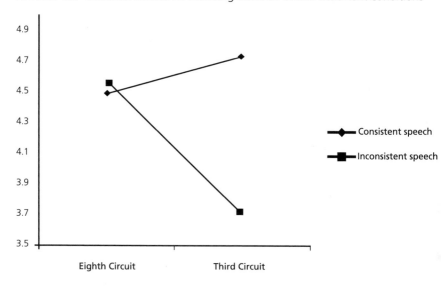

the plaintiff had standing when her view on abortion was inconsistent with theirs compared to participants in the Third Circuit. The mean for the standing/confidence variable in the Eighth Circuit was 4.49 where plaintiff was expressing inconsistent views, compared to 3.71 in the Third Circuit. This difference is also significant [t = 1.8 (Df = 43), p < .05].

The first thing to note about results from the ANOVA analysis is that participants' views on abortion influenced their decisions on the standing issue in systematic ways depending on the content of the view expressed by the plaintiff—but this was only true in the Third Circuit. In the Eighth Circuit, law students decided the standing issue the same way regardless of their agreement with the content of the views expressed by the spousal plaintiff. Also, in the Eighth Circuit conditions, participants were significantly more likely to conclude that the plaintiff had standing when she expressed views that were inconsistent with their own, in line with direct controlling authority in that circuit. The results from this analysis come closest to the pattern that would be predicted by a "constrained attitudinal" model of legal decision making.

The ANOVA results, however, tell us only how participants were acting in relation to speech that was consistent or inconsistent with their preferences on abortion. To test the influence of the other policy preferences that are potentially relevant to the standing decision, I conduct a logit analysis using the participants' responses to the dichotomous standing question as the dependent variable. In the analysis, I include several additional control variables, as well as content- and preference-specific variables for the abortion measure to see if I can make finer distinctions about how participants with alternative views are responding to particular speech content.

LOGIT ANALYSIS

Logit Model Specification

DEPENDENT VARIABLE

The dependent variable is participants' response to the standing decision question. The variable takes on a value of 0 when participants indicated that the plaintiff did not have standing to challenge the ordinance, and 1 when they decided that she did have standing.

INDEPENDENT VARIABLES

The speech content and jurisdiction manipulations were included as dichotomous variables in the analysis. Speech content takes on a value of 0 where plaintiff was expressing support for the pro-life candidate, 1 where she was expressing support for the pro-choice candidate. Circuit takes on a value of 0 where participants were told they were deciding a case that was pending in a district court in the Eighth Circuit, 1 if it was pending in a court within the jurisdiction of the Third Circuit.

Each of the measures of policy preference was also included in the model. The "abortion opinion" measure is dichotomous. It takes on a value of 0 for participants expressing pro-choice views, 1 for participants expressing pro-life views. The "flag-burning sanctions" variable was measured on a six-point scale with higher numbers indicating support for criminal sanctions. The "Pro-Hatch" variable was also measured on a six-point scale with higher numbers indicating support for regulations that restrict the political activity of public employees.

As mentioned earlier, opinions on abortion do not, in and of themselves, predict how participants will decide the standing issue. The relevant question is how participants' attitudes on abortion interact with the content of the speech in the condition to which they are assigned. Thus, the model includes a two-way interaction between abortion opinion and speech content.

The three-way interaction between abortion opinion, speech content, and circuit is also theoretically relevant. As demonstrated in the ANOVA analysis, participants may act differently in response to content with which they disagree under different levels of constraint. Including the three-way interaction allows me to test this possibility. All of the two-way interactions that are nested in the three-way interaction are also included in the model.[12]

There are two additional interactions in the model. The flag-burning variable, representing participants' level of support for free speech, and the Pro-Hatch variable were each interacted with the circuit manipulation. Again, this allows for the possibility that participants may be more inclined to act in accordance with their attitudes in the Third Circuit, where they are relatively free to do so because there is no direct legal authority on the standing question.

Finally, participants' ideology (seven-point scale), year in law school (three-point scale, 2L, 3L, and graduate), and gender were included in the model as control variables.

Logit Model Results

Coefficients for all the independent variables with robust standard errors are presented in table 4.5. Because all of the variables, except for the

TABLE 4.5 Logit coefficients for law students' standing decision in hypothetical case

INDEPENDENT VARIABLES	COEFFICIENT	ROBUST SE	SIGNIFICANCE
Constant	3.974*	2.478	0.05
Ideology	0.232†	0.160	0.08
Law year	−0.343	0.374	0.18
Gender	−0.384	0.552	0.25
Circuit	−3.106*	1.584	0.02
Speech content	−1.229†	0.935	0.10
Abortion opinion	−0.596	1.360	0.33
Flag-burning sanctions	0.598**	0.265	0.01
Pro-Hatch	0.298	0.474	0.42
Circuit × Flag-burning sanctions	0.185	0.335	0.29
Circuit × Pro-Hatch	0.298	0.473	0.27
Circuit × Content	2.540*	1.275	0.03
Circuit × Abortion opinion	2.412†	1.647	0.07
Content × Abortion opinion	−1.603	1.407	0.13
Circuit × Content × Abortion opinion	0.389	2.105	0.43
Wald chi-squared (14)	17.16		
Log likelihood ratio (14)	24.26*		
Count R-squared	0.84		
Adjusted count R-squared	0.35		

†significant at .10 level; *significant at .05 level; **significant at .01 level (one-tailed test)

control variables, are embedded in interactions, the coefficients from the model do not tell us much about their effect across the various treatment conditions. For instance, the fact that the flag-burning variable is statistically significant tells us only about its effect, where the circuit variable takes on a value of 0 (i.e., in the Eighth Circuit conditions). To test the effect of this variable in the Third Circuit (where the variable takes on a value of 1), a separate joint hypothesis test is necessary, accounting for the additive influence the interaction. Separate hypothesis and joint hypothesis tests were conducted to test each policy variable's influence in various theoretically relevant circumstances. These are set forth below where I discuss the statistical and substantive significance of particular variables.

None of the control variables were significant except ideology, which was marginally significant. Its direction indicates that liberal participants were more likely to find that the plaintiff had standing to challenge the ordinance than were conservative participants. This makes sense and may reflect the fact that the preference measures did not capture all of the ideological variance that could potentially impact the standing decision. Generally speaking, liberals are more likely to support broad conceptions of court access than are conservatives; I suspect the observed effect of the ideology variable reflects this difference.

I turn now to a discussion of results concerning the main variables of interest. I start with the Hatch Act and free-speech attitudes, saving for last the pattern of results observed for people with different views on abortion.

HATCH ACT—OPINIONS

The predicted probabilities set forth in table 4.6 indicate the likelihood that people with different views decided that the plaintiff had standing under the alternative treatment conditions used in the experiment. For instance, someone who supports Hatch Act restrictions had a .81 probability of deciding the plaintiff had standing when deciding the case in the Eighth Circuit. Someone who opposes such restrictions had a .85 probability of finding for the plaintiff under the same condition. Therefore we can see that the effect of the variable is quite small but in the predicted direction; in the Eighth Circuit, participants who support Hatch Act restrictions were less likely to decide the plaintiff had standing compared to those who did not. In the Third Circuit conditions, the effect of the variable was more pronounced, but in the wrong direction (i.e., participants who supported restrictions had a .77 probability of finding the plaintiff had standing versus .43 for those expressed opposition to restrictions on the speech of public employees).

The results of hypothesis and joint hypothesis tests demonstrate that the effect of this variable was *not significant* in either circuit condition (Wald = .04 n.s. 8th Circuit; Wald = 1.37 n.s. 3rd Circuit). Therefore, we can say that participants' views on regulations restricting the political speech of public employees did not significantly influence their decision on the standing question in the hypothetical case. Thus, findings indicate that participants were able to separate their preferences on this issue from the standing decision in line with traditional notions of legal decision making.

SUPPORT FOR FREE SPEECH

In contrast, participants' level of support for free speech did influence the standing decision in both the Eighth and Third Circuit conditions. Figure 4.3 sets forth the predicted probabilities of a standing decision

TABLE 4.6 Predicted probabilities of standing decision for decision makers with alternative views on Hatch Act restrictions, flag-burning sanctions, and abortion

OPINION/DECISION CONTEXT	PREDICTED PROBABILITY	STANDARD ERROR
Hatch Act opinions		
Eighth Circuit		
Pro Hatch Act	0.81	0.23
Anti Hatch Act	0.85	0.10
Third Circuit		
Pro Hatch Act	0.77	0.17
Anti Hatch Act	0.43	0.16
Free speech opinions		
(flag-burning sanctions)		
Eighth Circuit		
Anti Sanctions	0.91	0.09
Pro Sanctions	0.49	0.21
Third Circuit		
Anti Sanctions	0.68	0.13
Pro Sanction	0.27	0.17
Abortion opinions		
Eighth Circuit		
Pro-life content		
Pro-choicers	0.86	0.11
Pro-lifers	0.80	0.14
Pro-choice content		
Pro-choicers	0.71	0.09
Pro-lifers	0.27	0.21
Third Circuit		
Pro-life content		
Pro-choicers	0.57	0.11
Pro-lifers	0.86	0.12
Pro-choice content		
Pro-choicers	0.80	0.10
Pro-lifers	0.47	0.31

FIGURE 4.3 Predicted probabilities regarding free-speech opinions

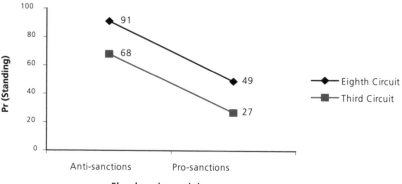

for participants who expressed strong support and opposition for flag-burning sanctions.

The effect of the variable is consistent with attitudinal hypotheses in both conditions. Participants who expressed support for free speech (opposition to sanctions) were more likely to conclude that the plaintiff had standing than those who did not support free speech. In the Eighth Circuit conditions, participants who expressed strong opposition to criminal sanctions for flag burning had a .91 probability of concluding the plaintiff had standing compared to .49 for participants who expressed strong support for such sanctions. The corresponding predictions for participants with similar views in the Third Circuit conditions were .68 and .27.

Contrary to expectation, the effect of this variable was not greater in the Third Circuit conditions. The magnitude of the difference for people with different views on free speech is almost identical in each circuit (42 in the Eighth Circuit vs. 41 in the Third). Table 4.7 sets forth the hypothesis and joint-hypothesis test for the free-speech variable and demonstrates that the observed effect was statistically significant in both the Eighth and Third Circuit conditions.

At first glance, the influence of free-speech preferences on participants' response to the standing question seems to lend support to attitudinal accounts of decision making. This finding, however, can also be explained by legal accounts of decision making. Specifically, although we know that free speech attitudes influenced participants' standing decisions, we do not know the precise nature of the influence; we cannot tell whether free-speech attitudes drove decisions from the "top down," or influenced participants' reasoning processes from the "bottom up."

TABLE 4.7 Hypothesis and joint hypothesis test for free-speech opinion variable across conditions

	WALD STATISTIC	SIGNIFICANCE
Eighth Circuit	5.08**	0.01
Third Circuit	2.67*	0.05

*significant at .05 level; **significant at .01 level (one-tailed test)

From a legal standpoint, it would be improper if participants' attitudes about free speech influenced their decisions in a top-down manner, that is, if they decided the case the way they did because they were sympathetic (or hostile) to the plaintiff's claim that the ordinance unjustly infringed her right to free expression. The influence of the variable, however, could also have been bottom-up. Recall that the specific legal test for standing is whether or not the plaintiff suffered an "injury" sufficient to challenge the ordinance. When considering this specific question, participants who supported free speech might have been more inclined to see the restriction of her speech as a cognizable legal harm.

Of course, from a strict legal standpoint, one may question whether this more benign bottom-up influence should have occurred in the presence of controlling authority on the issue. Still, this characterization of the variable's influence is more compatible with traditional notions of legal decision making. Since results are consistent with both top-down and bottom-up explanations, we cannot say which process is operating with regard to the observed influence of free-speech attitudes in this study.

OPINIONS ON ABORTION

To test the influence of participants' attitudes about abortion on the standing decision, four separate hypothesis tests were conducted to measure the influence of the abortion opinion variable in each treatment condition. The results of those tests appear in table 4.8. Table 4.8 also presents results of eight additional hypothesis tests measuring the effect of the speech content manipulation for participants with different views in each circuit, and the effect of the circuit manipulation for participants with different views given different speech content. The results of these tests, read in conjunction with the predicted probabilities set forth in figures 4.4 and 4.5, tell a different story about how participants with alternative views are reacting to content across the jurisdictional conditions.

Pro-Choicers. Consistent with results from the ANOVA analysis, participants with pro-choice views seem to be following a constrained attitu-

TABLE 4.8 Hypothesis and joint hypothesis tests for abortion opinion, speech content, and circuit manipulations under various theoretically relevant conditions

	WALD STATISTIC	SIGNIFICANCE
Is abortion opinion significant?		
Eighth Circuit/Pro-life content	0.19	0.33
Eighth Circuit/Pro-choice content	2.36†	0.06
Third Circuit/Pro-life content	2.63*	0.05
Third Circuit/Pro-choice content	0.26	0.31
Is speech content significant?		
Eighth Circuit/Pro-choicers	1.73†	0.10
Eighth Circuit/Pro-lifers	3.91*	0.02
Third Circuit/Pro-choicers	2.39†	0.06
Third Circuit/Pro-lifers	0.01	0.49
Is circuit significant?		
Pro-choicers/Pro-life content	4.34*	0.02
Pro-choicers/Pro-choice content	0.01	0.47
Pro-lifers/Pro-life content	0.02	0.45
Pro-lifers/Pro-choice content	1.8†	0.09

†significant at .10 level; *significant at .05 level (one-tailed test)

dinal model of decision making. In the Eighth Circuit, they made similar decisions when the plaintiff was expressing pro-choice views and when she was expressing pro-life views. In fact, pro-choice participants were slightly more likely to conclude that the plaintiff had standing where she was expressing views inconsistent with theirs in the Eighth Circuit. The predicted probability of a standing decision in the Eighth Circuit given pro-life content was .86, compared to .71 where the plaintiff was expressing pro-choice views.

In the Third Circuit, pro-choicers acted in accordance with their preferences. There participants who expressed pro-choice views had a .80 probability of deciding the plaintiff had standing when the content of the campaign sign was consistent with their views, compared to .57 when it was inconsistent (Wald = 2.39, $p < .06$). Moreover, in the Third Circuit conditions, pro-choicers were less likely to decide the plaintiff had standing when she was expressing pro-life views than participants who themselves expressed pro-life views. Predicted probabilities were .57

FIGURE 4.4 Predicted probabilities of decision makers with alternative views on abortion for different speech content in the Eighth Circuit

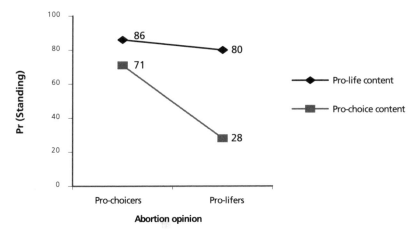

FIGURE 4.5 Predicted probabilities of decision makers with alternative views on abortion for different speech content in the Third Circuit

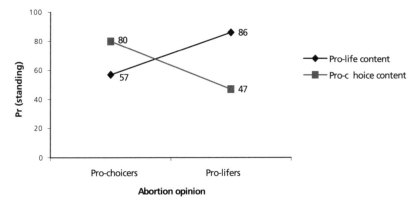

and .86, respectively, where the plaintiff was expressing pro-life content (Wald = 2.63, p < .05).

Perhaps the best evidence that participants with pro-choice views were following a constrained attitudinal model of decision making is the different way they treated pro-life content across conditions. In the Eighth Circuit, the predicted probability of pro-choicers saying the plaintiff had standing where she expressed pro-life views inconsistent with theirs was .86. The corresponding probability in the Third Circuit was .57 (Wald = 4.34, p < .02). Thus, participants were more likely to say that the plaintiff had standing when she was expressing a view that was inconsistent with their own where there was direct authority on the standing question favoring the plaintiff.

Pro-lifers. Results suggest that participants with pro-life views were acting in accordance with their preferences in the constrained and unconstrained conditions. In both circuits, pro-lifers were more likely to find plaintiff had standing where she was expressing pro-life views than when she was expressing pro-choice views. The predicted probability of a standing decision for participants who expressed pro-life views in the Eighth Circuit was .80 where plaintiff was expressing pro-life views, compared to .28 where she was expressing pro-choice views. The corresponding probabilities in the Third Circuit conditions were .86 and .47. Hypothesis test results indicate that the effect of content was significant for pro-lifers in the Eighth Circuit conditions (Wald = 3.91, $p < .02$), but the large standard errors noted above prevent us from saying the same is true about the difference observed in the Third Circuit conditions (Wald = .01, n.s.).

These results stand out in the analysis for several reasons. First, the finding that pro-lifers in the Eighth Circuit were being attitudinal— and, indeed, that they may have been more attitudinal than participants with similar attitudes in the Third Circuit—is at odds with experimental hypotheses suggesting participants should have been constrained by controlling authority. In direct contrast to expectations, it suggests pro-life participants were reacting against authority where it favored a plaintiff who was expressing views contrary to their own. It could be that the specific combination of factors (contrary speech with controlling authority favoring the plaintiff who is expressing those views) caused pro-lifers to buck prevailing authority under the precise conditions where they should have evidenced constraint.

Of course, the small N associated with the conditions where pro-lifers were given pro-choice content influences the confidence with which we can generalize this result to any group other than the law students in the sample. This is important to note because the experimental survey revealed that most of the law students were liberal on abortion and other social issues. Participants willing to express less popular, pro-life views may be individuals who are especially likely to go against the prevailing wisdom and challenge authority. Thus, further testing needs to be done to determine if the result would obtain in a sample where pro-lifers comprise a larger proportion of the sample.

If the finding is reflective of a more generalizable phenomenon, there are two possible explanations. It could be that pro-lifers see themselves as a "legal minority" because they are currently on the losing side of the abortion issue; the Supreme Court has recognized and reaffirmed a woman's fundamental right to choose. This perceived minority status might cause pro-lifers to resist controlling legal authority where they believe courts have not done a good job on the issue, especially when the issue is salient—as it was in the hypothetical fact pattern where the plaintiff was expressing pro-choice views.

A second possible explanation concerns the ideology of experimental participants with pro-life views. There is psychological evidence suggesting that people with conservative views may be especially prone to motivated decision processes (Jost et al. 2003). Thus, the jurisdictional manipulation that inhibited pro-choicers from making decisions consistent with their preferences may not have been effective to curb motivated decision processes among the more conservative pro-lifers in the sample.[13]

Because we cannot say which of these alternative processes is driving this unexpected result, or even that the finding would replicate in other samples, I will leave it as an intriguing observation inviting further investigation and consideration. It is important to note, however, that if pro-lifers and pro-choicers are responding to controlling authority in different ways, it would involve a more complex story than extant theories of legal decision making can currently account for. There is simply no theory that would predict such an outcome. Even though the way participants distributed in this study prevents us from making conclusive statements about whether this would happen on a broader scale, the possibility that it could suggests that we should consider the potential for differential responses to constraint in future research.

General Discussion

This study produced some interesting findings about the ability of law student participants to separate their preferences on substantive issues from the standing decision they were asked to make in this experiment. First, participants were clearly able to separate their views on regulations restricting the political activity of public employees from their reasoning about the standing issue.

It is equally clear that participants' level of support for free speech influenced their decisions in systematic ways. Participants who supported free speech were more likely to conclude the plaintiff had standing. As detailed above, this particular finding is consistent with purely attitudinal top-down accounts of decision making as well as more legally justifiable bottom-up accounts of influence.

Results of this study are somewhat mixed with respect to participants' abortion attitudes. Findings from the ANOVA were most consistent with the idea that participants were following a "constrained attitudinal" model of decision making. When we looked at how participants with different views responded to particular content, however, it appears that those results may have been driven by participants with pro-choice views in our sample.

Taken as a whole, the findings provide good evidence that the three-fourths of the sample that expressed pro-choice opinions were following a constrained attitudinal model of decision making with respect to their opinions on abortion. Although it appears that the pro-lifers were acting in accordance with their preferences in both the constrained and unconstrained conditions, we can have less confidence in that finding given the unequal distribution of participants with such views across treatment conditions.

The systematic differences in legal judgments for participants with the same preferences across conditions, and for subjects with different preferences within conditions, demonstrate that participants were interpreting the exact same authority quite differently. By themselves, these findings shed a good deal of light not only on how preferences can influence legal reasoning processes, but also on which preferences matter from a number of plausible alternatives, and under what theoretically relevant circumstances.

The analysis of responses to closed-ended questions, however, can only take us so far. It cannot tell us what specific arguments were influential in different circuit conditions or what authority people who came to different conclusions cited in support of their decisions. So, in the next chapter, I analyze open-ended responses participants gave to justify their decisions. I undergo this task because I believe that these experimental data have must have "more" to tell us. The logic is that it will be useful to see if there are systematic differences in what facts and authority participants relied on in this relatively closed system where they were responding to the identical legal arguments.

FIVE

JUSTIFYING OUTCOMES?

How Legal Decision Makers
Explain Threshold Decisions

In this chapter, I analyze the open-ended responses that law student participants gave to justify their decisions in the experiment testing the separability of preferences. Part of my purpose is to further demonstrate the utility of using experimental methods for studying legal reasoning processes. Although it is not a method commonly used by behavioral scholars interested in legal decision making, the control afforded by such methods can be extremely useful for answering interesting and important questions about differential reasoning processes. In essence, analyzing judgments in this way may shed light on how legal decision makers "get to where they want to go" in terms of drawing legal conclusions consistent with their policy preferences.

At the outset, I want to make it clear that this aspect of the analysis is exploratory and inductive. Rather than testing specific hypotheses, as I did in the previous two chapters, I explore several broad questions about participants' reasoning processes in this relatively "closed system" where they were responding to identical legal authority. Very generally, the questions guiding the analysis of open-ended responses are as follows:

1. Did participants who reached alternative conclusions on the standing issue cite systematically different arguments in justifying their decisions? If so, what arguments did they cite from those available in the brief?

2. Were some legal arguments more (or less) persuasive under the different levels of constraint created by the circuit manipulation? If so, what were they? Under what conditions did particular arguments have more or less impact?

3. Did participants with different policy views cite systematically different arguments? If so, what arguments appealed to decision makers with alternative views?

4. Can the analysis of open-ended justifications shed light on the specific nature of influence for attitudinal variables observed to influence the standing judgments in chapter 4? For instance, can they reveal whether the influence of free-speech attitudes was top-down or bottom-up? Can we tell from justifications whether participants were aware of the influence of abortion attitudes on their decisions?

In attempting to answer these questions, I present the incidence of selected facts and arguments mentioned by law student participants as well as statistics indicating what arguments were more likely to be cited by participants holding for particular parties under alternative jurisdictional conditions. I also present correlations between characteristics of decision makers and the invocation of particular arguments, being careful to address methodological issues that students of decision making must consider in analyzing such data. The analyses yield some interesting results that I hope will generate further hypotheses about the specific nature of attitudinal influence in legal reasoning processes. Not all of the questions I ask above are definitively answered, but the analysis of open-ended responses does provide at least some leverage on most of them, contributing to my general argument that there is much to gain by including experimental methods in a pluralistic approach to understanding legal decision making.

Because the basics of the experimental design were outlined in the previous chapter, I do not repeat them here. I do, however, go into a more detail in discussing the content of the legal arguments in the Mock Brief to clarify the coding scheme and make clear the alternative arguments from which participants had to draw in justifying their judgments. I also discuss aspects of the experiment that are particularly relevant to the analyses presented in this chapter.

Content of the Mock Brief

The facts and legal arguments in the Summary Brief were based on decisions from federal cases where the issue of spousal standing has been litigated. Since the defendants filed the motion, their arguments appeared first in the brief. Specifically, defendants relied on the specific language of the ordinance and the "weight of authority" in federal cases holding that injuries suffered by spousal plaintiffs were "too indirect" to confer standing. Defendants' brief also included two policy arguments having to do with municipal governments' interest in enacting restrictive ordinances like the one at issue and the potential of opening a door to much more litigation by recognizing the injury of spousal plaintiffs (often referred to as a "slippery slope" argument).

The plaintiff's main arguments as to the directness of the injury relied on the "chilling" of her free-speech (First Amendment) rights; included in this argument was a reference to the fact that the plaintiff had a prior history of political activity. In addition, the plaintiff's argument cited the potential loss of family income if her husband lost his job as an alternative ground for finding that she suffered a concrete injury in fact. There was also an allegation of retaliatory conduct—suggesting that her husband was being threatened because his supervisor was opposed to the particular abortion views she expressed. Finally, there was an argument that because the property was jointly owned by the plaintiff and her husband, the ordinance unfairly infringed on her property rights (this was the only argument not directly refuted by defendants in some way). The plaintiff almost exclusively relied on the only circuit court decision supporting her position—*City of Ferguson.*

At the end of the brief, participants were asked a series of closed- and open-ended questions including how they would decide the standing issue (closed-question format), how confident they felt in that judgment (closed-question format), and what facts and legal arguments in the brief led them to that decision (open-ended format). Participants were given approximately a half page to respond to each open-ended question. Subjects were told that the estimated time to read through the brief and respond to questions was forty minutes. This was generally sufficient time for subjects to complete the experimental materials: most participants took thirty to thirty-five minutes, and some took over an hour. There were no enforced time limits on the decision task.

Clearly these conditions differ from what judges do when rendering decisions. Typically, judges take weeks (not minutes) to make motion decisions; moreover, they may have significant help from clerks and/or legal assistants in drafting the explanations for such judgments. Also, participants were not specifically asked to draft opinions—just to list the evidence and authority influencing their judgments.

I would argue that this information is useful for several reasons. It can tell us what evidence, arguments, and authority legally trained decision makers were initially drawn to in the decision process. Initial impressions and preliminary judgments are important in the legal arena because they "frame" subsequent decision processes. Such preliminary judgments are common and often necessary for judges to simplify the decision task and/or delegate work to others (including law clerks) so they can proceed in a manner consistent with a judge's impression of what the law requires in particular circumstances. Moreover, once a decision maker makes this initial judgment based on a preliminary reading of the papers, it may be significantly harder to move him or her from that decision.

Summary Statistics and Preliminary Analysis of Responses to Self-Report Questions

The first thing to note about participant responses to self-report measures is that despite the systematic differences observed across speech content conditions where legal authority was identical, participants reported that the law played a more important role than facts in their decision making. In responses to questions asking about the relative influence of facts and law, measured on a six-point scale with higher values indicating more influence, the mean influence for facts reported by all participants was 3.18; the mean influence for law was 4.47. The relevant paired sample t-test indicates that this difference is highly significant [$t(113) = -11.11$, $p < .001$]. The finding suggests that participants were either unaware of the significant role that facts—like the content of the message on the campaign sign—played in their judgments or were unwilling to report such influence.

A second finding of note regarding participants' responses to self-report questions was that where there was direct controlling authority, participants reported being significantly more confident in their judgments. In a question measuring confidence on a three-point scale, with higher values indicating more confidence, the mean for the entire sample was 2.23. Participants in the Eighth Circuit had a mean of 2.34 compared to 2.12 for participants in the Third Circuit conditions [$t(113) = 2.07$, $p < .05$].

Coding Strategy for Open-Ended Responses

Several procedures were followed to guard against potential bias in coding the open-ended responses. First, there were some relatively objective measures (e.g., number of words) that were not subject to significant alteration by bias in coding. Second, open-ended justifications in Study B were kept separate from participants' answers to policy questions in Study A. Also, it was not obvious which experimental condition participants were in on the sheet where they responded to open-ended questions. Finally, responses to closed-ended questions about how participants would decide the motion were on a separate sheet of the instrument than questions asking them to list the reasons for their decisions.

It is important to note that the coding scheme took note of whether participants *mentioned* a particular argument without specifically noting how they said it influenced their decision. For instance, a statement such as "the argument about retaliation took away from the main issue in the case" was coded as a positive mention of retaliation, notwithstanding the fact that the participant specifically disavowed its influence in his or her decision. The logic is that coding for mention is easier than coding for how a particular argument influenced a decision maker, which in most cases was not entirely clear from how participants referred to aspects of the brief. Moreover, participants themselves may have been unaware of how particular parts of the brief influenced them. At the very least, coding for mentions indicates that participants took particular notice of content—enough to include it in the justification for their decisions.

Of course, it is possible that there were aspects of the brief that participants did not mention that were influential in their decisions. Indeed, this is part of what makes the inquiry so interesting. For example, we already know from the analysis of closed-ended responses presented in chapter 4 that participants were more likely to decide the plaintiff had standing where the content of the message she was expressing was consistent with their own views on abortion, especially in the unconstrained conditions. Analysis of the open-ended questions indicates that only 13 percent (15 out of 115) of participants specifically mentioned abortion or the direction of the spousal plaintiff's views on the issue. Moreover, the number of participants in the unconstrained conditions that mentioned abortion was not significantly different from the number of participants in the constrained conditions (8 versus 7 participants, respectively). Also, the proportion of pro-lifers and pro-choicers who mentioned the issue was the same (12 percent versus 13 percent). Finally, there was not a significant difference between the proportion of people mentioning abortion who decided the plaintiff should have standing (13.9 percent) and those who found she should not (10.3 percent).

These findings suggest that although abortion attitudes influenced participants in systematic ways, it was not at the forefront of the minds of most participants in justifying their decisions. Moreover, the fact that participants in each circuit condition were equally likely to mention abortion suggests they were similarly aware of its presence, and yet, consistent with a "constrained attitudinal" model of decision making, abortion opinion influenced participants in the unconstrained condition to a greater extent. Finally, the fact that participants with different views were equally likely to mention abortion suggests it was equally present in the minds of pro-life and pro-choice participants.

The analysis of such information, the kind that experimental methods can provide so effectively, has a great deal of potential to add to our understanding of differential reasoning processes that can lead to the development of new insights and testable hypotheses. With this in mind, I coded the open-ended responses of law student participants in this study along several dimensions described more fully below.

Descriptives and Bivariate Tests

Number of words—The number of words that participants used in explaining (1) what facts led them to their decision and (2) what legal arguments influenced them. The means on these measures were 42.5 words and 60.8 words respectively. Thus, consistent with self-report measures indicating that law had a greater impact on their reasoning, participants wrote significantly more in describing the legal influences on their decisions [$t(114)$ = 6.88, p < .001)].

Number of facts and arguments mentioned—The number of distinct facts and legal arguments participants mentioned in their answers. The means on these variables were 2.2 and 2.6, respectively.[1]

Facts, Arguments, and Authority Mentioned

Table 5.1 sets forth the coding scheme for various facts, arguments, and legal authority that participants mentioned in their justifications. Each participant was coded 1 on the relevant variable if they mentioned it in their reasoning, 0 if they did not.[2]

The incidence for each variable coded is in tables 5.2 and 5.3. Table 5.2 sets forth the incidence of facts and legal arguments mentioned. Table 5.3 presents the same information for legal authority participants used in justifying their decisions. I also indicate the total percentage of participants who mentioned each variable among participants deciding the case in favor of the plaintiff and defendant. The party Fisher's exact test indicates whether the difference in those percentages is statistically significant.[3]

The last three columns in tables 5.2 and 5.3 indicate the proportion of participants mentioning the variable in each of the relevant circuit

TABLE 5.1 Coding scheme for analysis of open-ended questions in Separable Preferences Experiment

VARIABLE MENTION	CODING QUESTION
Free speech	Did participant mention free speech, First Amendment rights, or the "chilling" of free expression?
Ordinance	Did participant mention the language or application of the restrictive ordinance?
Income	Did participant indicate that income was a factor in their decisions?
Abortion	Did participant mention "abortion" or that the plaintiff was "pro-life" or "pro-choice"?
Retaliation	Did participant mention the retaliation allegation in any way?
Joint home ownership	Did participant mention that the plaintiff owned home jointly with her husband?
Prior political activity	Did participant allude to the fact that the plaintiff had a history of prior political involvement?
Slippery slope	Did participant mention the policy argument that recognizing the spousal injury could open the door to a multiplicity of claims?
Municipal interest in restrictions	Did participant mention policy argument involving the municipal interest in restricting the political activity of public employees?
City of Ferguson	Did participant specifically mention or refer to the holding in the *City of Ferguson* case?
Other cases	Did participant specifically mention or refer to any case authority besides *Ferguson*?
Weight of authority	Did participant mention that most of the federal case law in the brief suggested that injury was "too indirect" to confer standing?
"Controlling authority" (relevant for participants in Eighth Circuit condition)	Did participant specifically mention the fact that there was "controlling authority" in the standing question in the Eighth Circuit?
"No controlling authority" (relevant for participants in Third Circuit condition)	Did participant specifically mention the fact that there was "no controlling" authority on the standing question in the Third Circuit?
Other facts/arguments	Did participant mention facts and/or legal arguments not included in the Mock Brief?

TABLE 5.2 Incidence of facts and arguments mentioned in sample, by decision and circuit condition

FACTS/ ARGUMENT MENTIONS	INCIDENCE OF TOTAL MENTIONS	PARTICIPANTS DECIDING CASE (%)			PARTICIPANTS DECIDING CASE (%)		
		FOR PLAINTIFF	FOR DEFENDANT	PARTY FISHER'S EXACT	IN THIRD CIRCUIT	IN EIGHTH CIRCUIT	CIRCUIT FISHER'S EXACT
Free speech	.75	86	41	.000***	74	75	n.s.
Joint home ownership	.56	62	38	.03*	54	56	.85
Prior political activity	.37	43	21	.04*	29	44	.12
Municipal interest in restriction	.26	21	41	.05*	33	19	.09†
Retaliation	.25	30	10	.05*	28	22	.52
Lost income	.22	22	24	.80	21	24	.82
Slippery slope	.16	9	34	.003**	21	10	.13
Abortion	.13	14	10	.75	14	12	n.s.

†$p < .10$; *$p < .05$; **$p < .01$; ***$p < .001$ (two-tailed test)

TABLE 5.3 Incidence of legal authority mentioned in sample, by decision and circuit condition

AUTHORITY MENTIONS	INCIDENCE OF TOTAL MENTIONS	PARTICIPANTS DECIDING CASE (%)		PARTY FISHER'S EXACT	PARTICIPANTS DECIDING CASE (%)		CIRCUIT FISHER'S EXACT
		FOR PLAINTIFF	FOR DEFENDANT		IN THIRD CIRCUIT	IN EIGHTH CIRCUIT	
City of Ferguson	.53	53	55	n.s.	33	77	.000***
Ordinance	.50	44	69	.03*	52	48	.71
Other cases	.30	33	20	.24	33	28	.54
Weight of authority	.26	13	59	.000***	29	19	.19
Controlling authority	.22	57	7	.03*	—	45	—
(Eighth Circuit condition)	(26 of 58)						
No controlling authority	.07	17	6	.07†	14	—	—
(Third Circuit condition)	(8 of 57)						

†p < .10; *p < .05; **p < .01; ***p < .001 (two-tailed test)

conditions. The circuit Fisher's exact test indicates whether those proportions are significantly different.

These analyses shed significant light on the first two sets of questions
at the beginning of this chapter:

*Did participants who reached alternative conclusions on the standing is-
sue cite systematically different arguments in justifying their decisions? If so,
what arguments did they cite from those available in the brief?*

Looking at the types of arguments cited by participants, it is clear that
those holding for the plaintiff favored some arguments in their justifications and those deciding for the defendants favored others. Participants
who decided the plaintiff had standing were more likely to mention
(1) free speech, (2) joint ownership of the marital home, (3) the fact that
the plaintiff had a history of prior political activity, and (4) the allegation
of retaliation. Those ruling in favor of the defendants were more likely to
mention (1) the municipal interest in restricting the speech of public employees, as well as the fact that (2) recognizing the spousal injury could
open the door to future litigation.

In terms of authority, those ruling in favor of the defendant were
more likely to cite or refer to (1) the language of the municipal ordinance
and (2) the weight of federal authority than were participants who ruled
in favor of the plaintiff. Interestingly, people tended to mention the fact
that there was "controlling authority" in the Eighth Circuit *and* the fact
that there was "no controlling authority" in the Third Circuit more often
in their justification of outcomes in favor of the plaintiff.

*Were some legal arguments more (or less) persuasive under the different
levels of constraint created by the circuit manipulation? If so, what were they?
Under what conditions did particular arguments have more or less impact?*

It is equally clear from these analyses that different arguments were more
persuasive under different circuit conditions. Participants mentioned the
City of Ferguson case more often in the Eighth Circuit condition, where it
was controlling. Mentions of the case occurred in similar proportions for
participants deciding the case for plaintiff (.53) and for defendants (.55).
This could be taken as evidence that a substantial number of participants
felt the need to address the case in some manner even if it did not help
their ultimate decision. Of the 62 participants who referred to *Ferguson*
in some way, 43 cited the case by name, and 19 referred to it indirectly.
Thirty-eight of the 62 participants who mentioned *Ferguson* cited reasons
to follow the case; 13 participants noted reasons to distinguish it.[4]

Consistent with the hypotheses on analogical perception tested in
chapter 3, participants' views on free speech were systematically related

to how they treated the case. Specifically, 62 percent of the participants who supported free speech cited reasons to follow *Ferguson,* compared to only 20 percent of participants who did not support free speech (Fisher's exact test = .04). Moreover, only 8 percent of participants supporting free speech cited reasons to distinguish the case from the scenario described in the Mock Brief; 26 percent of those supporting sanctions for flag burning distinguished the case (Fisher's exact test = .09).

Thirty percent of all participants mentioned some other case authority. Surprisingly, only 10 percent of all participants mentioned a different case by name. This could be because the "weight of authority" argument actually "blurred" the individual cases cited in the defendant's brief in the minds of participants—this is a very intriguing possibility worthy of further exploration.

Discussion of Comparisons

There is nothing too surprising in this summary of incidence and bivariate comparisons. In essence, one may argue, so what? Obviously people who hold for the plaintiff should be more likely to mention arguments made by the plaintiff and vice versa. I believe that it is a useful exercise for several reasons. First, it is valuable to note the proportion of participants responding to alternative arguments and authority they could use to justify decisions. In this respect, free speech seemed to carry a good deal of weight relative to other arguments in favor of the plaintiff, and the specific wording of the ordinance seemed the preferred argument among those holding for defendants.

Second, although there is some evidence that decision makers' predispositions played a role in how they treated authority like *Ferguson,* it is also clear from this analysis that participants did not mention only arguments and authority that were consistent with their decisions. There is significant evidence that they felt the need to address (or at least acknowledge) opposing evidence and arguments. The fact that 41 percent of participants who decided the standing issue in favor of the defendants referred to free speech is noteworthy, as is the fact that a good proportion (over 20 percent) of participants holding for the plaintiff mentioned policy arguments favorable to the defendants. One could point to this as evidence of the influence of legal norms encouraging thoughtful consideration of alternative evidence and authority.

Third, it is clear that some arguments and authority carried more (or less) weight depending on the circuit condition. The fact that 77 percent of participants in the Eighth Circuit conditions mentioned or referred to *Ferguson*, compared to only 33 percent in the Third Circuit conditions is particularly noteworthy. Also, the analyses suggest policy arguments about the potential for future litigation and municipal governments' interest in enacting such restrictions were more likely to be mentioned in relatively unconstrained conditions. This finding makes some sense and may prove a particularly interesting avenue for future research.

Did Certain Arguments Appeal to Different Types of Decision Makers?

I turn now to the third question set of questions asked at the beginning of this chapter:

Did participants with different policy views cite systematically different arguments? If so, what arguments appealed to decision makers with alternative views?

To investigate these questions, I present Pearson correlations between variable mentions and specific traits of decision makers in table 5.4. Specifically, I look at participants' policy views on the three questions relevant to the standing decision analyzed in chapter 4; I also look at correlations between the decision to invoke particular arguments and participants' gender, frequency of religious attendance, and ideology.

First, it is interesting that none of the correlations in table 5.4 is particularly high; indeed, the highest correlation in the entire chart is .22, indicating a moderate relationship, at best, between participant traits and the likelihood of mentioning particular arguments. Considering that participants had a multitude of arguments from which to choose, it is perhaps not too surprising that correlations are not higher. Still, one could take this as evidence that particular arguments were not strongly preferred by participants with specific characteristics. But we know that even if arguments were not strongly preferred by any particular type of individual, somehow participants made decisions consistent with their policy views on free speech (in both circuit conditions) and abortion (in the unconstrained conditions). Although the magnitude of correlations is not strong, several correlations are statistically significant, indicating a stronger relationship than one would expect by chance. I discuss them below to see if they can shed light on how specific decision makers reached legal conclusions comporting with their preferences.

In table 5.4, positive correlations indicate participants with the trait were more likely to mention the variables listed in each row. Thus, support

TABLE 5.4 Pearson correlations between variable mentions and participant traits

PARTICIPANT CHARACTERISTICS	PRO-HATCH	PRO-SPEECH	PRO-LIFE	FEMALE	INFREQUENCY OF RELIGIOUS ATTENDANCE	LIBERAL
Argument mentions						
Free speech	.01	.13	.03	.04	.12	.07
Joint home ownership	-.14	.12	.03	-.02	.10	-.05
Political activity	.02	.04	-.02	.01	.00	.11
Government interest	.02	-.01	-.06	.09	-.15†	-.15†
Lost income	-.21*	.03	.03	.11	.06	-.01
Slippery slope	.00	-.01	.11	.05	.05	-.18*
Abortion	-.15	.03	-.06	.03	-.01	.04
Authority mentions						
Ferguson	.00	.15†	-.12	.02	.00	.22*
Ordinance	.20*	-.05	-.12	.06	-.13	.10
Weight of authority	.13	-.17†	.10	-.02	-.02	-.12
Other cases	.05	-.03	.10	-.13	-.06	-.08

†correlation significant at *p* < .10; *correlation significant at *p* < .05 (two-tailed test)

for Hatch Act restrictions, as measured by the six-point policy question, was positively correlated with mentioning the language of the restrictive ordinance in participant justifications. It makes sense that those who support such restrictions would be particularly likely to mention or refer to the language of the ordinance. This particular trait was also and negatively correlated with mentioning lost income as a type of injury. This could reflect an unwillingness to acknowledge arguments that would result in the successful challenge of such provisions.

Opposition to flag-burning sanctions, the measure of support for free speech, was positively correlated with mentioning the *Ferguson* case. This also makes some sense as the holding in the case supported a finding for the plaintiff complaining about unfair restrictions. Similarly, this variable was negatively correlated with referring to the weight of federal authority, tending to suggest the opposite outcome.

As suggested by the bivariate relationships presented earlier, being pro-life was not strongly or significantly related to the invocation of any of the coded variables. Likewise, gender and frequency of religious attendance are not strongly correlated with any of the arguments or authority coded.

Looking at participants' ideology, however, does yield some interesting relationships. Liberalism is negatively correlated with mentioning both policy arguments. This makes sense given how these arguments were used in the case brief. Liberalism is also positively correlated with mentioning the *City of Ferguson* case; this particular finding resonates with the fact that those on the liberal side of the abortion debate (with pro-choice views) appeared to be particularly attentive to controlling case law in the last chapter.

A Methodological Aside

It is at this point in most scholarly inquiries that researchers offer regression analyses to see if relationships of the sort outlined above survive under multivariate analysis. I choose not to do so here for several reasons that are particularly worth discussing in the context of this inquiry. First, as mentioned above, this chapter is inductive. I had no specific hypotheses at the outset. So, while the bivariate relationships set forth suggest interesting hypotheses for future research—like the relative influence of policy arguments under different levels of legal constraint—to test them here would be somewhat inappropriate.

A second issue has to do with whether the standing decision should be treated as a *dependent variable,* explained by some combination of arguments cited, or an *independent variable*, helping explain the invocation of specific arguments, in a regression analysis of participants' decisions. Again the distinction between top-down and bottom-up avenues of influence is particularly relevant.

As referenced earlier Segal and Spaeth (1993, 2002) suggest a top-down process where outcome decisions come first and drive legal explanations that appear to, but do not actually, dictate voting. According to this characterization, legal reasoning is more rationalization than deliberation. On this view, the standing decision should be treated as an independent variable to help explain the invocation of particular arguments. Other judicial scholars have suggested a bottom-up, information-processing approach where preferences act as information filters, exercising their influence by affecting microdecisions that occur in the process of legal reasoning. This conception suggests the standing decision should be treated as a dependent variable, explained by evidence and arguments cited by participants. These distinct characterizations of the role attitudes play in decision making present a sticky methodological issue in the context of a study like this. Put simply, the direction of the causal arrow is unclear. Evidence presented in these experiments suggests that both top-down and bottom-up mechanisms could be at play in legal reasoning processes. For instance, analogical perceptions seem most likely to influence legal decisions in a bottom-up manner, while the influence of interrelated preferences may be more accurately categorized as top-down. After this inquiry, I am uncomfortable making any definitive statement about which type of process predominates. Now that we have seen that both top-down and bottom-up mechanisms can operate in legal decision making, it will be up to future researchers to specify causal assumptions and test them appropriately with empirical data.

A third problem is endogeneity in regressions where ideology and arguments are each used as predictors of decision making. Obviously, it would be ideal if researchers could separate the independent influence of ideology and legal arguments cited in a single regression analysis—the problem is that many would argue that the two are related—that ideology can lead decision makers to accept or reject certain arguments. Moreover, the same could be said about consistency of speech[5] and/or the circuit manipulation in the context of this experiment.[6] Thus, there is a difficulty in putting these variables in a regression equation with evidence and arguments cited, but there could also be an omitted variable problem in leaving them out.

Clearly these are important issues that need to be addressed carefully in future research. Besides having empirical implications, they raise important theoretical questions that judicial scholars should seriously consider. These are vital questions we should be thinking about anyway; I would argue that the great potential of experimental methods for understanding the questions we are interested in suggests that we do so sooner rather than later.

Nature of Influence: What Does This Analysis Tell Us?

Although there is not enough certainty to specify a causal direction for regression analyses, it is possible that participants' open-ended responses could shed light on the nature of attitudinal influence observed in this inquiry. The one question I have not yet addressed is what this analysis says about the influence of free-speech and abortion attitudes affecting participants' standing judgments:

Can the analysis of open-ended justifications shed light on the specific nature of influence for attitudinal variables observed to influence the standing judgments in the last chapter? For instance, can they reveal whether the influence of free-speech attitudes was top-down or bottom-up? Can we tell from justifications whether participants were aware of the influence of abortion attitudes on their decisions?

As we saw in chapter 4, free-speech attitudes had the most consistent effect on participants' standing decisions, influencing judgments in both constrained and unconstrained conditions; I suggested there was a legally justifiable reason for such influence, making it the "least separable" of the preferences tested in this study. One could argue that the fact that 75 percent of all participants specifically mentioned free speech in justifying their decisions lends support to the idea that the influence of such attitudes was bottom-up rather than top-down. That is, in considering whether the plaintiff had suffered a cognizable legal injury, those who supported free speech were more likely to see restriction of her first amendment rights as an "injury"; those who were more likely to support restrictions on speech were less likely to see it as such in the context of reasoning through applicable doctrinal authority. This could also explain why the influence of the free-speech variable was statistically and substantively significant in both the constrained and unconstrained conditions. Participants in both circuit conditions were, after all, considering the same legal question about the plaintiff's "injury," and so they were equally likely to have such analysis shaded by their personal preferences, notwithstanding the presence of controlling authority on the issue.

In contrast, the influence of abortion opinions could only have been top-down. Put simply, there is no legally justifiable way to explain systematic differences observed across content conditions where the plaintiff was expressing views that were consistent (and inconsistent) with those of law student participants. The relevant question is whether experimental subjects were *aware* of the influence of abortion attitudes on the decisions they were rendering. The simple answer is that there was little evidence that they were specifically attending to abortion in their justifications. First, open-ended responses uniformly referenced appropriate doctrinal authority from the brief. Second, only 13 percent of all participants mentioned abortion specifically, and only one participant in the entire sample explicitly expressed any self-conscious concern that sympathy for the views expressed by the plaintiff may have influenced his/her standing analysis.

Still, we know that abortion opinions influenced decisions in systematic ways. I believe that, taken in its entirety, the evidence from this study lends support to the idea that, consistent with psychological research, the influence of abortion attitudes in this experiment was real but largely unconscious. In the process of reasoning through the standing question, participants somehow "found a way" to justify decisions consistent with their sympathy (or lack of sympathy) for the views expressed by the plaintiff, especially in the unconstrained condition, where they had more latitude to do so.

Of course, it is possible that decision makers were actively making decisions consistent with abortion attitudes but trying to obfuscate the illegitimate influence of such attitudes in justifying their decisions. Although I cannot fully refute this idea with data available from this study, I think this alternative explanation is less tenable for several reasons. First, consistent with the strong socialization processes described in chapter 1, participants reported that the law played a more important role than facts in their judgments and went to greater length in describing the legal rationale for their decisions. This suggests that participants themselves believed they were making decisions based on the doctrinal authority in the brief.

Second, although abortion was mentioned by only about 13 percent of experimental participants in open-ended justifications, it was present to some extent in the minds of participants. The fact that there is very little differentiating those who mentioned abortion from those who did not suggests pro-lifers and pro-choicers and those in constrained and unconstrained conditions were equally aware of its presence. Thus, it was not that participants were trying to hide its influence on their decision processes—the analyses indicate that they were aware of abortion at some level—it was just not in the forefront of the minds of most participants in justifying their standing decisions. This seems to indicate that they were aware of abortion content, but perhaps not aware of the impact that their own abortion views had on their decision making.

Finally, the "link" between participants' abortion attitudes and the standing decision they were asked to make in this experiment was not altogether obvious. Participants were asked a battery of eight policy questions in Study A, including the three measures hypothesized to influence their standing decision. In the instructions, they were informed that Study A and Study B were independent. They had no way of knowing answers on the policy questions would be used in analyzing their responses to the instrument following the legal brief. Even if law students did harbor some suspicion that the two studies were related in some way, it would be very hard to know *which* of the policy questions were relevant, or that several of them, in fact, would be used in the analysis.

Moreover, guarding against the influence of one policy attitude in rendering the standing decision may have inhibited participants from checking the influence of the others. This could explain why, of the three attitudes tested, opinions on Hatch Act restrictions had the least leverage. One could argue its link to the standing judgment was the most "obvious" in the context of this study, and so participants were careful to guard against its influence. The questions about flag-burning sanctions used as the measure of free-speech and abortion restrictions were not as closely related to the standing judgment that participants were asked to render. This is especially true where participants were completely unaware that there were alternative versions of the brief where the content of the message on plaintiff's campaign sign was manipulated.[7]

The discovery of systematic differences on some attitudinal variables, notwithstanding the fact that participants may have been "guarding against" the influence of others, is strong evidence for the potential of policy preferences to influence legal judgments in systematic ways. Moreover, the analyses of open-ended justifications suggest law students were not fully aware of the various influences on their decision making.

Conclusion

At the very least, this study demonstrates that, taking law students at their word, there were sufficient ways to justify policy-based conclusions using legal doctrine. Moreover, the delineation of differences noted in this inquiry gives us a richer understanding of legal justifications that different decision makers used in reaching alternative conclusions in this study. I hope that such observations can lead to the development of interesting hypotheses and that in going about the study this way I have strengthened the case for using experimental methods in studying legal decision making.

SIX

MOTIVATED REASONING AS
AN EMPIRICAL FRAMEWORK
Finding Our Way Back to Context

In the part 1 of this book, I argued that existing models of attitudinal influence in legal decision making provide incomplete and unsatisfactory accounts of legal behavior that do not comport with the subjective experience of decision makers. In part 2, I tested two mechanisms of influence taken from intuitions about how legal experts consider evidence and arguments in real-world cases using highly stylized decision norms. I also explored the *limits* of such influence by looking for evidence of constraint in studies testing each of the hypothesized mechanisms of influence. I hope I have convinced readers that motivated reasoning accounts have the potential to fill gaps left by other models of decision making and offer a richer, more complete understanding of the precise role of attitudes in decisional behavior.

In this concluding chapter, I have two goals. The first is to summarize findings from the empirical chapters highlighting what we have learned about each of the mechanisms and potential avenues for future investigation. Consistent with Kinder and Palfrey's (1993) characterization of experimental research, findings from both studies provide important insights into cognitive processes of legal decision makers *and* significant fodder for future research. My second goal is to outline the broad contours of what a research paradigm incorporating motivated reasoning as empirical framework might look like. Ideally, it would be interdisciplinary; the approach should appeal to researchers from different disciplines interested in legal cognition. Moreover, the research agenda should be organized around substantive questions and assumptions rather than any particular empirical method. I suggest several lines of inquiry and ways scholars may take motivated reasoning inquiries outside the experimental lab using methods that are more familiar to political scientists and legal scholars. I also point to existing research addressing questions that should be of interest to researchers who might be attracted to using motivated reasoning as an empirical framework.

Summary of Results

Like most research that studies political phenomena from a new perspective, this inquiry raises at least as many questions as it answers. Overall, however, this study advances our knowledge of how preferences interact with case facts and norms of decision making to influence legal reasoning processes. I hope we will see more attempts to understand the interaction of these forces in future research; motivated reasoning provides an excellent framework to pursue this inquiry.

Consistent with results presented here, future research adopting this perspective will probably reveal a more complex picture of decision making than "purely legal" or "purely attitudinal" models of decision making suggest. The influence of preferences may be more resistant to constraining decisional norms in some issue areas than others. Or, as suggested in the experiment on separable preferences, there could be individual differences in how decision makers respond to controlling authority.

As with all empirical inquiries, researchers invoking this framework will need to be explicit about their expectations, and allow for the distinct possibility that those expectations are wrong and that other factors may come into play in unexpected ways. All of these things happened here. But, consistent with experimental hypotheses, findings revealed significant evidence of attitudinal influence in the context of norms actively used and subjectively experienced by legal decision makers.

First, in line with what was suggested in the doctrinal analysis of Commerce Clause cases from chapter 2, the experiments on analogical perception demonstrated that perceptions of precedent can be shaded by policy predispositions. This mechanism is consistent with bottom-up characterizations of attitudinal influence. The effect was observed for lay observers of court outputs as well as experimental participants with legal training. Significantly, however, the influence of policy attitudes was constrained by objective similarity in both samples. The interaction between policy attitudes and case outcomes was significant only in the "middle range" of cases for undergraduates in the first experiment and law students in the second.

There was evidence in Experiment 2 that lay observers and law student participants used a different "metric" of distance, perhaps due to their differential familiarity with the case scenario presented in that study. Clearly, law students drew sharper distinctions than did undergraduates and acted more skeptically in judging the similarity of all cases. Moreover, contrary to expectations, law students seemed particularly sensitive to whether outcomes were consistent with their preferences in making similarity judgments. Rather than being attenuated, the effects of motivated perceptions were *heightened* in our sample of legally trained decision makers. This finding is inconsistent with legal models of decision making suggesting that legal training should inhibit the influence of attitudinal factors. Indeed, it tends to support attitudinal conceptions of influence suggesting that legally trained participants viewed cases through an outcome-oriented lens. Still, the confining influence of case facts moderated this effect in the legal sample, suggesting objective similarity can act as a meaningful constraint on motivated perceptions.

The analogy experiments also showed that attitudes influenced lay observers in unexpected ways. Undergraduates who favored the expansion of legal rights used more lenient criteria in judging the similarity of all cases. Also, there was evidence in Experiment 1 that participants' positive feelings toward a highly sympathetic defendant (the Boy Scouts) may have influenced judgments as well. Interestingly, both of these unexpected main effects were most evident in cases that were "furthest away" from the target dispute, suggesting that policy preferences may influence judgments in these respects where there is significant latitude for them to operate. Further inquiries can be designed to test the boundaries and reliability of these unexpected main effects that could be important in shaping public perceptions of judicial outputs.

The experimental results discussed in chapters 4 and 5 shed light on how motivated decision processes influenced legally trained decision makers as participants reasoned about a case involving multiple issues. Specifically, an experiment was designed to test whether law students were able to separate their preferences about substantive issues from a seemingly neutral standing decision they were asked to make in a hypothetical case involving the restriction of political speech regarding abortion.

From a legal standpoint, there was no justifiable reason that participants' agreement with the plaintiff's views on abortion should have influenced their determination of the standing question. Yet, consistent with top-down conceptions of attitudinal influence, there were systematic differences in participants' judgments depending on their sympathy for views expressed by the spousal plaintiff. Significantly, this effect was tempered by the jurisdictional conditions where participants were rendering their judgments. Participants were less likely to make decisions consistent with their abortion attitudes where there was controlling legal authority limiting their ability to so do. This was especially true for the majority of the sample expressing pro-choice views.

Findings suggested that participants with pro-life views made decisions consistent with their preferences in the constrained and unconstrained jurisdictional conditions. In fact, evidence showed that the small number of pro-lifers assigned to conditions where there was controlling authority contrary to their views were especially likely to make attitudinal judgments against the plaintiff, in direct conflict with that authority. This differential response to constraint by people with alternative views was not anticipated. Although the unequal distribution of people with alternative views across treatment conditions suggests findings should be treated with caution, the significant result raises the possibility that there are systematic differences in decision makers' response to controlling authority. This is an idea that is not addressed in extant theories of decision making. The potential for such behavior could merit further consideration and empirical investigation.[1]

The separability of preferences experiment also tested the influence of two other attitudes that could have influenced participants' standing decisions in the hypothetical case. Consistent with traditional characterizations of legal decision making, participants' views of Hatch Act restrictions did not influence their standing judgments in systematic ways. The influence of free-speech attitudes, however, was strong and consistent with attitudinal hypothesis in both the constrained and unconstrained jurisdictional conditions. Participants who supported free speech were more likely to say the plaintiff spouse had standing controlling for other factors.

The analysis of open-ended justifications that law students gave for their judgments in chapter 5 shed more light on the precise nature of attitudinal influence for the variables investigated in this study. We saw that, notwithstanding differences across speech-content conditions, participants reported the law influenced their judgments more than the facts did. Only about 13 percent of all participants specifically mentioned abortion or the direction of the plaintiff's views in their justifications. Therefore, although their own attitudes about abortion had a systematic effect on participants' standing judgments, it was not in the forefront of most of their minds in explaining such decisions.

Free speech, on the other hand, was specifically referenced in some way by about 75 percent of all participants in the experiment, strongly suggesting that the influence of this particular variable was bottom-up rather than top-down. That is, when considering whether the plaintiff suffered an "injury" in her own right, those who supported free speech were more likely to conclude that she had, and those who did not support free speech were more likely to conclude that she had not when reasoning through the legal authority in the brief.

We also saw the influence of legal norms in participants' justifications and responses to closed-ended questions. Law students reported being significantly more confident in their judgments in conditions where there was controlling authority; they were also more likely to cite specific authority when it was controlling. Moreover, findings demonstrate that participants felt the need to acknowledge opposing evidence in their justifications, consistent with norms suggesting they should consider arguments raised by opposing litigants in the context of adversarial decision making.

Findings demonstrate that particular arguments were favored by experimental participants holding for the plaintiff (free speech), and different arguments seemed to be mentioned by those holding for the defendants (specific language of the restrictive ordinance). Interestingly, policy arguments seemed to carry the most weight in conditions where there was no direct controlling authority. Finally, findings indicate that participants with specific attitudes were drawn to distinct legal arguments.[2]

In testing a sincere model of attitudinal influence, results here speak most directly to debates about influence of legal and attitudinal factors in decision making. Findings, however, may also have import for those who study decision making from a strategic perspective. Looking at how individuals respond to case facts and authority under different levels of constraint may reveal the relative ease with which strategic actors will convince others of their views as we move to the group context of appellate decision making. Moreover, looking at the influence of particular attitudes may point toward arguments that will hold sway in that environment.

Arguably, the debate between sincere and strategic conceptions of judicial behavior has been fueled by the failure of judicial scholars to address cognitive processes. Without knowing *how* judges reach conclusions consistent with their preferences, political scientists, skeptical of doctrinal explanations judges give for their own behavior, have been quick to jump to strategic accounts of decision making. While this study does not disprove strategic explanations, evidence of constraint uncovered here lends support to the idea that accuracy goals predominate in the minds of decision makers and attitudinal outcomes may be the result of very human psychological processes rather than any conscious decision to flout the law in pursuit of policy.

What Does Motivated Reasoning Research Look Like?

Clearly, we have just begun to scratch the surface of discovering the cognitive mechanisms behind findings of preference-oriented decision making. It is inquiry that would benefit from the contributions of researchers with varied interests and expertise. I hope that findings in this study will be of interest to scholars across subfields in political science. Besides being directly relevant for those interested in courts and judicial decision making, the questions addressed should speak to political scientists interested in political psychology and the effect of personal preferences on politically relevant behavior, especially in the presence of norms designed to reduce their influence. I also believe that this subject matter has the potential to reach across disciplinary lines. Findings here may be of particular interest to psychologists interested in a direct application of analogical reasoning to a politically relevant domain and legal scholars who show signs of becoming increasingly open to social science techniques.

Although legal scholars have been slow to take up the systematic investigation of attitudinal influence, it is an inquiry they avoid at their own peril. Those who are trained in traditional modes of decision making are especially well equipped to test avenues of attitudinal influence and their limits. Their failure to do so allows researchers from other disciplines to set the research agenda and characterize findings in their own way. Rather than dismissing evidence tending to demonstrate policy-oriented behavior, legal scholars should confront the issue head-on; their failure to take up this inquiry represents a missed opportunity at this critical stage in our collective knowledge.

Just as important, behavioral scholars, who have been the forerunners in contributing to our understanding of the role preferences play in legal decision making, should reassess the excessively critical stance they have taken in favor of a more complex understanding of attitudinal influence. At the very least, they should take a step back to consider *why* preferences matter as much as they do in legal decision processes.

Following Pritchett's (1948) seminal study, it seems that behavioral scholars took pride in their critical stance in demonstrating that policy preferences were a strong determinant of judicial voting behavior. Fueled by consistent findings of attitudinal influence, they were dismissive of doctrinal accounts of decision making; behavioral scholarship developed with little regard for the legal factors judges cited as determinative. Once behavioral researchers started to go in this direction, I think they may have lacked the empirical framework to bridge the gulf that developed between legal and attitudinal accounts of decision making. Political scientists became *as invested* in policy-driven explanations as legal theorists were in doctrinal accounts. Scholars became entrenched in their home discipline's assumptions and methodologies; thus, two fields that purported to explain the same decisional phenomenon grew further apart.

This trend has reversed itself a bit in the last ten years as studies employing behavioral methods have started to make their way into law reviews (see for example, Ruger et al. 2004; George 1998; and Brace, Hall, and Langer 1999). For the most part, however, differences between the disciplines remain. It is important to note that progress in this respect is *not* merely a question of when legal scholars will "come around" to behavioral ways of thinking. Consistent with one of the main arguments motivating this inquiry, judicial scholars need to take judges' doctrinal accounts more seriously if they want to understand *how and when* policy attitudes will influence the outcome choices that are the focus of their analyses.

Although I have been somewhat critical of scholars, including Segal and Spaeth, for invoking motivated reasoning in a superficial manner, I have to credit them with coming up with the insight that offers an empirical framework to bridge the gap between legal and attitudinal accounts of decision making. Motivated reasoning accounts allow for legal "accuracy" and "directional" policy goals that can exist in the minds of decision makers simultaneously. Moreover, this conception of influence is not an all-or-nothing proposition. The account posits attitudinal influence, but suggests "outer limits" on the ability of decision makers to reach conclusions consistent with their preferences.

Thus, the goal of research using motivated reasoning as an organizing framework is not to discover whether preferences or legal considerations always predominate in the minds of decision makers, but to discover the "conditions under which" each is likely to play a role in decisional behavior. In this way, the motivated reasoning approach accommodates legal and attitudinal influences in decision-making behavior. As discussed in chapter 1, not all scholars agree that such an accommodation is necessary. But in order to have a more realistic and, indeed, *more correct* account of attitudinal influence, I think it is clear that researchers must address the tension between legal and attitudinal explanations of decision making.

Motivated reasoning provides a well-developed theoretical and empirical framework to undertake this inquiry. Findings from cognitive and social psychology can and should go a long way in informing our theory and hypotheses. But researchers must also be mindful of the stylized environment where decision makers act. Directional biases shown to influence lay subjects may operate differently or be attenuated in the minds of legally trained individuals following stylized norms. Moreover, not every legal decision rule has a ready cognate in the psychological literature, so findings cannot be assumed to transfer directly from the laboratory to the courtroom or judicial chamber.

Still, we must always remember that judges are human (Frank 1931a, 1931b). Given the pervasiveness of motivated cognition in common decisional domains, it is not unreasonable to think they may be subject to directional biases in thinking about cases. To seriously investigate this proposition, however, researchers must consider the evidence and authority that decision makers *actually use* in reasoning about disputes. This means taking legal norms much more seriously than extant behavioral studies have done thus far. It also means being open to numerous empirical methods likely to advance our understanding of what is going on in the minds of decision makers.

Here I employed, and went to some length to justify, experimental methods that have been widely used in psychology to explore cognitive processes. In making my case for experiments, however, I did not mean to suggest that other approaches are without merit or that experiments are the only way to investigate constraint and motivated biases in legal decision making; they are not. Our investigations can only benefit from the interest and efforts of scholars from various fields using multiple methods of inquiry. Experiments are but one technique that empirical scholars can use to understand constraint and biases in our legal system. As such, they should be part of our methodological toolbox, subject to critical evaluation, but accepted for the potential contribution they can make to our knowledge of decision-making processes.

Moreover, it is important to note that what distinguishes motivated reasoning as an empirical framework is not the method researchers utilize, but the assumptions they adopt in formulating hypotheses and the substantive questions they investigate. Specifically, the approach posits that understanding the mix of conscious and unconscious goals in the minds of decision makers and how norms and context facilitate and frustrate those goals is the key to understanding legal behavior. Scholars engaged in these kinds of inquiries are doing work consistent with the paradigm I describe. As detailed below, there are already judicial scholars undertaking such questions using alternative methods.

Most critically, the motivated reasoning approach requires that researchers be explicit about the role of alternative motives and the factors that can limit their realization in our investigations of decision making. The vagueness that has characterized the issue of intention in legal decision making can no longer stand, particularly now that we have a framework that allows for the influence of alternative goals. We need to be more explicit about the role of alternative motives and the factors that can limit their realization in our theories of decision making. Rather than assuming that accuracy or policy goals always prevail, researchers need to identify specific choices where the two are in tension, make predictions about the observable implications of each, and conduct analyses to ascertain the relative influence of competing motives in those choices.

Case votes are probably not the optimal decisions to investigate for this purpose. As mentioned earlier, there are many component choices that judges make that dictate outcome decisions. Segal and Spaeth may be right when they argue that judges are free to convince themselves of the merit of whatever authority gets them to desired outcomes where they have multiple issues and alternative arguments to choose from. This remains to be tested. Even if they are right, however, this is not an especially satisfying answer for people interested in uncovering cognitive mechanisms. It would be much more interesting to see how decision makers are able to convince themselves of the soundness of particular arguments that people with opposing views deem to be without merit.

Assuming this is an interesting and worthwhile goal, I describe some of the empirical questions scholars incorporating this framework can investigate using methods with which political scientists and legal scholars may be more comfortable. My purpose is to suggest future directions for studies using this approach to understanding decisional behavior.

Future Research Directions

The two avenues investigated in this inquiry do not exhaust the ways that preferences can influence legal decision making. It is in thinking about alternative mechanisms of influence that legal scholars can make a significant contribution to this literature. Indeed, looking at existing doctrinal analyses with particular questions in mind can help us develop theory and testable empirical propositions. For instance: What are the conditions under which judges have more and less latitude to decide cases in ways consistent with their preferences? Are there certain issues where we might expect attitudes to operate more than others? Are there individual differences in the ways particular judges treat arguments and controlling authority that suggest motivated reasoning is at play in judges' decisional behavior?

There is legal and empirical scholarship addressing some of these important issues already. For instance, with regard to judicial latitude in decision making, one well-worn distinction in legal scholarship is the relationship between rules and standards (Schauer 1991; Schlag 1985). Conventional wisdom holds that judges are constrained in the presence of "black-letter rules" and have more latitude to make decisions consistent with their preferences in the presence of more flexible legal standards. One way to test this proposition empirically to see if legal decision criteria constrain decision makers as conventional wisdom suggests might be to find two alternative jurisdictions where the same issue (for instance, a specific standard of evidence) is governed by different decisional criteria, one jurisdiction where a rule is at play and the other a legal standard. Presumably decisions on that issue in each jurisdiction could be compared using regression techniques to see if judicial attitudes come into play in one jurisdiction more than the other.

Bartels (2005) has looked at "issue salience" as a factor moderating the influence of attitudinal influence in decision making. He uses hierarchical regression techniques speaking to whether certain issues invite attitudinal decisions more than others. Presumably legal scholars should have insights into what issues are particularly likely to trigger attitudinal responses and motivated decision-making phenomena. In line with the doctrinal analysis presented in chapter 2, looking at periods reflecting significant shifts in Supreme Court doctrine may reveal more attitudinal behavior due to ambiguity in the state of the law. Alternatively, we may see more evidence of constraint once issues are well settled. Time-series techniques could be used to investigate decisions in a specific issue area over time to test this proposition.

Collins (2007, 2008) has done some interesting research looking at whether the judges on the Supreme Court are swayed more by amicus briefs from groups whose views are consistent with their ideological preferences than by amicus briefs from groups whose views are not. These inquiries go to the sort of arguments and evidence judges are most likely to be drawn to in light of their preferences. In this vein, it should also be possible to use content analysis techniques to trace how judges with different views "treat" particular precedents using citation services to find relevant cases. Such inquires may lead to interesting insights: Do liberal justices cite reasons to follow cases with outcomes consistent with their preferences more frequently than conservative judges looking at the same cases? Are such tendencies tempered by group decision processes, and specifically the presence of judges with opposing views in opinion coalitions?

Just as this study does not test all possible avenues of preference-based decision making, it does not exhaust the factors that may constrain motivated decision processes. Significantly, many of the institutional protections against the operation of unconscious goals that I mentioned in chapter 1, including professional accountability and the group nature of decision making, remain to be investigated. Here the insights of psychologists and political psychologists should be particularly useful.

As mentioned in the introduction, there is a significant body of research in social psychology on these issues. Specifically, Tetlock and his colleagues (ex. Tetlock 1983; Tetlock, Skitka, and Boettger 1989; see Lerner and Tetlock 1999 for review) have investigated accountability concerns which are beginning to be addressed more seriously in the judicial literature (Bartels 2005; Baum 2006). Moreover, Moscovici and others (Moscovici 1980; Moscovici and Zallvaloni 1969; Janis 1982; Nemeth 1986) have addressed issues of majority and minority influence in group decision making (see Morehead 1998 for a review). Gruenfeld (1995) did a particularly interesting study using content analysis and the concept of integrative complexity to investigate the influence of dissent on majority opinions on the Supreme Court. Moreover, she and her colleague (Gruenfeld and Hollingshead 1993) have a study on sociocognition in work groups that should be particularly useful for scholars interested in investigating factors impacting collegial decision making on appellate courts (i.e., Collins and Martinek 2007).

Researchers doing empirical work along these lines are already studying legal decision processes in a manner consistent with the framework I suggest. The motivated reasoning approach has great potential to attract scholars from various perspectives interested in legal decision making for differing reasons. It is also an approach that can accommodate, and indeed invites, multiple methods of inquiry. Most important, the approach moves us beyond unrealistic all-or-nothing conceptions of attitudinal influence that have divided scholars interested in understanding the influences on legal behavior for far too long. It is time that empirical scholars find our way back to context and embrace the complexity inherent in the phenomena we are investigating. Motivated reasoning provides a way to do so without sacrificing our theoretical or empirical rigor. The approach can substantially improve our understanding of legal and attitudinal influences in legal decision making.

Appendixes

MATERIALS RELATED TO EXPERIMENTS ON ANALOGICAL PERCEPTION

Article Describing Target Case—Experiment 1

Supreme Court Will Hear Case about Gay Boy Scout Leader

WASHINGTON—Today the United States Supreme Court agreed to hear arguments in the case of *Boy Scouts of America v. Dale*. The case arises from plaintiff James Dale's claim that the Boy Scouts engaged in unlawful discrimination when they removed him as scout master of a troop in New Jersey and revoked his membership upon learning he was a homosexual.

Gay rights activists argue that the conduct of the scouting organization was a violation of Dale's civil rights and that his sexual orientation does not affect his ability to serve as a scout master. Lawyers for the Boy Scouts of America argue that they are a voluntary organization, and are free to restrict membership in a manner consistent with their beliefs and values.

It is difficult to predict how the justices will decide the Boy Scouts case, but some legal experts point to a previous decision that might guide the Court's reasoning: Indian Guides v. Henman. *In that case the Court ruled that the Indian Guides, a national boys' organization,* engaged in unlawful discrimination [or acted within its legal rights] *when they refused to let a* gay man [or woman or black man] *serve as a youth leader.* [Source case manipulation: see following for examples of relationship variations.]

The Court will hear arguments in *Boy Scouts v. Dale* in late April and should issue its decision before the end of the current term.

TABLE A.1 Undergraduate sample characteristics: Analogical perception, Experiment 1

	NUMBER IN SAMPLE	PERCENTAGE
Gender		
Male	79	38
Female	129	62
Ideology		
Liberals	78	38
Conservatives	89	42
Moderates	41	20
Party affiliation		
Democrats	69	33
Republicans	98	47
Independents	41	20
Race		
Black	23	11
White	164	78
Asian	13	6
Hispanic	2	< 1
Mixed	5	2

Relationship Manipulations Used in Experiment 1

EMPLOYER VARIATION

It is difficult to predict how the justices will decide the Boy Scouts case, but some legal experts point to a previous decision that might guide the Court's reasoning: Henman v. Selko Inc. *In that case the Court held that Selko Inc., an advertising company that produces commercials for NASCAR auto races, engaged in unlawful discrimination* [or acted within its legal rights] *when they refused to hire a* gay man [or woman or black man] *for a management position because of his sexual orientation.*

INSURANCE COMPANY VARIATION

It is difficult to predict how the justices will decide the Boy Scouts case, but some legal experts point to a previous decision that might guide the Court's reasoning: Manson Insurance Co. v. Henman. *In that case the Court held that Manson Insurance, a company that provides health insurance coverage to individuals,* engaged in unlawful discrimination [or acted within its legal rights] *when it systematically denied coverage for illnesses that affect* gay men [or women or black men].

Relevant Questions—Experiment 1

SIMILARITY QUESTIONS

Scouting Organization

How similar would you say the case of *Boy Scouts v. Dale* is to the other case mentioned in the news article which involved a boy's organization that would not allow a *gay man [or woman, or black man]* to be a youth leader?

1—very dissimilar   3—fairly similar
2—fairly dissimilar   4—very similar

Employer

How similar would you say the case of *Boy Scouts v. Dale* is to the other case mentioned in the news article which involved an advertising company that would not hire a *gay man [or woman, or black man]* to be a manager?

Insurance Company

How similar would you say the case of *Boy Scouts v. Dale* is to the other case mentioned in the news article which involved an insurance company that would not offer coverage for illnesses that affect *gay men [or women, or black men]*?

SCOUT LEADER QUESTION

In your opinion, is it acceptable or unacceptable for a gay man to be a Boy Scout Leader?

1—completely unacceptable   4—slightly acceptable
2—moderately unacceptable   5—moderately acceptable
3—slightly unacceptable   6—completely acceptable

Article Describing the Target Case—Experiment 2

NJ Supreme Court Will Hear Case about Access to Religious-Based Treatment Program

TRENTON 2/1/03—The New Jersey Supreme Court is scheduled to hear arguments next week in the case of *Wazzer-Din v. Goodwill Home and*

TABLE A.2 Undergraduate sample characteristics: Analogical perception, Experiment 2

	NUMBER IN SAMPLE	PERCENTAGE
Gender		
Male	52	54
Female	44	46
Ideology		
Liberals	30	31
Conservatives	49	51
Moderates	17	18
Party affiliation		
Democrats	31	32
Republicans	53	55
Independents	12	13
Race		
Black	4	4
White	84	88
Asian	2	2
Hispanic	3	3
Mixed	3	3

Mission of Passaic. The case arises from a claim that the Goodwill Home and Mission engaged in unlawful discrimination when it denied plaintiff, Wazzer-Din, admission to its domestic abuse treatment program because of his religious views.

The main issue in the case is whether the Goodwill program qualifies as a "public accommodation" under New Jersey's anti-discrimination statute (also known as the LAD—Law Against Discrimination). The New Jersey statute is one of the broadest in the country, protecting individuals from discrimination on the basis of race, religion, and sexual orientation in a number of contexts.

Specifically, the LAD defines "places of public accommodation" by illustration. The list of places subject to the New Jersey law includes, "any tavern, hotel, motel, camp or resort whether for entertainment of guests or accommodation of those seeking health or relaxation; as well as any producer, manufacturer, or concession of any kind dealing with goods and services of any kind." N.J.S.A10:5–4.

TABLE A.3 Law student sample characteristics: Analogical perception, Experiment 2

	NUMBER IN SAMPLE	PERCENTAGE
Gender		
Male	36	47
Female	41	53
Ideology		
Liberals	35	45
Conservatives	32	42
Moderates	10	13
Party affiliation		
Democrats	30	39
Republicans	32	42
Independents	15	19
Race		
Black	8	10
White	62	81
Asian	3	4
Hispanic	1	< 1
Mixed	3	4
Year in law school		
2L	37	48
3L	20	26
Graduates	20	26

The list also includes "hospitals" and "clinics." The New Jersey Supreme Court has held that "other accommodations similar to those enumerated were intended to be covered." *Fraser v. Robin Day Camp,* 210 A.2d 208 (1965). There is a specific exemption, however, for "educational facilities operated by a bona fide religious or sectarian institution." N.J.S.A. 10:5–12(f).

Plaintiff Wazzer-Din argues that the home's refusal to treat him because of his Islamic faith is a violation of his civil rights under the LAD. The Goodwill program is acknowledged to be the most successful of its kind in the area. Participants live at the home during three weeks of intensive treatment and therapy. Wazzer-Din's lawyers emphasize that the program has admitted people of other faiths in the past and that it often accepts contributions from residents in the form of publicly funded food stamps and income from supplemental social security checks.

Lawyers for the Goodwill Home emphasize that the program receives no direct government funding. They acknowledge that the program has admitted people of different faiths in the past, but assert that because the program is based, in part, on religious instruction, all residents, regardless of faith, must express an openness to Christian teachings. They argue that under the First Amendment's guarantee of free association, the faith-based home should be free to restrict program participants in a manner consistent with its values and beliefs.

It is difficult to predict how the New Jersey Supreme Court will decide the Wazzer-Din case, but some legal experts point to a recent public accommodation decision that might guide the court's reasoning: Promised Hope v. Lafon, *742 A.2d 536 (2001). In that case the court ruled that Promised Hope, a Christian organization,* engaged in unlawful discrimination [or acted within its legal rights] *when it refused to let an* Islamic [or a gay or a black] man *take part in its residential drug treatment program.* [Source case manipulation: see following for examples of relationship variations.]

The court will hear arguments in *Wazzer-Din v. Goodwill Home and Mission of Passaic* next Tuesday and should issue its decision before the end of the current term.

SERVICE ORGANIZATION VARIATION

It is difficult to predict how the New Jersey Supreme Court will decide the Wazzer-Din case, but some legal experts point to a recent public accommodation decision that might guide the court's reasoning: Cherry Hill Kiwanis v. Lafon, *742 A.2d 536 (2001). In that case, the court ruled that a local chapter of the Kiwanis organization, a civic group that encourages community service,* engaged in unlawful discrimination [or acted within its legal rights] *when it refused to let an* Islamic [or a gay or a black] man *become a member.*

INSURANCE COMPANY VARIATION

It is difficult to predict how the New Jersey Supreme Court will decide the Wazzer-Din case, but some legal experts point to a recent public accommodation decision that might guide the court's reasoning: Marine Insurance Co. v. Lafon, *742 A.2d 536 (2001). In that case the court ruled that Marine Insurance, a company that provides health care insurance to individuals,* engaged in unlawful discrimination [or acted within its legal rights] *when it systematically denied coverage for illnesses that affect* Islamic [or gay or black] men.

Relevant Questions—Experiment 2

SIMILARITY QUESTIONS

Religious Organization

How similar is the *Wazzer-Din* case described in the article to *Promised Hope v. Lafon* (the case where the religious organization was found to have *engaged in unlawful discrimination [or to have acted within its legal rights]* when it refused to let an *Islamic [or gay or black] man* take part in its drug treatment program)?

1—Very Similar	5—Somewhat Dissimilar
2—	6—
3—Somewhat Similar	7—Very Dissimilar
4—	

Community Service Organization

How similar is the *Wazzer-Din* case described in the article to *Cherry Hill Kiwanis v. Lafon* (the case where the community service organization was found to have *engaged in unlawful discrimination [or to have acted within its legal rights]* when it refused to let an *Islamic [or gay or black] man* become a member)?

Insurance Company

How similar is the Wazzer-Din case described in the article to *Marine Insurance Co. v. Lafon* (the case where the community service organization was found to have *engaged in unlawful discrimination [or to have acted within its legal rights]* when it refused to let an *Islamic [or gay or black] man* become a member)?

POLICY QUESTION—FAITH-BASED SERVICES

Some people believe that when religious organizations provide treatment services or charity to the underprivileged, they should do so without regard to religious beliefs; others believe that faith-based organizations should be able to offer preferential services to their members if they want.

Please indicate the extent to which you *personally agree or disagree* with the following statement:

Faith-based organizations should have the right to restrict their services to clients who share their religious beliefs.

1—disagree strongly	4—agree slightly
2—disagree somewhat	5—agree somewhat
3—disagree slightly	6—agree strongly

DEMOGRAPHIC QUESTIONS—USED IN ALL SAMPLES

1. Are you male or female?
2. How would you describe your general political views? Would you call yourself a liberal or a conservative? (7-point scale)
3. What about your political party preference? Do you consider yourself a Democrat, a Republican, or an Independent? (7-point scale)
4. What racial or ethnic group do you consider yourself to be a member of?

1—Black, African American	4—Hispanic
2—White, European American	5—Mixed
3—Asian	

SUPPLEMENTAL REGRESSION ANALYSES FOR EXPERIMENTS ON ANALOGICAL PERCEPTION

The following are supplemental regression analyses on similarity judgments analyzed in chapter 3. They confirm findings from the ANOVAs presented in that chapter. I include them here for those who want to see the effects of control variables including ideology, race, and political knowledge. All analyses are ordinary least-squares.[1]

Independent variables were measured in the same way in both experiments (see appendix A-1 for specific questions). I will discuss how each variable used in the regression analyses was coded before discussing results. The same variables were used in regressions in both experiments except where specifically referenced.

Each analysis includes the following control variables: ideology (measured on a seven-point scale, with higher numbers reflecting more conservative views); gender (coded 0 male, 1 female); race (coded 1 African American, else 0); political interest (measured on a five-point scale with lower numbers indicating more interest). For the analyses in Experiment 2, I also include a measure of religiosity indicating how frequently participants attend religious services (lower numbers reflect more frequent attendance). In the pooled analysis, student type is coded 0 for undergraduates, 1 for law students.

Outcome is dichotomous; all analyses with discrimination outcomes were coded as 1, and nondiscrimination outcomes were coded as 0. Predisposition is also dichotomous, with those opposed to discrimination coded as 1, else 0. Given the way outcome and predisposition are coded, the interactive term represents the effect for participants against discrimination in cases where there was a finding of discrimination consistent with their preferences.

Distance is measured in Experiment 1 using our a priori classification scheme (close cases were coded as 1; cases in the middle range were coded as 2; and far cases were coded as 3). Consistent with the ANOVA in Experiment 2, the distance measure is the relationship manipulation (close cases [coded as 1] are those involving religious treatment services; medium cases [coded as 2] are cases with community civic organization defendants; and far cases [coded as 3] are those with insurance company defendants]. For Experiment 1, I present results of analyses for undergraduates in all cases as well as results for disaggregated analyses in close, medium, and far cases. These analyses are included in table A.4.

For Experiment 2, I present results for the pooled sample in all cases as well as undergraduates in all cases and close medium and far cases (table A.5). I conclude with law students' judgments in all cases; and in close, medium, and far cases in Experiment 2 (table A.6). I discuss these results, including the meaning of significant terms and interactions, to show that the results are consistent with those from the ANOVAs presented earlier.

OLS Regression Analyses—Experiment 1

All Cases. The analysis of all cases presented in table A.4 demonstrates that case distance was the only statistically significant factor in participants' judgments of similarity. The negative direction of its influence is consistent with experimental hypotheses. Participants tended to see cases classified as further from the target dispute as less similar than cases categorized as being closer to the target dispute. None of the other measured variables or manipulations is significant in the analysis of similarity judgments in all cases. To see how relevant variables operate in categories of interest, I performed regressions in close, medium, and far cases. The "distance" variable subsequently drops out in these analyses.[2]

Disaggregated Analyses. The last three columns in table A.4 represent analyses in cases coded as close, medium, and far from the target dispute. Consistent with results presented in chapter 3, the interaction between policy preference and predisposition is only significant in the middle range of cases. Its positive direction indicates that in the middle range of cases, those who were against discrimination found cases with discrimination outcomes as closer to the target dispute than cases with no finding of discrimination consistent with their preferences.

The analysis of close cases in Experiment 1 shows none of the measured variables is significant in participants' similarity judgments, suggesting that objective distance and case facts are driving participants' similarity ratings.

Supplemental Regression Analyses *183*

TABLE A.4 Ordinary-least-squares regression: Similarity judgments, Experiment 1

VARIABLE	ALL CASES	CLOSE CASES	MEDIUM CASES	FAR CASES
Constant	2.90***	2.85***	2.86***	2.12**
	(.38)	(.50)	(.58)	(.45)
Ideology	−0.01	0.04	−0.08	−.004
	(.04)	(.07)	(.07)	(.06)
Gender	0.14	0.23	0.65*	−0.41
	(.14)	(.22)	(.28)	(.22)
African American	0.11	0.72	−0.63	−0.27
	(.21)	(.37)	(.54)	(.25)
Interest	−0.03	−0.18	0.05	0.09
	(.07)	(.11)	(.14)	(.09)
Outcome	−0.32†	−0.05	−1.10**	−0.22
	(.17)	(.29)	(.37)	(.25)
Predisposition	0.27	0.12	−0.53	1.04**
	(.18)	(.28)	(.36)	(.28)
Outcome ×	0.12	−0.21	1.17*	−0.37
Predisposition	(.25)	(.42)	(.48)	(.37)
A priori distance	0.19**	—	—	—
	(.08)			
N	208	79	61	68
R-squared	0.10	0.10	0.26	0.32

†significant at $p < .10$ level; *significant at $p < .05$ level; **significant at $p < .01$ level; ***significant at $p < .001$ level

The significant outcome coefficient in the middle range of cases reflects the influence of outcome on persons who express opposition to gay scout leaders (where predisposition equals 0). It demonstrates that those opposed to gay scout leaders were less likely to judge cases where there was an outcome of discrimination as similar to the target dispute compared to cases where there is no finding of discrimination. Again, this is wholly consistent with hypotheses in the middle range of cases.

In far cases, the significant coefficient for predisposition reflects its influence in cases without discrimination outcomes. Thus, for those cases where there was a finding of no discrimination (i.e., where outcome = 0), participants who favored gay scout leaders were more likely to see cases as similar compared with individuals opposed to gay scout leaders. At first glance, this seems to go against motivated reasoning hypotheses, but it also resonates with the main effect for predispositions observed for far cases in Experiment 1, suggesting that people who oppose discrimination will use more lenient criteria in judging case similarity, regardless of outcome.

The only control variable that is significant in the analysis of undergraduate judgments in Experiment 1 is gender in the middle range of case. This is interesting as two of the three cases in that category involve female victims of discrimination. It seems that females were more likely to see those cases as similar to the *Dale* scenario than were male participants in the sample. As referenced in chapter 3, ideology is not significant in similarity judgments in Experiment 1. This is probably because there is a very specific measure of preference (indicating whether participants are for or against gay scout leaders) included in the analysis. Also, political interest is not significant, demonstrating no significant differences in similarity judgments between those who were interested in politics (and therefore might have heard about the *Dale* decision) and those who were less interested.

OLS Regression Analyses—Experiment 2

POOLED ANALYSIS—ALL CASES

In the pooled analysis, the effects for distance (operationalized as relationship between parties) and student type that were observed in chapter 3 are clear in table A.5. The significant student type variable indicates that law students (coded as 1 in the analysis) tended to see cases as less similar than did undergraduates. The distance coefficient again shows that participants tended to judge cases deemed "further away" as less similar to the target dispute than cases that were closer on objective dimensions. The significant coefficients for outcome, predisposition, and the interaction between them demonstrate that motivated reasoning was present in the entire sample for all cases. The direction of each variable is consistent with hypotheses. Those who favored exclusion see cases with discrimination outcomes as less similar (outcome is significant where predisposition equals 0); participants against discrimination see nondiscrimination outcomes as less similar (predisposition is significant where outcome equals 0); and, as indicated by the significant interaction, those who are against discrimination see cases with discrimination outcomes as more similar to the target dispute consistent with their preferences.

TABLE A.5 Ordinary-least-squares regression: Similarity judgments, Experiment 2 (pooled sample and undergraduates)

VARIABLE	POOLED SAMPLE	UNDER ALL CASES	UNDER CLOSE CASES	UNDER MEDIUM CASES	UNDER FAR CASES
Constant	5.61***	5.27***	4.85**	3.82**	4.12***
	(.61)	(.84)	(1.67)	(.1.40)	(1.10)
Ideology	0.04	0.06	−0.30	−0.07	0.23
	(.07)	(.11)	(.28)	(.23)	(.14)
Gender	0.24	0.24	0.58	0.85	−0.54
	(.24)	(.34)	(.81)	(.63)	(.50)
African American	0.10	2.02**	—	1.95	1.42
	(.44)	(.80)		(1.20)	(1.01)
Religiosity	−0.17	−0.09	.13	0.11	−0.24
	(.09)	(.13)	(.32)	(.26)	(.17)
Interest	0.16	0.12	0.31	−0.06	0.44
	(.12)	(.18)	(.45)	(.36)	(.28)
Outcome	−1.12***	−1.10**	−0.98	−0.65	−1.21†
	(.31)	(.44)	(1.01)	(.81)	(.66)
Predisposition	−0.81**	−0.80†	−1.34	−0.12	−0.57
	(.33)	(.46)	(.93)	(.97)	(.67)
Outcome ×	1.75***	1.71**	0.78	0.79	2.50**
Predisposition	(.45)	(.67)	(1.50)	(1.23)	(.99)
Student type	−1.24***	—	—	—	—
	(.23)				
Distance (relationship)	−0.38**	−0.36†	—	—	—
	(.14)	(.20)			
N	173	96	27	32	37
R-squared	0.26	0.18	0.20	0.23	0.43

†significant at $p < .10$ level; *significant at $p < .05$ level; **significant at $p < .01$ level; ***significant at $p < .001$ level

ANALYSIS OF UNDERGRADUATE SAMPLE IN EXPERIMENT 2

All Cases. The second column in table A.5 shows that, consistent with the analysis in the pooled sample objective case, similarity is important in participants' judgments. The distance variable is marginally significant (p < .08), indicating that undergraduates judged cases categorized as further away as less similar to the target dispute than those that were closer. Also, there seems to be significant motivated reasoning by undergraduates in the analysis of all cases. Again, those who favored exclusion of people of other faiths see cases with discrimination outcomes as less similar (outcome is significant where predisposition equals 0); participants against discrimination see nondiscrimination outcomes as less similar (predisposition is marginally significant where outcome equals 0); and the significant interaction demonstrates that those who are against exclusion see cases with discrimination outcomes as more similar to the target dispute consistent with their preferences. Also, race is significant in the analysis of all cases, demonstrating that African American undergraduates saw all source cases as being similar more often than did other undergraduates. The effect is not significant in the disaggregated analyses for medium and far cases,[3] although the direction for the race variable is the same.

Disaggregated Analyses. Disaggregated analyses in the last three columns of table A.5 are once again consistent with results presented in chapter 3. We see that motivated reasoning appears to be most prevalent in far cases in this sample. Those who favored exclusion see cases with discrimination outcomes as less similar (outcome is significant where predisposition equals 0); and the interaction is significant, indicating that those against exclusion saw cases with discrimination outcomes as more similar to the target dispute in the distant category.

ANALYSIS OF LAW STUDENT SAMPLE IN EXPERIMENT 2

All Cases. The first column of table A.6 shows significant motivated reasoning in the analysis of all cases for law student subjects. Those who favored exclusion see cases with discrimination outcomes as less similar (outcome is significant where predisposition equals 0); Participants against discrimination see nondiscrimination outcomes as less similar (predisposition is significant where outcome equals 0); and those who are against discrimination see cases with discrimination outcomes as more similar to the target dispute consistent with their preferences, as indicated by the significant interaction. Moreover, race is significant and negative, indicating that African American law students were less likely than other law students to judge all cases as similar. This is contrary to what we saw in the undergraduate analysis, where African Americans were more likely to see cases as similar; but the small number of participants identifying as African American in each sample (4 in the undergraduate sample and 8 among the law students) cautions against making too much of this difference. Also, the analysis of all cases shows that participants who attended religious services less frequently tended to see all source

TABLE A.6 Ordinary-least-squares regression: Similarity Judgments, Experiment 2 (law students)

VARIABLE	ALL CASES	CLOSE CASES	MEDIUM CASES	FAR CASES
Constant	5.32**	2.54	4.62	3.42*
	(.86)	(1.81)	(.1.29)	(1.31)
Ideology	0.01	0.23	−0.14	0.06
	(.10)	(.07)	(.21)	(.17)
Gender	0.22	0.17	0.72	0.27
	(.34)	(.79)	(.69)	(.76)
African American	−1.01*	−0.33	−2.15†	−0.78
	(.50)	(1.07)	(1.16)	(1.08)
Religiosity	−0.22†	−0.14	0.16	−0.43
	(.13)	(.26)	(.30)	(.27)
Interest	0.17	0.40	−0.11	0.17
	(.15)	(.36)	(.27)	(.25)
Outcome	−1.33**	−0.75	−.60*	−0.85
	(.41)	(1.03)	(.74)	(.73)
Predisposition	−1.21**	−1.17	−2.07*	−0.84
	(.47)	(1.10)	(.92)	(.79)
Outcome ×	2.31***	1.74	2.76*	2.01
predisposition	(.25)	(1.49)	(1.12)	(1.18)
Distance (relationship)	0.59**	—	—	—
	(.20)			
N	77	25	28	24
R-squared	0.30	0.23	0.45	0.31

†significant at $p < .10$ level; *significant at $p < .05$ level; **significant at $p < .01$ level

cases as less similar to the target dispute (religiosity variable is marginally significant).

Disaggregated Analyses. The disaggregated analyses presented in the last three columns of table A.6 are wholly consistent with experimental hypotheses indicating motivated reasoning processes are most pronounced in the middle range of cases for law student participants in Experiment 2. Results indicate that in that category of cases, participants who favored exclusion see cases with discrimination outcomes as less similar (outcome is significant where predisposition equals 0); participants against discrimination see nondiscrimination outcomes as less similar (predisposition is significant where outcome equals 0); and those who are against discrimination see cases with discrimination outcomes as more similar to the target dispute consistent with their preferences, as indicated by the significant interaction. The directions of the outcome, predisposition, and interaction variables in close and far cases are also consistent with motivated reasoning, although none of them are significant, consistent with what we saw in chapter 3, where motivated reasoning processes were strongest in the middle range of cases.

MATERIALS RELATING TO EXPERIMENT TESTING THE SEPARABILITY OF PREFERENCES

Instructions: Study B (Estimated Time: 40 Minutes)

In this study we are looking at reactions to a new kind of legal brief. Due to high case volume, many state and federal jurisdictions have proposed using a "Summary Brief" format where parties agree to strict page limits within a single document submitted to the court in order to get expedited decision on motions.

What follows is an actual Summary Brief submitted to the federal district court for the *Eastern District of Missouri (located in the 8th Circuit) [or Eastern District of Pennsylvania (located in the 3rd Circuit)]* as part of a pilot study.

Please read the brief carefully, as if you were the judge responsible for rendering a decision on the motion. At the end of the brief, you will be asked how you would decide the motion and what information from the Summary Brief led you to your decision. You may mark up the brief if you wish.

THE MOCK BRIEF

DENISE BRUNELL, Plaintiff,

vs.

CITY OF GAYSON AND RICK HUMPREY, CITY MANAGER, Defendants.

Case No. 5:01CV00876 ERW

ISSUE:

Does the spouse of a city firefighter have standing to challenge an ordinance prohibiting public employees from engaging in campaign activity on behalf of local candidates?

SUMMARY OF MOTION PROCEEDINGS:

This action was brought pursuant to 42 U.S.C. § 1983. Plaintiff, Denise Brunell, is seeking injunctive relief, damages, and a declaratory

TABLE B.1 Law student characteristics in Separable Preferences Experiment

	NUMBER IN SAMPLE	PERCENTAGE
Gender		
Male	51	44
Female	64	56
Ideology		
Liberals	50	43
Conservatives	47	41
Moderates	18	16
Party affiliation		
Democrats	44	38
Republicans	49	43
Independents	22	19
Race		
Black	9	8
White	94	82
Asian	7	6
Hispanic	1	1
Mixed	4	4
Year in law school		
2L	48	42
3L	46	40
Graduate	21	18

judgment that a Gayson City ordinance, § 7.2 of the City Charter, violates her right to political expression under the First Amendment. This matter is currently before the court on the defendants' Motion for Summary Judgment.

Defendants, the City of Gayson and City Manager Rick Humprey, argue in this Summary Brief that plaintiff's claims should be dismissed because she has not suffered an injury in fact. Plaintiff has submitted an Argument in Opposition stating that she has suffered the requisite injury to challenge the ordinance.

[NOTE—The following Summary of Facts was prepared by an objective third-party referee. Each of the parties involved in the dispute has reviewed the statement. Both sides have agreed to its inclusion in this Summary Brief stating that it is an accurate representation of the facts which may be used in the interest of getting an expedited ruling on the Motion.]

STATEMENT OF FACTS:

The City of Gayson is located in *St. Louis County, Missouri [or Chester County, Pennsylvania].* In 1994 the city approved the current charter with the following provision:

§ 7.2—Employees. Participation in City Elections.
Neither the City Manager nor any person holding an administrative office or position under the city manager's supervision shall be a candidate for mayor or city council member or engage, directly or indirectly in sponsoring, electioneering, or contributing money or other things of value to any person who is a candidate for mayor or city council. All such persons shall retain the right to vote as they choose and to express their opinions on all political subjects. Any person violating the provisions of this section shall be removed in the manner provided by the personnel code.

The provision was adapted from a model charter drafted by the National Civic League. It was designed to protect city employees from undue coercion by local candidates for public office. The City Manager, Rick Humprey, stated in his deposition that the provision has been important in maintaining a degree of impartiality for city government in what has been a somewhat volatile political environment. [Humprey Deposition (Hump. Dep.) at 78].

Plaintiff's husband, John Brunell, is employed as a city firefighter in Gayson. The couple has lived in the city since 1998. Prior to moving to Gayson, plaintiff was active in city politics. She previously worked on the campaign of a councilwoman in the town where she used to reside. She has also made telephone calls on behalf of local political candidates. [Brunell Depostion (Brun. Dep.) at 8]. Although not directly subject to disciplinary action herself, Denise Brunell claims that she has been reluctant to engage in political campaign activity since moving to Gayson because she is fearful that her husband will lose his job.

The most recent election for city council in the City of Gayson was hotly contested. The campaign centered on the controversial issue of abortion. Candidates debated a proposed zoning ordinance that would have had the effect of closing down a clinic that performed abortion services within the city. The Democratic incumbent, Ruth Bandree, declared that she would not support the ordinance because it would make it more difficult for city residents to obtain legal abortion services. The

Missouri [Pennsylvania] Right to Life Party sought to sponsor a candidate for Gayson City Council who supported the proposed ordinance. Based on this single issue, they were able to get enough signatures to win a place on the election ballot. Rita Moray entered the race for city council running as the Right to Life candidate.

Although she did not become active in campaigning activities during the election, plaintiff demonstrated her support for the *Right to Life [or Democratic]* candidate by placing a sign in her front yard, reading: *"Support Life—Vote Moray for City Council" [or "Support Choice—Vote Bandree for City Council"].*

When her husband's supervisor learned of the sign, he told John Brunell he would have to remove it or be subject to disciplinary action under § 7.2 of the City Charter. John Brunell explained that his wife posted the sign in the yard and that although he generally agreed with his wife's political views, it was an expression of her political support for the candidate, not his. His supervisor reiterated the order emphasizing that the charter provision prohibits city employees from supporting candidates for city council, "directly or indirectly."

After discussing the matter with his wife, John Brunell removed the sign from the front yard to avoid adverse disciplinary action. He also registered a complaint with his union, the International Association of Firefighters for *St. Louis [or Chester]* County (Local 2665), and his wife, Denise Brunell, filed this action challenging the constitutionality of § 7.2. Specifically, plaintiff argues that the ordinance infringes upon her First Amendment rights to political expression by threatening her husband's employment. She also asserts that her husband has been unfairly targeted because the current city manager is personally opposed to the political views she sought to express in the sign that was posted on the couple's property.

[NOTE—The following sections of the Summary Brief were submitted by each of the parties to the dispute. They encompass the legal arguments each party makes in support of their stated position. Arguments are strictly limited to 1,500 words. Each side was able to review the argument of the other side before making their final submissions. Both parties have agreed that these arguments may be considered by the Court in the interest of getting an expedited ruling on the Motion.]

LEGAL ARGUMENT:
Defendant's Summary Argument in Support of Motion to Dismiss

The facts in this case are clear. There is no issue of material fact that would preclude summary judgment in this matter. *Cellotex Corp. v. Ca-*

trett, 477 U.S. 317, 91 L. Ed. 265, 106 S. Ct. 2548 (1986). Defendants are entitled to summary judgment because plaintiff has not suffered any cognizable injury that would give her standing to challenge §7.2 of the City Charter. Any and all injuries she claims to suffer through the operation of the provision are speculative and indirect.

The weight of applicable legal authority clearly supports defendants' position. At least two United States courts of appeal and one federal district court have held that the type of injury plaintiff claims to have suffered is insufficient to confer standing. These cases expressly hold that spouses do not have standing to challenge narrowly tailored ordinances that restrict the political activity of public employees. Therefore, plaintiff's claims should be dismissed in their entirety.

Provisions similar to the one in this case have been upheld as a limited restriction on public employees' right to engage in political behavior. *Reeder v. Kansas City Board of Police Commissioners,* 733 F.2d 548 (8th Cir. 1984); *Margill v. Lynch,* 733 F.2d 22 (1st Cir. 1977). Federal judges have recognized that "when the government deals with an employee in its role as an employer it has broader latitude in First Amendment matters than when it deals with citizens in its role as sovereign." *Firefighters, Local 3808 v. Kansas City,* 220 F.3d 969, 973 (8th Cir. 2000) (citing *Wabanausa County v. Umbehr,* 518 U.S. 668, 135 L.Ed. 2d 843, 116 S. Ct. 2342 [1996]).

Narrowly tailored provisions limiting the political activities of public employees in local elections have been justified as a rational way for municipalities to "(1) protect against the erosion of public confidence in the impartiality of the provision of government services (2) preserve fairness in city elections and (3) preserve the efficiency of the operation of the city." *Reeder* at 542. The political climate surrounding the last city council election in Gayson makes it clear § 7.2 was fundamentally important in achieving all of these valid municipal interests.

Plaintiff's assertion that her husband was unfairly targeted because the City Manager does not share her views on abortion is not only irrelevant to the standing issue raised in this motion, it is completely unfounded. The ordinance is content-free on its face and in its application. Moreover, § 7.2 is narrowly tailored. It only applies to election activity on behalf of local candidates for mayor and city council.

By its express terms, § 7.2 applies only to city employees. There is no question that plaintiff herself is not a city employee, and therefore not subject to direct disciplinary action under the Charter. The only injury plaintiff could suffer through the operation of the provision is entirely indirect through the loss of her husband's employment. Although indirect injury can sometimes constitute injury in fact, such injuries do not confer standing where they are "speculative and incidental." *Ben Oehreleins & Sons v. Hennepin County,* 115 F.3d 1372 (*8th [or 3rd] Cir.* 1997).

At least three federal courts have held the type of injury plaintiff alleges is not sufficiently direct to confer standing. In *Biggs v. Best, Best & Krieger,* 189 F. 3d 989 (9th Cir. 1999), the husband and daughter of a city attorney were vocal community activists regarding a local environmental issue. A city council member informed the attorney that she would be fired unless "members of her family were silenced" on the issue. *Biggs* at 996. The attorney, her husband, and her daughter all brought claims against members of the city council in federal court. The claims of the husband and daughter were dismissed by the trial judge.

Upon review, the Court of Appeals for the Ninth Circuit upheld the decision stating that the husband and daughter did not have standing to raise claims on their own, but only to raise, derivatively, the same claims as the city attorney. The court noted that "although the loss of [the city attorney's] salary was not insubstantial" in terms of its effect on the family's economic condition, the injuries to her husband and daughter were "too indirect" for them to have standing to raise separate individual claims. *Biggs* at 998.

The Tenth Circuit issued a similar ruling in *Horstkoetter v. Department of Public Safety,* 159 F.3d 1265 (10th Cir. 1998). In that case, a state trooper's wife challenged a policy prohibiting troopers from engaging in political campaign behavior. Her husband was threatened with disciplinary action because she wanted to post a campaign sign in their yard. The court noted that under the policy there was no possibility of disciplinary action against the spouse herself. It acknowledged that the trooper's wife was indirectly injured by the application of the policy to her husband because she was faced with a loss of income that would have affected the entire family. However, the court ruled that the wife had no claim of her own because her injuries were "speculative and incidental." *Horstkoetter* at 1279. The Court reasoned that if the law was valid as to the activities of the husband, it would also be valid to discipline him on account of the activities of his wife.

Plaintiff cites *International Association of Firefighters v. City of Ferguson,* 283 F.3d 969 (8th Cir. 2002) in support of her argument. Several things are noteworthy about the court's ruling in that case. First, it stands alone as the only court of appeals decision finding spousal standing to challenge the constitutionality of restrictions on political behavior of public employees. Second, the case is factually distinguishable from the current matter.

In *City of Ferguson,* a plaintiff spouse interested in running for local office wrote several letters to the mayor asking if her husband, a city firefighter, would be subject to discipline under a local ordinance if she ran for city council. After three of her letters went unanswered, she filed an action in federal court seeking a declaratory judgment that the ordinance interfered with her First Amendment rights. A Missouri District Court dismissed her claim for lack of standing, but the Eighth Circuit reversed the ruling, holding she could maintain the action under the circumstances presented.

The facts giving rise to this case are clearly distinguishable from *City of Ferguson.* First, plaintiff in this matter is not seeking political office. She sought to post a sign on property that was jointly owned by her and her husband, a municipal employee. There is no question that public employees may be disciplined under such circumstances (see *Horstkoetter,* supra). Moreover, Denise Brunell did not directly inquire as to whether her husband would be subject to discipline for her conduct before she posted the campaign sign. Had she done so, the City Manager would have promptly responded to her inquiry. Thus, there is no history of indifference toward plaintiff's First Amendment rights on the part of the city as was the case in *City of Ferguson.*

Finally, in *Knoll v. City of Chesterfield,* 71 F. Supp. 959 (W.D.N.Y. 1999), the court ruled that the wife of a city police officer did not have standing to challenge an ordinance prohibiting public employees from campaigning on behalf of mayoral candidates. In that case, the plaintiff's husband was threatened with disciplinary action unless he removed a campaign sticker that his wife put on their family car. In dismissing the wife's First Amendment claim, the court soundly reasoned:

> Plaintiff's pleadings do not allege the imminent threat of injury by the city upon Lynette Knoll. While Robert's choices have ramifications impacting Lynette . . . the city's alleged conduct is not directed at Lynette and threatens no direct injury to her.
>
> To expand the concept of standing to encompass familial economic interdependence would allow, for example, an employee's spouse and dependents to bring derivative causes of action in almost any suit based on the employee's termination or suspension without pay. *Knoll* at 961.

As the court's decision in *Knoll* suggests, expansion of the doctrine of standing to encompass the type of injury alleged by the plaintiff in this case is not only illogical, but dangerous. It would open the door to a multitude of litigation based on indirect economic injury when spouses lose their jobs. Rather than start down the slippery slope the plaintiff's argument ultimately entails, this court should abide by the reasoning of the majority of federal courts that have considered this issue and dismiss plaintiff's claims for lack of standing.

Plaintiff's Argument in Opposition to Motion to Dismiss

Plaintiff, Denise Brunell, respectfully files this Argument in Opposition to Defendants' Motion for Summary Judgment. It is clear that plaintiff has suffered an injury in fact, giving her sufficient standing to challenge § 7.2 of the Gayson City Charter. Contrary to the arguments raised by defendants, Denise Brunell's injuries are real and personal to her. Moreover, the claims raised by plaintiff in this action are distinct and separate from those of her husband.

Currently there is a conflict among the federal circuits concerning whether or not the spouses of public employees have standing to challenge provisions like § 7.2 based on allegations that such provisions violate their own First Amendment rights. The most recent decision on the matter is *International Association of Firefighters v. City of Ferguson,* 283 F.3d 969 (8th Cir. 2002), cert. denied, 2003 LEXIS 602 (January 13, 2003). In that case the United States Court of Appeals for the Eighth Circuit recognized that spouses of public employees suffer "real and tangible" injury when inhibitory provisions like § 7.2 overreach to infringe on their rights of political expression. 283 F.3d at 975.

This district lies in the Eighth Circuit, making City of Ferguson *controlling legal authority* [*or: The issue of spousal standing has not yet been litigated in the Third Circuit where this district is located. Thus, regardless of where the "weight of authority" lies, this court is free to follow whatever precedent it finds most compelling under the circumstances raised by this litigation. Plaintiff respectfully argues that the court should follow the sound logic of the Eighth Circuit in* City of Ferguson.] Defendants' attempts to distinguish this case from *City of Ferguson* are entirely unsuccessful. The material facts giving rise to the current dispute are, in fact, more similar to *City of Ferguson* than any other case where spousal standing has been at issue. In that case the plaintiff spouse of a city firefighter was reluctant to run for local office where a municipal ordinance threatened her husband's employment for "endorsing or campaigning or supporting candidates for city office in any manner." *City of Ferguson* at 970. The wife challenged the ordinance in federal court, claiming it was over-broad because it inhibited her willingness to run for office as she was fearful her husband could lose his job on account of her political activities.

In holding that the plaintiff had standing to challenge the provision, the Eighth Circuit specifically stated that she had suffered an injury in fact. The court reasoned that it was her own political rights that were inhibited by the threat of substantial economic harm that would come to her (and her entire family) should her husband lose his job. Specifically, the court reasoned, plaintiff's "apprehension that the city might act aversely if she exercised her . . . [First Amendment] rights was not unreasonable. The threatened consequence of her exercising the rights, the discipline or discharge of her husband, would substantially damage her life and economic condition." *City of Ferguson* at 973.

The situation is exactly akin to this case. John Brunell's livelihood was threatened because of a sign his wife posted expressing her personal political beliefs. Later plaintiff agreed to the removal of the sign—effectively silencing her political voice—because of the direct threat to her family's only means of support. Defendants' implication that it was the type of political activity plaintiff sought to engage in (running for office vs. posting a sign) that was important in *City of Ferguson* is completely misleading. It was the fact that plaintiff's First Amendment rights were inhibited that was important, not the specific sort of activity she sought to engage in.

Moreover, in this case, as in *City of Ferguson,* the plaintiff has a substantial history of engaging in local political activity. Denise Brunell's efforts on behalf of candidates for municipal office in the city where she used to live were frequent and extensive. Upon moving to Gayson, plaintiff testified that her willingness to engage in local election activity was inhibited by the threat to her husband's employment. She stated at her deposition that she was reluctant to work on behalf of local candidates because of the ordinance. [Brun. Dep at 14.] Federal courts have held that where municipal provisions act to inhibit the First Amendment rights of citizens, this "chilling" effect coupled with a realistic apprehension of state action, is sufficient to confer standing. *Shaggs v. Carle,* 110 F.3d 831 (Fed. Cir. 1997).

Here not only was there a reasonable apprehension that plaintiff's husband would lose his job if plaintiff exercised her First Amendment rights, her political voice was effectively silenced when John Brunell's supervisor ordered that the sign she posted be removed from the couple's property. Under these circumstances it can hardly be argued that the injury was "speculative." Rather, the threat of imminent disciplinary action was made clear to the plaintiff and her husband.

Contrary to the defendants' assertions, the political context surrounding the order is hardly irrelevant. Plaintiff has long been a supporter of the Right to Life [Abortion Rights] Movement. In May of last year she volunteered for an organization involved in the cause. She testified at her deposition that she was an active and visible participant in the organization for several months prior to posting the campaign sign. [Brun. Dep. at 43].

Plaintiff believes that she and her husband have been unfairly targeted in an effort to silence her politically. At his deposition, City Manager Rick Humprey denied such targeting occurred, but he did state that he was aware of plaintiff's activity prior to the posting of the campaign sign and that he was "diametrically opposed" to her views on abortion. [Hump. Dep. at 97]. At the very least Humprey's comments raise the real possibility that § 7.2 was applied in a discriminatory manner to prevent plaintiff from expressing deeply held political beliefs that were unique and personal to her. This clearly belies defendants' argument that plaintiff's injuries are wholly derived from her husband's claims and bolsters plaintiff's assertion that she has suffered a real and substantial injury in her own right.

In *City of Ferguson* the court clearly agreed with this characterization of the plaintiff spouse's claims. It stated that plaintiff's claims were not "merely duplicative" of her husband's, noting that the plaintiff spouse had "an interest of her own to defend. Not only is it her own political activity that she seeks to protect, but her own personal and economic status as well." *City of Ferguson* at 973.

In this case John Brunell's income acts as the primary and exclusive means of support for the Brunell family. Any depletion of his earnings as a result of disciplinary action or dismissal would prove catastrophic to the economic condition of plaintiff and her entire family. As the court said in *City of Ferguson,* "plaintiff is herself injured by having to give up or hesitating to exercise her First Amendment rights and by the consequent loss of her husband's ability to provide the mutual support that the law imposes as a duty on both spouses." *City of Ferguson* at 973.

Finally, it is worth noting that two of the cases cited by defendants are distinguishable from this matter in a very important respect. In *Horstkoetter v. Department of Public Safety,* 159 F.3d 1279 (10th Cir. 1998), the home where the state trooper's wife posted the campaign sign was exclusively owned by her husband. Likewise the car in *Knoll v. City of Chesterfield*, 71 F. Supp. 959 (W.D.N.Y. 1999) belonged to the public employee spouse. Thus, in each of these cases the government argued that disciplining public employees for political material that was posted on property was justifiable.

In this case the property where the sign was posted is jointly owned by John and Denise Brunell. John Brunell could not legally prohibit his wife from posting a sign on property she has an equal right to use and enjoy. Likewise the city ordinance should not inhibit her use of the property because it is jointly owned with her husband. The *Horstkoetter* court itself acknowledged this fact, suggesting that it would be unfair to discipline employees for spousal activity they had no legal right to control. *Horstkoetter* at 1279.

While it is true that federal courts have recognized that municipalities have a limited interest in curbing the political speech of public employees, this interest does not extend to violating the First Amendment rights of their spouses. It is clear that here plaintiff has suffered a substantial injury though the operation of a provision that overreaches to inhibit her First Amendment rights. The injury is quite real and entirely personal to her. Plaintiff respectfully asks this court to abide by the Eighth Circuit's sound reasoning in *City of Ferguson* and deny defendants' Motion to Dismiss.

Policy Questions Used in Analyses

ABORTION MEASURE

Some people believe that state governments have a valid interest in restricting a woman's access to abortion in order to protect the life of an unborn child; others believe restrictions on abortion interfere with a woman's right to determine what happens to her own body.

Please indicate the extent to which *you personally* agree or disagree with the following statement:

State governments should have substantial authority to regulate women's access to abortion services.

1—disagree strongly	4—agree slightly
2—disagree somewhat	5—agree somewhat
3—disagree slightly	6—agree strongly

HATCH ACT MEASURE

Some people believe the government should be able to restrict the political activities of public employees such as postal workers and police officers in order to preserve impartiality in the provision of government services; others believe such policies are an unjustified restriction on employees' rights to political expression.

Please indicate the extent to which *you personally* agree or disagree with the following statement:

Government should be able to restrict political activities of public employees.

1—disagree strongly   4—agree slightly
2—disagree somewhat   5—agree somewhat
3—disagree slightly   6—agree strongly

FREE-SPEECH MEASURE

Some people believe the American flag is an important symbol that should be treated with respect and that people who burn the flag should be subject to criminal sanctions; others believe criminalizing such behavior would unjustly violate citizens' right to express dissatisfaction with the government.

Please indicate the extent to which *you personally* agree or disagree with the following statement:

People who burn the American flag should be subject to criminal sanctions.

1—disagree strongly   4—agree slightly
2—disagree somewhat   5—agree somewhat
3—disagree slightly   6—agree strongly

Experimental Instrument

1. Was the information in the Summary Brief presented clearly?
1—very unclear   4—
2—   5—
3—   6—very clear

2. Were the facts in the STATEMENT OF FACTS section of the Summary Brief presented objectively?
1—biased in favor of plaintiff   4—
2—   5—biased in favor of defendants
3—presented objectively

3. Generally speaking, was the LEGAL ARGUMENT section of the brief balanced?
1—yes
2—no

4. Based on your reading of the Summary Brief, do you think the court should find that the plaintiff, Denise Brunell, has standing to challenge the city ordinance?
1—yes
2—no

5. On the following scale, please rate how confident you feel about your answer to the previous question, based on the facts and legal argument presented in the Summary Brief.
1—not very confident
2—somewhat confident
3—extremely confident

6. How much of a role did the FACTS presented in the Summary Brief play in your decision?

1—no role	4—
2—	5—major role
3—	

7. How much of a role did the LEGAL ARGUMENTS cited by the parties play in your decision?

1—no role	4—
2—	5—major role
3—	

8. In the blank space below, briefly indicate (in a few sentences) what FACTS influenced your decision and how they influenced you as they did.

9. In the blank spaces below, briefly indicate (in a few sentences) what LEGAL ARGUMENTS influenced your decision and how they influenced you as they did.

NOTES

Introduction

1. 542 U.S. 1 (2004).

2. *Newdow,* 542 U.S. 1 at 9 (quoting, complaint).

3. A "threshold issue" is one a court must decide before it can hear a matter or invoke a particular standard of review. See chapter 4 for further discussion.

ONE Outlining a Theory of Motivated Cognition in Legal Decision Making

1. Some of the most significant early studies using bloc analysis techniques include: Pritchett (1941), looking at patterns of agreement for all justices on the Court from 1939 to 1941; Spaeth (1961), discussing levels of "ideational" agreement between particular pairs of justices; and Ulmer (1965), explaining subgroup formation in terms of fluid case "coalitions" and more stable policy "cliques."

2. For instance, scaling-study respondents may be asked questions such as: (1) Would you be willing to work in the same office as someone of another race? (2) Would you invite someone of a different race over to your home for dinner? (3) Would you accept it if your son/daughter dated someone from another race? (4) Would you accept it if your child married someone from a different race?

3. Some of the most prominent research efforts demonstrating the importance of preferences in judicial voting behavior have used scaling techniques. Examples include Ulmer's (1960) study looking at civil liberties cases in the 1950s; Schubert's (1962) study creating the "C" (civil liberties), "E" (economic liberalism), and "F" (fiscal) scales to explain votes of the justices during the Court's 1960 term; Rohde and Spaeth's (1976) book using cumulative scaling techniques to predict the votes of justices in cases arrayed along "freedom," "equality," and "New Dealism" scales, and Segal and Spaeth's (1993) study looking at the voting behavior of judges on the Supreme Court over eleven issue areas.

4. Segal and Spaeth's model is specifically designed to explain the behavior of Supreme Court justices. The authors leave open the possibility, however, that the model has broader application, stating, "it is our judgment that the attitudinal model will explain the decision making of other courts to the extent the environment on these courts approximates that of the Supreme Court" (1993, xv).

5. There is a series of impressive experiments by Rachlinski and his colleagues with federal magistrate and specialized judges that looked at things like susceptibility to anchoring and prospect theory in damage awards and settlement negotiations (see, for

instance, Guthrie, Rachlinski, and Wistrich 2001; Wistrich, Guthrie, and Rachlinski 2005). Significantly, however, judges in these studies are not asked to divulge their political preferences.

6. See, for example, Tetlock (1981, 1984), looking at cognitive styles of U.S. senators and members of the British House of Commons through content analysis of speeches and debates; Winter (1987), looking at motives of U.S. presidents by analyzing inaugural speeches; and Kaarbo and Hermann (1998), comparing cognitive styles of prime ministers using spontaneous utterances reported in the media.

7. This is changing a bit with the advent of sophisticated software systems designed to detect linguistic patterns in large volumes of text. Prior to the availability of such programs, a handful of systematic content analyses were conducted, mostly by psychologists interested in decision-making phenomena (see, for instance, Gruenfeld 1995; Gruenfeld, Kim, and Preston 1998; and Tetlock, Bernzweig, and Gallant 1985).

8. The influence of this self-selection is further magnified by the institutional and self-selection noted by Posner (discussed below) regarding the "types" of individuals that become judges. See Eagly and Johnson (1990) for general discussion of self- and institutional selection processes.

9. "Resocialization" is a term used in sociology to describe the process by which certain institutions indoctrinate new members. In its most extreme form, it can involve an attempt to "break down" prior personality traits, beliefs, and/or modes of behavior and replace them with role-appropriate traits, beliefs, and behavior. Many law schools still use the Socratic method to accomplish this task (which some consider only slightly less harrowing than techniques used by the military to resocialize new recruits). Admittedly, the resocialization that occurs in law school is not as all-encompassing as that which might occur in other institutions like the military. But the comparison is not wholly inappropriate; moreover, it is not entirely original (see Scott Turow's *One L* for a popular account of the resocialization that occurs in the first year of law school).

10. Political scientists refer to this as the "d-term" or "duty" term in models of voting behavior. Of course, judicial votes generally yield more influence. Therefore, the utility judges derive from voting is a composite of values, one of which is purely consumptive.

11. See, generally, Moscovici 1980; and Nemeth 1986; see also Gruenfeld 1995; and Gruenfeld, Kim, and Preston 1998 for evidence that the presence of dissent causes judges in the majority to evidence more integrative complexity in their decisions.

12. Segal and Spaeth acknowledge, but never really address, limits on people's ability to construct justifications in service of their preferences. Taking this proposition a bit more seriously than they do would suggest that the law *can* serve as a constraint on specific decisions judges make where there is "no seemingly reasonable justification to support [them]" (Segal and Spaeth 1996b, 1075, quoting Kunda 1990, 480).

13. The influence of preferences in analogical perception is consistent with bottom-up characterizations of motivated behavior. As we will see, the second mechanism, involving the separability of preferences, is more closely related to Segal and Spaeth's top-down conception of the role that political attitudes play in policy-driven decision making.

14. Experimental and quasi-experimental methods have been used to study the influence of judicial decisions on public opinion, however (see Bass and Thomas 1984; Mondak 1994; and Hoekstra and Segal 1996).

TWO A Motivated Reasoning Approach to the Commerce Clause Interpretation of the Rehnquist Court

1. The justices on the Court during this period were Chief Justice Rehnquist and Associate Justices Stevens, O'Connor, Scalia, Kennedy, Souter, Thomas, Ginsberg, and Breyer.

2. This law-and-order dimension also could have been relevant in *Lopez,* making the vote in that case more complex than initially portrayed. I choose not to complicate matters to make my point by assuming that *Lopez* is, more or less, ideologically straightforward; the legislation at issue in the case involved gun possession rather than sanctions for alleged criminal behavior.

3. Indeed, this dimension may have been particularly relevant given that many of the interest groups involved in the case were ideologically conservative organizations, arguing that Congress had "gone too far" in appeasing feminist interests by creating this federal cause of action.

4. Later in this chapter, I provide doctrinal evidence that this was, indeed, the case in *Raich.*

5. Segal and Spaeth put Scalia and Kennedy at one "polar extreme" in supporting states in conflicts against the federal government—with decision rates at or above 59 percent in favor of state outcomes. The justices on the liberal wing of the Court support state outcomes only between 5 and 33 percent of the time.

6. Although some rational-choice theorists may argue that they are interested only in explaining what helps decision makers form winning coalitions, making the explanation of this sort of concurring behavior unnecessary, the failure of strategic models to address this sort of vote and opinion is extremely problematic.

7. See the majority's discussion of the School Safety Act at issue in *United States v. Bass,* 404 U.S. 336 (1971) (*Lopez,* 514 U.S. 549 at 561).

8. Justice Thomas writes separately in all three cases, concurring in *Lopez* and *Morrison* and issuing a separate dissent in *Raich.* Justice Kennedy (joined by Justice O'Connor) also writes a concurrence in *Lopez.* Justices Stevens and Souter dissent separately in *Lopez.* Justice Breyer issues a separate dissent in *Morrison* that is joined (at least in part) by the other dissenting justices. Finally, as mentioned above, there is a separate concurrence by Justice Scalia in *Raich* detailing his distinct reasoning in the case.

9. This is somewhat problematic as Kennedy and Scalia do not write separately in all three cases. It would be better, of course, if I had each justice's unique view of the relevant facts and legal authority for each case. I assume, consistent with legal conceptions of decision making, however, that where the justices do not write separately, they agree with the legal analyses in the majority opinions they have endorsed. This is not ideal, but it is the best anyone can do given the nature of Supreme Court decision making.

10. It is important to note that even the stricter "substantial effects" test announced in *Lopez* leaves significant latitude to decision makers in concluding what is (and is not) appropriately tied to interstate commerce. As detailed more fully below, this is evident in *Lopez* itself, as well as in the Court's subsequent Commerce Clause decisions.

11. See, especially, *Lopez,* 515 U.S. 549 at 602–3. "Guns are both articles of commerce and articles that can be used to restrain commerce. Their possession is a consequence, either directly or indirectly of commercial activity" (Stevens, J., dissenting).

12. This sort of accusation is actually quite common in Supreme Court doctrine and in the opinions of judges on lower federal and state courts where they disagree.

13. As set forth below, Justice Scalia also implies he sees the *Raich* scenario as substantially similar to *Wickard,* although he does not rely on the case to the same extent as the justices in the majority.

14. Indeed, Scalia writes, "I write separately because my understanding of the doctrinal foundation on which th[e] holding rests is, if not inconsistent with that of the Court, at least more nuanced" (*Raich,* 545 U.S. 1 at 33 [Scalia, J., concurring]).

15. To underscore this point, the majority acknowledges differences in the two cases, which they do not see as problematic in their reasoning: "respondents suggest that *Wickard* differs from this case in three respects. . . . Those differences, while factually accurate, do not diminish the precedential force of this Court's reasoning" (*Raich,* 545 U.S. 1 at 20).

16. See, especially, the discussion of cognitive consistency below.

17. Indeed, O'Connor goes further in the dissent, arguing that even if the activity were economic in nature, because it occurs entirely within California, supporters of federal authority would have to show a "substantial effect" on the interstate market, which they had not done in the case. Here, O'Connor seems to be contradicting some of the earlier language she endorsed in Justice Kennedy's concurrence from Lopez, making it somewhat unclear where she stands on the regulation of intrastate economic activity.

18. "Not only is it impossible to distinguish 'controlled substances manufactured and distributed intrastate' from 'controlled substances manufactured and distributed interstate,' but it hardly makes sense to speak in such terms. Drugs like marijuana are fungible commodities. As the Court explains, marijuana that is grown at home and possessed for personal use is never more than an instant from the interstate market—and this is so whether or not the possession is for medicinal use or lawful use under the laws of a particular State" (*Raich,* 545 U.S. 1 at 40 [Scalia, J., concurring in judgment]).

19. Indeed, the dissenting justices strongly criticize what they see as the selective invocation of the doctrine Scalia relies on from that case as "seizing upon our language in *Lopez*" to reach conclusions that turn that decision into "nothing more than a drafting guide" (*Raich* 543 U.S 1 at 37–38 [O'Connor, J., dissenting]).

20. Looking at national supremacy cases from the Court's 1986–99 terms, Segal and Spaeth report that Justices Kennedy and Scalia support "prostate" outcomes 59 percent and 61 percent of the time, respectively. This compares with Justices Thomas, who supports prostate outcomes 78 percent of the time, O'Connor at 69 percent, and Chief Justice Rehnquist at 67 percent (Segal and Spaeth 2002, 421).

THREE   Seeing What They Want?

1. Psychologists and philosophers have long been interested in the role of analogy in creative thought (see Koestler 1964). A classic narrative portrayal of the importance of analogy in scientific innovation is James D. Watson's *The Double Helix,* which describes the work of his research team in delineating the structure of DNA.

2. As referenced earlier, it is difficult to pinpoint the goals of a particular decision maker in any particular case. Based on the substantial evidence demonstrating preference-consistent decision making, many behavioral scholars have assumed that judges are primarily motivated by directional policy goals (see Segal and Spaeth 1993,

2002; and Epstein and Knight 1998). Others (Baum 1997) suggest that professional accountability and the desire to "get it right" may be important in judges' motivations. In this experiment, I test the former conception of goals by measuring how preferences interact with outcomes to influence similarity judgments, but I also allow for the latter, hypothesizing the interaction will influence perception in some, but not all, cases.

3. As explained further below, in the first experiment the theoretical categories worked well. Based on the manipulation check and number of interactions observed, it seems clear that participants were engaging in a "gestalt" process in judging analogical similarity. In the second experiment, a manipulation check indicates that the classification scheme did not work as well. Indeed, the relationship manipulation was the only manipulation to which participants were attending in making similarity judgments. So the process was not gestalt, but clearly in line with what the competing psychological theory would predict—a "feature-matching" process with relationship used as the dominant feature. As set forth further in the next section, I adjust my analyses in the second experiment to accommodate this difference in a manner that is wholly consistent with testing the general theory of motivated perception outlined above.

4. The case was actually decided over a year before the experiment took place. Admittedly, this is a potential problem because, in hindsight, subjects who were aware of the decision may have been inclined to see things as the Court did. I decided to use the case anyway, reasoning that most undergraduates would not be aware of the specifics of Supreme Court jurisprudence; although they may have had some awareness of the case when it was decided, they were probably not familiar with the details of the Court's decision. Moreover, subjects may not have been aware of the stage the case was in when they heard about it and, thus, may have believed that it was still pending in the judicial system. Finally, even if subjects knew the case had been the subject of a final determination in favor of the Boy Scouts, it is not clear exactly how such knowledge would influence perceptions of case similarity. As a precaution, we controlled for political interest to see whether there was a significant difference between those who were likely to know about the case and those who were not. As it turned out, this variable was not significant in a supplemental regression analysis (see appendix A-2).

5. I also asked subjects several questions about their views of homosexuality and the government's role in preventing discrimination on the basis of sexual orientation. I use subjects' response to the gay scout leader question as the measure of predisposition, however, because it is the most specific indication of how participants felt about the issue underlying the target case. The logic behind this decision is that answers to general policy questions predict attitudes about specific disputes less well than more targeted questions. Knowing how someone feels about gay rights, in general, may not tell us much about how that individual will respond to a specific instance when it is in conflict another democratic value, in this case, free association.

6. These variables figure in regression analyses that confirm the ANOVA results presented in this chapter and are included in appendix A-2. None of the additional measures were significant in the analyses of similarity judgments. This, in itself, is not too surprising as there is a very specific measure of policy preference in the analysis. Moreover, inclusion of these variables does not change the pattern of results in the full or disaggregated samples for the primary variables of interest (see appendix A-2).

7. *Wazeerud-Din* involves the additional layer of values concerning separation of

church and state. This is, in part, what makes it such a useful dispute for this inquiry. One might argue that it involves a new legal question about how far the Supreme Court's free association holding in *Dale* should extend: Does it include religious treatment programs receiving indirect assistance from the government? Presumably undergraduate and law students will have some opinion on this issue, although it is not yet clear how it will be resolved in the courts. Testing whether there are systematic differences in similarity judgments based on these opinions would provide compelling evidence of motivated perception.

8. Although the sample contains more "rising 2Ls" than I would have preferred, I still am confident that the substantial socialization students undergo during their first year of law school justifies their inclusion in the legally trained sample. See Becker (1964), justifying a similar participation requirement for law students in an experimental study.

9. Again, these variables were used as controls in a confirmatory regression analyses (see appendix A-2).

FOUR Reasoning on the Threshold: Testing the Separability of Preferences in Legal Decision Making

1. Specifically, jurisdiction involves whether or not a court has the constitutional and statutory authority to hear a case. Justiciability issues concern whether adversarial disputes meet certain criteria making them appropriate for judicial resolution. There are actually several separate doctrines related to justiciability including standing, mootness/ ripeness, and the political question doctrine.

2. These examples set forth a "sincere" use of the threshold doctrine where judges' decision on the threshold issue allows them to hear claims they believe have merit and dismiss claims that do not. There are also suggestions in the literature that judges may use threshold issues more strategically to hear cases when they are opposed to the plaintiff's claim because they think the case is "weak" on the merits. Although this strategic use of the doctrine is entirely plausible, it is beyond the scope of the current chapter.

3. Specifically, they argue that this occurs in litigation concerning the division of labor between and state and federal judicial systems involving issues like national supremacy, comity, sovereign immunity, and choice of law (1993, 19–31).

4. The requirement arises from the "case and controversies," language in article III of the Constitution and also from prudential considerations judges have developed about what makes disputes appropriate for judicial resolution. The logic behind the standing doctrine is that it is important for the person litigating the matter to have a substantial interest in its outcome so she will have incentive to present the best arguments in the context of an adversarial proceeding.

5. Such ordinances are actually quite common. Their purpose is to protect public employees from undue pressure from local political candidates and to preserve the appearance of impartiality in the provision of government services.

6. In each case, the plaintiff alleged that her husband was being retaliated against because the current city manager was averse to the political views she was expressing in the campaign. The allegation was consistent across all treatment groups. It was made when the plaintiff was expressing support for the pro-life candidate and when she was supporting the pro-choice candidate. Although it could be argued that this argument

sensitized participants to the content of the political message more than they would have been had the allegation not been included, the claim adds to the realism of the brief. Allegations of retaliatory disciplinary conduct are not uncommon in the real world. Raising such concerns is, in fact, what effective representation entails where the seeds of such an argument are there to be made. The important question is whether decision makers with different policy views respond to the argument in systematically different ways.

7. This chapter analyses answers to the closed-ended questions. Analyses of participants' answers to the open-ended questions appear in chapter 5. They were included to see what part of the brief participants with different views cited in support of their decisions.

8. I also conducted a three-way ANOVA with predisposition, speech content, and circuit as individual factors, using the small treatment groups. Results from the three-way ANOVA are substantively the same as those observed in the logit analysis, presented in this chapter.

9. Admittedly, it is somewhat contrived because decision makers do not generally indicate their confidence level when rendering judgments. I am confident, however, that the measure captures a meaningful underlying construct. Moreover, the distribution of responses to the confidence question was substantially similar for participants who concluded the plaintiff had standing and those who did not. This suggests that the scaled measure influenced participants on both sides of issue in the same way. I use what some may consider the more theoretically justifiable dichotomous standing judgment as the dependent variable in the logit analysis that follows.

10. This variable was created by splitting responses on the abortion question at its midpoint; participants who expressed pro-choice views (1–3 on the abortion scale) were classified as having consistent attitudes when they were in a condition where the plaintiff was expressing pro-choice views. Similarly, those who expressed pro-life views (4–6 on the abortion scale) were classified as having consistent attitudes when they were in conditions where the plaintiff was expressing pro-life views. Participants were classified as having inconsistent views where their expressed abortion opinion was incongruent with the speech of the plaintiff in the condition to which they were assigned.

11. There is also a marginally significant main effect for speech consistency. Because the speech consistency variable is embedded in a significant higher-level interaction, however, it eludes substantive interpretation (Keppel 1982).

12. These include interactions for circuit × speech content and for circuit × abortion opinion, as well as for the content × abortion opinion interaction.

13. This explanation is somewhat consistent with the findings in the analogical perception experiments from chapter 3, demonstrating that perceived differences were more pronounced among participants with conservative views on discrimination, especially in the undergraduate samples.

FIVE   Justifying Outcomes?

1. This was an extremely difficult variable to code as legal arguments sometimes appeared in response to the fact question and vice versa—as such it is probably the most subjective of all the measures—consequently, it does not appear again in the analyses.

2. Besides aspects of the brief mentioned above, I included an "other facts/legal arguments" category. This was a catch-all category for facts and legal arguments not

included in the coding scheme. I was quite liberal in coding this variable. Fifty-seven percent of participants mentioned some other fact and/or argument. In most cases, these facts or arguments were quite closely related to things in the scheme. For instance, a number of people specifically mentioned infringement of plaintiff's property rights as a basis for standing (which was usually mentioned with joint ownership of the marital home). Others mentioned things like the fact that Ferguson was the most recent circuit court decision on spousal standing and should carry additional weight for that reason.

Other responses were more surprising. For instance, several participants indicated that the couple had the option of moving to another city rather than be subject to the restrictions of the ordinance. Others suggested that there should be a "spousal exception" to the standing doctrine (or the applicability of the ordinance) specifically to protect the sanctity of the marital relationship.

3. This statistic is the equivalent of a chi-square test statistic; Fisher's exact test is appropriate when comparing the proportions of two binary variables.

4. These options were not exhaustive or mutually exclusive, although most participants did one or the other.

5. Where speech was consistent with one's view, participants may have been more likely to accept certain arguments having to do with freedom of speech than where speech was inconsistent.

6. Being in a circuit with direct controlling authority makes it more likely participants will mention that authority in their justifications.

7. When participants were debriefed, they were very surprised to learn that they had been given "different versions" of the Mock Brief. Indeed, when one subject was informed of experimental hypotheses and alternative conditions, he/she reported having absolutely no recollection of whether she was in a condition where plaintiff was expressing pro-life or pro-choice views—specifically stating that it did not influence his/her judgment on the standing question at all!

SIX Motivated Reasoning as an Empirical Framework

1. While unexpected, differential responses to constraint have also been uncovered in other empirical research looking at responses to legal authority (see, for example, Randazzo, Waterman, and Fine 2006, finding differential responses to statutory authority).

2. Notwithstanding the methodological issues raised in chapter 5 about endogeneity and the direction of the causal arrow, I hope researchers will pursue these sorts of inquiries in future work, being careful to specify their assumptions with appropriate theory and empirical methods. My purpose in discussing these methodological concerns was to promote carefully considered empirical tests of attitudinal influence, not to stifle them.

APPENDIX A-2 Supplemental Regression Analyses for Experiments on Analogical Perception

1. The main analyses of interest—disaggregated regressions in close, medium, and far case categories—have fewer than one hundred observations. Maximum likelihood estimates generally require at least that many cases to take on their appropriate functional form (Long 1997, 54). In the analyses of similarity judgments in Experiment 2, OLS is appropriate as the dependent variable utilized is undergraduates' and law

students' judgments on a seven-point scale. In Experiment 1, where the judgments were measured on a four-point scale, I use OLS rather than ordered probit due to the number of cases in disaggregated analyses. As referenced below, however, I also conduct an ordered probit of all 208 observations in Experiment 1. The results are substantially similar to those in the OLS analysis presented here.

2. An ordered probit of all cases yields results that are the same as the OLS regression in terms of the direction and significance of relevant variables with one exception. Predisposition is marginally significant in the ordered probit analysis (specifically, $p = .10$ instead of .12 as indicated in the OLS analysis).

3. There were not enough African Americans in the close-case category to measure the influence of the variable.

REFERENCES

Arkes, Hal R., and Caroline Blumer. 2000. "The Psychology of Sunk Cost." In *Judgment and Decision Making: An Interdisciplinary Reader,* edited by Terry Connolly, Hal R. Arkes, and Kenneth R. Hammond, 97–113. New York: Cambridge University Press.

Baas, Larry, and Dan Thomas 1984. "The Supreme Court and Policy Legitimation: Experimental Tests." *American Politics Quarterly* 12:335–60.

Bartels, Brandon L. 2005. "Heterogeneity in Supreme Court Decision Making: How Case Level Factors Alter Preference Based Behavior." Paper presented at the Annual Meeting of the Midwest Political Science Association, Chicago.

Baum, Lawrence. A. 1997. *The Puzzle of Judicial Behavior.* Ann Arbor: Michigan University Press.

———. 2006. *Judges and Their Audiences: A Perspective on Judicial Behavior.* Princeton, N.J.: Princeton University Press.

Becker, Theodore L. 1964. *Political Behavioralism and Modern Jurisprudence.* Chicago: Rand McNally.

———. 1966. "Surveys and Judiciaries, or Who's Afraid of the Purple Curtain?" *Law and Society Review* 1:133–43.

———. 1969. "A Survey Study of Hawaiian Judges: The Effect of Decisions on Judicial Role Variations." *American Political Science Review* 60:677–80.

Bem, Daryl J. 1972. "Self Perception Theory." In *Advances in Experimental Social Psychology, Volume 6,* edited by Leonard Berkowitz, 2–62. New York: Academic Press.

Bickel, Alexander. 1986. *The Least Dangerous Branch.* New Haven: Yale University Press.

Bonneau, Chris W., and Thomas H. Hammond. 2005. "Conceptualizing Sincere and Strategic Behavior on the U.S Supreme Court." Paper presented at the Annual Meeting of the Midwest Political Science Association, Chicago.

Brace, Paul, Melinda Gann Hall, and Laura Langer. 1999. "Judicial Choice and the Politics of Abortion: Institutions, Context and the Autonomy of Courts." *Albany Law Review* 62:1265–303.

Braman, Eileen. 2006. "Reasoning on the Threshold: Testing the Separability of Preferences in Legal Decision Making." *Journal of Politics* 68, no. 2:308–21.

———. 2008. "Catching up to Move Ahead: Identifying and Filling Theoretical Gaps on Precedental Constraint on the Supreme Court." *Law and Courts* 18:13–16.

Braman, Eileen, and Thomas E. Nelson. 2007. "Mechanism of Motivated Reasoning?: Analogical Perception in Discrimination Disputes." *American Journal of Political Science* 51, no. 4:940–56.

Cardozo, Benjamin N. 1921. *The Nature of the Judicial Process.* New Haven: Yale University Press

———. 1924. *The Growth of the Law.* New Haven: Yale University Press.

Christensen, Larry. 1997. *Experimental Methods.* Boston: Allyn and Bacon Press.

Collins, Paul. M. 2007. "Lobbyists before the U.S. Supreme Court Investigating the Influence of Amicus Briefs." *Political Research Quarterly* 60, no. 1:55–77.

———. 2008. *Friends of the Supreme Court: Interest Groups and Judicial Decision Making.* New York: Oxford University Press.

Collins, Paul M., and Wendy L. Martinek. 2007. "The Small Group Context: Designated District Court Judges on the United States Courts of Appeals." Paper presented at the Annual Meeting of the Southern Political Science Association, New Orleans.

Cooper, Joel, and Russell H. Fazio. 1984. "A New Look at Dissonance Theory." In *Advances in Experimental Social Psychology, Volume 17,* edited by Leonard Berkowitz, 229–67. New York: Academic Press.

Cross, Frank B. 1997. "Political Science and the New Legal Realism: A Case of Unfortunate Interdisciplinary Ignorance." *Northwestern University Law Review* 92:251–326.

Eagly, Alice H., and Blair T. Johnson. 1990. "Gender Style in Bureaucracy: A Meta-Analysis." *Psychological Bulletin* 180:233–56.

Easterbrook, Frank H. 1982. "Ways of Criticizing the Court." *Harvard Law Review* 95:802–32.

Edwards, Harry T. 1998. "Collegiality and Decision Making on the D.C. Circuit Court." *Virginia Law Review* 84:1335–71.

Epstein, Lee, and Jack Knight. 1998. *The Choices Justices Make.* Washington D.C.: CQ Press.

———. 2000. "Toward a Strategic Revolution in Judicial Politics: A Look Back, a Look Ahead." *Political Research Quarterly* 53:624–61.

Ferguson, Joshua, Linda Babcock, and Peter M. Shane. 2008. "Do a Law's Policy Implications Affect Beliefs about Its Constitutionality?" *Law and Human Behavior* 32:219–27.

Fischhoff, Baruch. 1977. "Perceived Informativeness of Facts." *Journal of Experimental Psychology: Human Perception and Performance* 3:349–58.

Frank, Jerome. 1931a. "Are Judges Human? Part One: The Effect on Legal Thinking of the Assumption that Judges Behave Like Human Beings." *University of Pennsylvania Law Review* 80:17–53.

———. 1931b. "Are Judges Human? Part Two: As Through a Class Darkly." *University of Pennsylvania Law Review* 80:233–67.

Gentner, Dedre. 1998. "Analogy." In *Companion to Cognitive Science,* edited by William Bechtel and George Graham, 107–13. Malden, Mass.: Blackwell.

Gentner, Dedre, Brian Bowdle, Phillip Wolff, and Consuelo Boronot. 2001. "Metaphor Is Like Analogy." In *The Analogical Mind: Perspectives from Cognitive Science,* edited by Dedre Gentner, Keith J. Holyoak, and Boicho N. Nokinov, 199–253. Cambridge: MIT Press.

George, Tracey. E. 1998. "Developing a Positive Theory of Decision Making on the U.S Court of Appeals." *Ohio State Law Journal* 58:1635–96.

George, Tracey E., and Lee Epstein. 1992. "On the Nature of Supreme Court Decision-Making." *American Political Science Review* 86:323–37.

Gibson, James. 1978. "Judges' Role Orientations Attitudes and Decisions: An Interactive Model." *American Political Science Review* 72:911–24.

———. 1991. "Decision Making in Appellate Courts." In *The American Courts,* edited by John Gates and Charles Johnson, 255–78. Washington: CQ Press.

Gillman, Howard. 2001. "What's Law Got to Do with It? Judicial Behavioralists Test the 'Legal Model' of Judicial Decision-Making." *Law and Social Inquiry* 36:465–504.

Green, Donald P., and Alan S. Gerber. 2002. "Reclaiming the Experimental Tradition in Political Science." In *Political Science: The State of the Discipline,* edited by Ira Katznelson and Helen V. Milnor, 3:805–32. New York: Norton.

Gruenfeld, Deborah. 1995. "Status, Ideology and Integrative Complexity on the U.S. Supreme Court: Rethinking the Politics of Political Decision Making." *Journal of Personality and Social Psychology* 68:5–20.

Gruenfeld, Deborah, and Andrea B. Hollingshead. 1993. "Sociocognition in Work Groups: The Evolution of Integrative Complexity and Its Relation to Task Performance." *Small Groups Research* 24:383–405.

Gruenfeld, Deborah, Peter Kim, and Jared Preston. 1998. "Interdependence of Competitive Groups: How Power, Legitimacy, and Precedent Affect Integrative Complexity of the Majority." Paper presented at the Annual Meeting of the Academy of Management, San Diego.

Guthrie, Chris, Jeffery J. Rachlinski, and Andrew J. Wistrich. 2001. "Inside the Judicial Mind." *Cornell Law Review* 86:777–830.

Hall, Melinda Gann, and Paul Brace. 1989. "Order in the Courts: A Neo-Institutional Approach to Judicial Consensus." *Western Political Quarterly* 42:391–407.

Hammond, Thomas H., Chris W. Bonneau, and Reginald S. Sheehan. 2005. *Strategic Behavior and Policy Choice on the U.S. Supreme Court.* Stanford, Calif.: Stanford University Press.

Heider, Fritz. 1958. *The Psychology of Interpersonal Relations.* New York: Wiley Press.

Hinch, Melvin J., and Michael C. Munger. 1997. *Analytical Politics.* New York: Cambridge University Press.

Hoekstra, Valerie, and Jefffery S. Segal. 1996. "The Shepherding of Local Public Opinion: The Supreme Court and *Lamb's Chapel.*" *Journal of Politics* 58: 1079–102.

Holyoak, Keith J., and Paul Thagard. 1995. *Mental Leaps: Analogy in Creative Thought.* Cambridge: MIT Press.

Iyengar, Shanto, and Donald R. Kinder. 1987. *News That Matters.* Chicago: University of Chicago Press.

James, Dorothy B. 1968. "Role Theory and the Supreme Court." *Journal of Politics* 30:160–86.

Janis, Irving L. 1982. *Groupthink.* 2nd ed. Boston: Houghton Mifflin.

Johnson, Charles A. 1987. "Law, Politics, and Judicial Decision-Making." *Law and Society Review* 21:325–40.

Johnson, Frank. 1976. "The Constitution and the Federal District Judge." *Texas Law Review* 54:903–16.

Jost, John T., Jack Glaser, Arie W. Kruglanski, and Frank J. Sulloway. 2003. "Political Conservatism as Motivated Social Cognition." *Psychological Bulletin* 129:339–75.

Kaarbo, Juliet, and Margaret G. Hermann. 1998. "Leadership Styles of Prime Ministers: How Individual Differences Affect the Foreign Policymaking Process." *Leadership Quarterly* 9:243–63.

Kahn, Ronald. 1994. "The Supreme Court as a (Counter) Majoritarian Institution: Misperceptions of the Warren, Burger and Rehnquist Courts." *Detroit College of Law Review* 1994:1–60.

Keppel, Geoffery. 1982. *Design and Analysis: A Researcher's Handbook.* 2nd ed. Englewood Cliffs, N.J.: Prentice Hall.

Khong, Yueng Foong. 1992. *Analogies at War: Korea, Munich, Dien Bien Phu, and the Vietnam Decisions of 1965.* Princeton: Princeton University Press.

Kinder, Donald, and Thomas R. Palfrey. 1993. "On Behalf of an Experimental Political Science." In *Experimental Foundations of Political Science,* edited by Donald Kinder and Thomas R. Palfrey, 1–42. Ann Arbor: University of Michigan Press.

Knight, Jack, and Lee Epstein. 1996. "The Norm of *Stare Decisis*." *American Journal of Political Science* 40:1018–35.

Koestler, Arthur. 1964. *The Act of Creation.* New York: Penguin.

Kunda, Ziva. 1990. "The Case for Motivated Reasoning." *Psychological Bulletin* 108:480–98.

———. 1999. *Social Cognition: Making Sense of People.* Cambridge: MIT Press.

Lacy, Dean. 2001. "A Theory of Nonseparable Preferences in Survey Responses." *American Journal of Political Science* 45:239–58.

Lerner, Jennifer S., and Phillip E. Tetlock. 1999. "Accounting for the Effects of Accountability." *Psychological Bulletin* 125:255–75.

Llewellyn, Karl. N. 1962. *Realism in Theory and Practice.* Chicago: University of Chicago Press.

Long, J. Scott. 1997. *Regression Models for Categorical and Limited Dependent Variables.* London: Sage.

Lord, Charles G., Mark R. Lepper, and Elizabeth Preston. 1984. "Considering the Opposite: A Corrective Strategy for Social Judgment." *Journal of Personality and Social Psychology* 47:2131–43.

Lord, Charles G., Lee Ross, and Mark R. Lepper. 1979. "Biased Assimilation and Attitude Polarization: The Effects of Prior Theories on Subsequently Considered Evidence." *Journal of Personality and Social Psychology* 37:1098–21.

MacCoun, Robert. 1998. "Biases in the Interpretation and Use of Research Results." *Annual Review of Psychology* 49:259–87.

McGraw, Kathleen. 2000. "Contributions of the Cognitive Approach to Political Psychology." *Political Psychology* 21:805–32.

McGuire, William J. 1985. "The Nature of Attitudes and Attitude Change." In *The Handbook of Social Psychology*, 3rd ed., edited by Gardner Lindzey and Elliot Aronson, 2:233–346. New York: Random House.

Mendelson, Wallace. 1963. "The Neo-Behavioral Approach to the Judicial Process: A Critique." *American Political Science Review* 57:593–603.

Mondak, Jeffery J. 1994. "Policy Legitimacy and the Supreme Court: The Sources and Context of Legitimation." *Political Research Quarterly* 47:675–92.

Morehead, Thomas. 1998. "Small Groups." In *The Handbook of Social Psychology*, 4th ed., edited by Daniel T. Gilbert, Susan T. Fiske, and Gardner Lindzey, 415–69. New York: McGraw Hill.

Moscovici, Serge. 1980. "Toward a Theory of Conversion Behavior." In *Advances in Experimental Social Psychology*, edited by Leonard Berkowitz, 13:209–39. New York: Academic Press.

Moscovici, Serge, and M. Zallvaloni. 1969. "The Group as a Polarizer of Attitudes." *Journal of Personality and Social Psychology* 12:125–35.

Murphy, Walter F. 1964. *Elements of Judicial Strategy.* Chicago: University of Chicago Press.

Murphy, Walter F., and Joseph Tanenhaus. 1972. *The Study of Public Law.* New York: Random House.

Nelson, Thomas E., Rosalie Clawson, and Zoe Oxley. 1997. "Media Framing of a Civil Liberties Conflict and Its Effect on Tolerance." *American Political Science Review* 91:567–83.

Nemeth, Charlan Jeanne. 1986. "Differential Contributions of Majority and Minority Influence." *Psychological Review* 92:23–32.

Peppers, Todd C. 2006. *Courtiers of the Marble Palace: The Rise and Influence of the Supreme Court Law Clerk.* Palo Alto, Calif.: Stanford University Press.

Posner, Richard A. 1990. *The Problems of Jurisprudence.* Cambridge: Harvard University Press.

———. 1995. *Overcoming Law.* Cambridge: Harvard University Press.

———. 2003. *Economic Analysis of Law.* 6th ed. New York: Aspen.

———. 2008. *How Judges Think.* Cambridge: Harvard University Press.

Pound, Roscoe. 1905. "The Decadence of Equity." *Columbia Law Review* 5: 20–35.

———. 1913. "Justice According to Law." *Columbia Law Review* 13:696–713.

———. 1931. "The Call for a Realist Jurisprudence." *Harvard Law Review* 44: 697–711.

Pritchett, C. Herman. 1941. "Division of Opinion among Justices of the U.S. Supreme Court, 1939–1941." *American Political Science Review* 35:890–98.

————. 1948. *The Roosevelt Court: A Study in Judicial Politics and Values.* New York: Macmillan.

Provine, Marie D. 1980. *Case Selection in the United States Supreme Court.* Chicago: University of Chicago Press.

Randazzo, Kirk A., Richard W. Waterman, and Jeffrey A. Fine. 2006. "Checking the Federal Courts: the Impact of Congressional Statutes on Judicial Behavior." *Journal of Politics* 68:1006–17.

Richards, Mark J., and Herbert M. Kritzer. 2002. "Jurisprudential Regimes in Supreme Court Decision Making." *American Political Science Review* 96:305–20.

Rohde, David, and Harold J. Spaeth. 1976. *Supreme Court Decision Making.* San Francisco: W. H. Freeman.

Ross, Lee. 1977. "The Intuitive Psychologist and His Shortcomings: Distortions in the Attribution Process." In *Advances in Experimental Social Psychology, Vol. 10,* edited by Leonard Berkowitz, 173–200. New York: Academic Press.

Ross, Michael R., Cathy McFarland, and Garth J. Fletcher. 1985. "Attribution and Social Perception." In *Handbook of Social Psychology,* edited by Gardner Lindzey and Elliot Aronson, 2:73–122. New York: Random House.

Rowland, C. K., and Robert A. Carp. 1980. "A Longitudinal Study of Party Effects on Federal District Court Policy Propensities." *American Journal of Political Science* 24:291–305.

————. 1996. *Politics and Judgment in Federal District Courts.* Lawrence: University Press of Kansas.

Ruger, Theodore W., Pauline T. Kim, Andrew D. Martin, and Kevin M. Kim. 2004. "The Supreme Court Forecasting Project: Legal and Political Science Approaches to Predicting Supreme Court Decision Making." *Columbia Law Review* 104:1150–208.

Schauer, Fredrick. 1991. *Playing by the Rules: A Philosophical Examination of Rule-Based Decision Making in Law and Life.* Oxford: Oxford University Press.

Schlag, Pierre 1985. "Rules and Standards." *University of California Law Review* 33:379–430.

Schubert, Glendon. 1962. "The 1960 Term of the Supreme Court." *American Political Science Review* 56:90–107.

Schwartz, Edward P. 1992. "Policy, Precedent and Power: A Positive Theory of Supreme Court Decision Making." *Journal of Law, Economics, and Organization* 8:219–53.

Schwartz, Thomas. 1977. "Collective Choices, Separation of Issues and Vote Trading." *American Political Science Review* 71:999–1010.

Segal, Jeffrey A. 1984. "Predicting Supreme Court Cases Probabilistically: The Search and Seizure Cases." *American Political Science Review* 78:891–900.

Segal, Jeffrey A., and Albert D. Cover. 1989. "Ideological Values and the Votes of U.S. Supreme Court Justices." *American Political Science Review* 83:557–65.

Segal, Jeffrey A., and Harold J. Spaeth. 1993. *The Supreme Court and the Attitudinal Model.* New York: Cambridge University Press.

————. 1996a. "The Influence of Stare Decisis on the Votes of United States Supreme Court Justices." *American Journal of Political Science* 40:971–1003.

————. 1996b. "Norms, Dragons, and Stare Decisis: A Response." *American Journal of Political Science* 40:1064–82.

————. 2002. *The Supreme Court and The Attitudinal Model Revisited.* New York: Cambridge University Press.

Shapiro, Martin M. 1993. "Public Law and Judicial Politics." In *Political Science: The State of the Discipline,* edited by Ada W. Finifter 365–81. Washington D.C.: American Political Science Association.

Sheehan, Reginald S., William Mishler, and Donald R. Songer. 1992. "Ideology, Status and the Differential Success of Direct Parties before the Supreme Court." *American Political Science Review* 86:464–71.

Sheppard, Stephen M. 1998. *The History of U.S. Legal Education.* Hackensack, N.J.: Salem Press.

Sherwin, Emily. 1999. "A Defense of Analogical Reasoning in Law." *University of Chicago Law Review* 66:1179–97.

Slotnick, Elliot. 1991. "Judicial Politics." In *Political Science: Looking to the Future,* edited by William Crotty, 4:67–97. Evanston: Northwestern University Press.

Sniderman, Paul. 2000. "Taking Sides: A Fixed-Choice Theory of Political Reasoning." In *Elements of Reason: Cognition Choice and the Bounds of Rationality,* edited by Arthur Lupia, Matthew McCubbins, and Samuel Popkin, 67–84. New York: Cambridge University Press.

Spaeth, Harold J. 1961. "An Approach to the Study of Attitudinal Differences as an Aspect of Judicial Behavior." *American Journal of Political Science* 5:165–80.

————. 1963. "An Analysis of Judicial Attitudes in Labor Relations Decisions of the Warren Court." *Journal of Politics* 25:290–311.

Spaeth, Harold J., and Jeffrey A. Segal. 1999. *Majority Rule or Minority Will: Adherence to Precedent on the U.S. Supreme Court.* New York: Cambridge University Press.

Spiller, Pablo T., and Rafael Gely. 1992. "Congressional Control or Judicial Independence: The Determinants of U.S. Supreme Court Labor Relations Decisions." *Rand Journal of Economics* 23:463–92.

Spriggs, James F., II, and Paul J. Wahlbeck. 1997. "Amicus Curiae and the Role of Information at the Supreme Court." *Political Research Quarterly* 50:365–86.

Stevens, Robert. 1983. *Law School: Legal Education from the 1850s to the 1980s.* Chapel Hill: University of North Carolina Press.

Stone-Sweet, Alec. 2002. "Path Dependence, Precedent and Judicial Power." In *On Law Politics and Judicialization,* edited by Martin M. Shapiro and Stone-Sweet, 112–35. New York: Oxford University Press.

Suedfeld, Peter, and Phillip E. Tetlock. 1977a. "War, Peace, and Integrative Complexity." *Journal of Conflict Resolution* 221:427–42.

————. 1977b. "Integrative Complexity of Communications in International Crises." *Journal of Conflict Resolution* 21:169–84.

Sunstein, Cass. 1993. "On Analogy in Legal Reasoning." *Harvard Law Review* 106:741–49.

Taber, Charles. 1998. "The Interpretation of Foreign Policy Events: A Cognitive Process Theory." In *Problem Representation in Foreign Policy Decision Making,* edited by Donald A. Sylvan and James F. Voss, 29–52. New York: Cambridge University Press.

Taber, Charles, and Milton Lodge. 2006. "Motivated Skepticism in Political Information Processing." *American Journal of Political Science* 50:755–69.

Taber, Charles, Milton Lodge, and Jill Glathar. 2001. "The Motivated Construction of Political Judgments." In *Citizens and Politics: Perspectives from Political Psychology*, edited by James Kuklinski, 198–226. New York: Cambridge University Press.

Tanenhaus, Joseph. 1966. "The Cumulative Scaling of Judicial Decisions." *Harvard Law Review* 79:1583–94.

Tesser, Abraham, and John Campbell. 1983. "Self Definition and Self-Evaluation Maintenance." In Psychological Perspectives on the Self, edited by Jerry Suls and Anthony Greenwald, 1–31. New York: Guilford Press.

Tetlock, Philip E. 1981. "Personality and Isolationism: Content Analysis of Senatorial Speeches." *Journal of Personality and Social Psychology* 41:737–43.

———. 1983. "Accountability and the Complexity of Thought." *Journal of Personality and Social Psychology* 45:74–83.

———. 1984. "Cognitive Style and Political Belief Systems in the British House of Commons." *Journal of Personality and Social Psychology* 46:365–75.

Tetlock, Philip E., Jane Bernzweig, and Jack L. Gallant. 1985. "Supreme Court Decision-Making: Cognitive Style as a Predictor of Ideological Consistency of Voting." *Journal of Personality and Social Psychology* 48:1227–39.

Tetlock, Phillip E., L. Skitka, and R. Boettger. 1989. "Social and Cognitive Strategies for Coping with Accountability Conformity, Complexity and Bolstering." *Journal of Personality and Social Psychology* 57:632–40.

Turow, Scott. 1977. *One L.* New York: Putnam.

Tversky, Amos. 1977. "Features of Similarity." *Psychological Review* 84:327–52.

Ulmer, S. Sidney. 1960. "Supreme Court Behavior and Civil Rights." *Western Political Quarterly* 13:288–311.

———. 1965. "Toward a Theory of Subgroup Formation in the U.S. Supreme Court." *Journal of Politics* 27:133–52.

———. 1973. Social Backgrounds as an Indicator to the Votes of Supreme Court Justices in Criminal Cases: 1947–1956 Terms. *American Journal of Political Science* 17:622–30.

Velleman, Daniel. 1994. *How to Prove It: A Structural Approach.* Cambridge: Cambridge University Press.

Walker, Thomas G., and Deborah J. Barrow. 1985. "The Diversification of the Federal Bench: Policy and Process Ramifications." *Journal of Politics* 47:596–617.

Ward, Artemus, and David L. Weiden. 2006. *Sorcerers' Apprentices: 100 Years of Law Clerks at the United States Supreme Court.* New York: New York University Press.

Watson, James D. 1969. *The Double Helix.* New York: Signet.

Welch, Susan, Michael Combs, and John Gruhl. 1988. "Do Black Judges Make a Difference?" *American Journal of Political Science* 32:126–36.

Winter, David. 1987. "Leader Appeal, Leader Performance and the Motive Profiles of Leaders and Followers: A Study of American Presidents and Elections." *Journal of Personality and Social Psychology* 52:196–202.

Wistrich, Andrew, Chris Guthrie, and Jeffrey Rachlinski. 2005. "Can Judges Ignore Inadmissible Information?" *University of Pennsylvania Law Review* 153: 1251–345.

CASES

Biggs v. Best, Best and Krieger, 189 F.3d 989 (9th Cir. 1997).

Boy Scouts of the United States of America v. Dale, 530 U.S. 640 (2000).

Elk Grove Unified School District v. Newdow, 542 U.S. (2004).

Gonzalez v. Raich, 454 U.S. 1 (2005).

Heart of Atlanta Motel v. United States, 379 U.S. 241 (1964).

Horstkoetter v. Department of Public Safety, 159 F.3d 1265 (10th Cir. 1998).

International Association of Firefighters v. City of Ferguson, 283 F.3d 969 (8th Cir. 2002).

National Labor Relations Board v. Jones and Laughlin Steel Corp., 301 U.S. 1 (1937).

United States v. Lopez, 514 U.S. 549 (1985).

United States v. Morrison, 529 U.S. 598 (2000).

Wazeerud-Din v. Goodwill Home and Missions Inc., 737 A.2d 683 (N.J. Super. AD 1999).

Wickard v. Filburn, 317 U.S. 111 (1942).

INDEX